THE LAND OF MY FATHER'S BIRTH

Memoir of the Liberian Civil War

Nvasekie N. Konneh

Royal House Communication Consortium Inc.

The Land of My Father's Birth
Memoir of the Liberian Civil War
All Rights Reserved.
Copyright © 2013 Nvasekie N. Konneh
v2.0 r1.1

Cover Photo © 2013 JupiterImages Corporation. All rights reserved - used with permission.

Royal House Communication Consortium Inc.

ISBN: 978-0-578-11300-5

PRINTED IN THE UNITED STATES OF AMERICA

This book is dedicated to the memory of my Dear Mother, Haja Machemeh Donzo who departed this world on January 3, 2012.

Table of Contents

Acknowledgements

WORKING ON THIS book has been a very tedious and an engaging experience for me. While I take credit and blame for everything, I am truly indebted to some people who provided some important and useful advises and suggestions. First of all, we thank the Creator for his protection and guidance.

Among those whose expert advices and suggestions I must acknowledge include Pastor Yadeh Chea, Dr. Abdoulaye Dukule, Prof. K. Moses Nagbe, Vamba Sherif, Rietske Zuidema, Manseen Logan. All of these read through the manuscript and gave their critical views on it. Ophelia Lewis for pointing me to the direction of Manseen Logan whose proof-reading and editorial service proved to be very valuable. Without those critical assessment of the manuscript and useful advises the book might have not come out to be what it is now. I am greatly indebted to Professors James Fairhead, Tim Geysbeek, Svend E. Holsoe and Melissa Leach for their seminal efforts in Liberian studies, a book titled, **"African American Exploration of West Africa"** which greatly broadened my understanding of Benjamin Anderson's famous visit to Mousadou, the capital of the **"Western Mandingo Country,"** which would have been part of Liberia had it not been because of the French colonial expansion in West Africa. I am very greatful to Uncle Raphael Saye for his oral historical accounts of his and my father's Mano background as well as Movaba Fofana for his oral history accounts of Quardu-Gbonie Mandingo homeland of Lofa County.

There are countless others whose supports for me as a writer and community activist have been very crucial over the years. In as much I would have loved to name them all, there is not enough space to name all of them. However, there are few names I will surely be guilty if I don't acknowledge. In that order, my friend and partner Mariam Sherif and my three children, Nvasekie Jr., Machemeh, and Foday, come first. Without their patience and sacrifices, my work as a community activist and this project could not have been possible. Added to this list will be my uncle, Dr. Fode Donzo, my good friend, brother and partner, Kalifala "KD" Donzo as well as Mohammed Keita, Ansumana Jabateh, Mohamed Konneh (Richmond), Uncle Karfala Toure, Voffee Jabateh and Musa A. M Sheriff, my official photographer. Brother Valee Sanoe and Mike Jabateh, thank for everything. I know you will always have my back in time of difficulty. For my friends and brothers, Musa "Paul" Bility and Foday Donzo (Dr. D), this is my version of our stories going way back to where we come from, Saclepea. I will be thrilled if this book inspires you enough to write your own versions of our stories some days. Bless be the Most High God for keeping us alive to tell these stories.

Introduction

THIS BOOK HAS been a project in the making since the early days of the Liberian Civil War. It started as a diary. It is a reflection on both the happy memories of the past and painful experience of the war. It comprises of three parts. The first part, **Days of Sweet Memories,** is made up of chapters exploring childhood experiences and family history. Then the war came and since then I have been on an endless journey, a journey that took me to the Ivory Coast and back to Liberia in the early 90s, hoping that the war was over and I could put the pieces of my life back together. After a few years of trying to put my life back together in Liberia, the journey continued on to the US through the US government sponsored DV Lottery Visa program in 1995. Having arrived on the shore of the United States, my journey continued into the US Navy in which I served for nine consecutive years. Six of those years were spent on two mighty warships, USS Detroit and USS Dwight D. Eisenhower in Earle, New Jersey and Norfolk, Virginia respectively. In a nutshell, this book provides bits and pieces of my personal experiences in Liberia before the war that rocked the country for more than a decade continuing through Abidjan, Dakar, Conakry, New York, Philadelphia, Paris, as well as Jerusalem.

Liberians refer to the days before the war as "Normal Days." Those were the days when we didn't have to think about running from one place to another for survival while dodging bullets. Those were the days when our neighbors were not our enemies. Though we might have had some disagreements and dislike for each other, we managed to coexist. Those were the days where whenever we thought of war it was in some distant lands we could only see through pictures or listen to on the radio. For me, those days were full of sweet memories. Sometimes I wish to relive those happy days but they are gone forever. There are many young Liberians who did not live to see and experience those normal days. They were either too young when the war started or were born during the war and went with their parents to various places of refuge. Some of them were even born in those places of refuge. They can't remember what those normal days looked like. For those of us who lived those normal days, it is good to share our experiences with those who did not live them.

When Charles Taylor spoke for the first time on BBC, announcing that the National Patriotic Front of Liberia (NPFL) had launched the war to get rid of the dictatorial regime of President Samuel Doe, I supported him, like many Liberians who were yearning for change. I thought it was a necessary move to change the status quo. Unfortunately, when we started hearing the alarming news of ethnic cleansing on the part of the "liberators," making them no different from the Doe regime that was targeting the Manos, Gios, and others, it felt like a bitter taste in my mouth. I found myself in a dilemma. I strongly believed that Doe was a dictator and I thought that the war was necessary to bring about democratic change, but then I realized that there would be no place for me and many others in that change on the account of our ethnicity and religion. How could I support the war when part of its agenda was to drive the "foreigners," meaning people that looked like me, out of Liberia? This was the question on my mind when I joined the exodus of hundreds of thousands of people fleeing the country to Sierra Leone, Guinea, Ivory Coast and elsewhere in Africa and beyond.

The Mandingo tribe is one of the largest in West Africa and can be found in nine of the 16 West African countries, but we face a unique predicament in Liberia because despite the fact that our presence in Liberia predates that of the Americo-Liberians, some of our fellow Liberians continue to regard us as foreigners. This was the main reason why we were targeted in the war. This and other related matters are found in Part II, **"Revelation Time."**

I have been in the US for more than ten years, having started my American experience in Harlem, New York. Now I call East Lansdowne, Pennsylvania my home, thanks to the US Navy which transferred me here at the end of my first four years of sea duty on board the USS Detroit. Of these years in the US, nine were spent in the US Navy. Taking this into consideration, I can say with all fairness that the Navy has formed the major part of my American experience. The sea duty on USS Detroit and USS Dwight D. Eisenhower saw me through two deployments in Europe and the Middle East. In between, there was a shore duty in Philadelphia, the City of Brotherly Love. Being in the US Navy was another kind of American experience that is different from that of just being an immigrant in America. Meeting and interacting with people from different parts of this great country, with some (like me) from other countries and traveling to all those distant places were incredible experiences. Some of those people I met in the ships have become life-long friends; we have kept in touch with each other.

Most people will say they join the Navy to see the world. While on my first ship, I saw my fair share of the world. My navy experiences in particular and American experience in general are in Part III, **So Far Away on the Distant Sea.**

Despite the fact that I was serving in the military, my heart and soul have been involved in the cause of social justice in Liberia. I became very active as an activist while on shore duty assignments in Philadelphia. While the navy was my day job which sustained me, community engagement and service was like a second job. This second job, which was a voluntary one, was done out of love for my people and nation, Liberia and humanity. When Charles Taylor incarcerated the Liberian journalist, Hassan Bility and others, I along with many others mobilized hundreds of people to demonstrate at the Liberian Embassy and at the US Capitol in Washington DC.

Part III continues with a chat with a Jewish boy at a McDonald's restaurant in Hafai, Israel. It also reveals the search for my friend,

Fatim Diop in Dakar; as well as reflects on the hype surrounding the new millennium and the surprise New Year Eve military coup in Ivory Coast led by a man who happened to be the father of one of my Ivorian friends, Nicole Guei.

As I write about my experiences, I'm aware that some Liberians will be sensitive to much of what I have explained about my experience as a Mandingo in the Liberian civil war. While I respect their feelings, I wish to note that my intention is not to exploit ethnicity in any negative shape or fashion but to accurately describe how things unfolded during the war from my angle of vision. If there was no ethnic targeting during the war, my perspective on what transpired might have been different. Since ethnicity and religion were major factors in the war, and my ethnic group was one of the targeted, I find it a disservice to Liberia and to posterity to shy away from telling that story like it is. In the same way, I don't see anything wrong with the fact that a Mano, Gio, or Krahn person may want to write about how the war affected him or her on the basis of ethnicity. Of course, there are others who were victimized not because of any ethnic affiliation but because of their political affiliation. Still others were victimized because of their religious affiliations. There were still others that got caught up in cross fires between opposing forces. One way or the other, we all have been victims of the war. The more we tell our stories, the more liberating it will be for our souls. Hopefully, when we all tell our stories based on the reality of our experiences we will finally appreciate and empathize with each other, strive to make sure that such terrible incidents never occur in our country again and work together to build a society on the foundation of mutual respect.

By extension, this theme is critical to the future of Africa. After more than 50 years of independent rule in Africa (more than a hundred years in the case of Liberia), we have not yet evolved into a functioning democracy where individuals will not be judged constantly on their ethnicity or religious backgrounds. It is unfortunate that in many countries in Africa people keep reminding each other of their ethnicities and keep victimizing each other on the basis of it. Some of us have traveled and experienced freedom and democracy in the West. We observe the benefits accruing from equality, but when we return to Africa we seek refuge, for instance, in ethnicity. Of course, the West did not come by its significant respect for equality through sudden flight. The citizens made a purposeful effort to work at it, knowing that cultivating a sense of equality is just as important as cultivating a sense of security for each one in the society. We Africans, too, can begin the process. It will surely pay off. With the election of President Barack Obama, the first African-American as president of the United States, who also has a root on the African continent, it is my hope that we are all inspired to cultivate and sustain respectable values in our individual countries and societies in Africa.

Nvasekie N. Konneh
E. Lansdowne, Pa
August 15, 2012

Part I
Days of Sweet Memory

1

From Beyla to Saclepea

WHEN MY FATHER, Ngoamilleh Konneh and his family left Saclepea in the early 1990s and went to Guinea as a result of the war, he didn't have the slightest idea that he would be seeing Saclepea, his birth place, for the last time. He didn't have the slightest idea that he would live in Guinea for three consecutive years and then be flown from Conakry to Monrovia where he would die in 1994. Born and raised in Saclepea, my father lived there his whole life. He used to visit places near and far but he would always return to Saclepea, the place he loved more than anywhere else. In his life, he dabbled into many things, all with the hope of providing for his family. He was a tailor, grocery shop owner and farmer; sometimes buying and selling produce such as cocoa, coffee, palm kernels, as well as owning diamond creeks. He did all these with strong determination but did not get rich. Until the war, he lived a modest life as head of a very big family. He came back to Liberia towards the end of 1993, frail and beaten down by a sickness he could not survive.

My father was the son of a Mandingo man and a Mano woman. His mother, Mah Tolor, was from Tengben, a town within Saclepea Mah County District. Grandma Tolor was the daughter of Glay Vlahnkhan, a local chief and his wife, Kpoyee Wheyee. Glay Vlahnkhan, my great grandfather from the Mano side of the family used to live in Geinwee, another town, but he later on moved his family to Tengben where Grandma Tolor and her siblings were born. Among grandma's siblings were Mah Gomah (Dekpa Tee), Mehnsah, Nya, Mah Tenwei and Yelelei, the youngest.

Grandma Tolor had two children, my father and his sister Bendu Kenneh. My father and his sister Bendu shared a mother but had different fathers. Grandma Tolor was married to my grandfather, Nvakaifa Konneh but when my father was a toddler, she and grandpa divorced. It was after their divorce that grandma married to Sekou Kenneh with whom aunty Bendu was born. When grandma died several years later, as tradition required, one of her younger sisters was given as a replacement to Oldman Sekou Kenneh. This sister of Grandma Tolor was called Seiney, her Mano name but she was also called by her Mandingo name, Mawata.

On the Mandingo side of the family, my grandfather was Nvakaifa. My father was his third child, the first two being aunty Mandenyen and Uncle Vasayou. It was Uncle Vasayou's mother, Madagbeh Dukuly who raised my father after the divorce of his mother and my grandpa. Grandma Madagbeh was one of the three Mandingo wives of my grandfather. She was in fact his first wife. He added four Mano women bringing the total to seven. These Mano women, as I am told, were given to my grandpa by their parents because it was customary for people to give their daughters to powerful people in society. Since Grandpa Nvakaifa was a kamoh who prayed and blessed many of the powerful people of those days, some of these women were given by their parents in appreciation for the holy works grandpa performed for them. He married one of Johnny Voker's relatives who bore him Uncle Vafomo, named after Sheik Kafumba Konneh's father, Alhaji Famo Konneh. By family tradition, Alhaji Famo was a paternal uncle of Grandpa Nvakaifa but grandpa was older than him. He was a successful travelling salesman, primarily residing in Sanniquellie. Grandpa Nvakaifa persuaded him to settle in Saclepea. Over the years, he became very successful and powerful in his own right. His legacy lives through his son, Sheik Kafumba Konneh, Chairman of the National Muslim Council of Liberia and also a prominent figure within the nation's Interfaith Mediation Committee which played a major role in the Liberian peace process. Uncle Sekou, the father of the famous ULIMO General Pepper & Salts is a son of another Mano woman but his mother died when he was a baby. As a result of this, he was raised by Grandma Madagbeh Dukuly.

My father's elder brother, Vasayou had three wives, including my mother, Machemeh Donzo. With Uncle Vasayou, my mother had my brothers Bankalie and Funcia. My brother Abu's mother was Muatata. When Uncle Vasayou passed away, his three wives, my mother, Muatata, and Mabana stayed with my father as a continuation of the marriage. In the Mandingo tradition, it is permissible that when a brother dies, his wife or wives stay with the younger brother as a continuation of the marriage. This has to be done with the consent of the women. This is done in the interest of the children so they won't be strangers in another man's household. By continuing the marriage with my father, my brothers Bankalie, Abu and Funcia grew up knowing my father Ngoamilleh Konneh as their father. My eldest brothers didn't get to know their biological father, Vasayou. They were too young when he passed away. It is said that Grandpa Nvakaifa cried and wished that God had taken him instead of his first son. He was in his advanced age and it is generally expected that the children would bury their parents, not the other way around.

When his brother passed away, my father had his young wife, Manyamuay Koisiah. He was compelled to marry his brother's three wives because his younger brothers, Uncle Sekou and Vafomo were not of marriage age. That brought the total number of my father's wives to four. He had fifteen additional children plus the previous three. Together, my father and his wives raised 18 children under one roof.

Even though in all of my official records I have listed Saclepea as my birth place, according to my mother, I was actually born in Dumpea, a diamond mining town in Zoe Geh District, also in Nimba County. It is about an hour drive from Saclepea. In Dumpea, my father had a diamond mine where he employed men to dig diamonds for him. He also had a grocery store. My mother was one of his four wives that stayed with him while in Dumpea. I was delivered by traditional midwives; therefore, there was no official record of my birth such as a birth certificate. According to my mother, I was born in the year Saran was murdered. This is supported by Muafeta, one of my paternal aunts. When it comes to information of who was born where, when, and who is older than who, Muafeta is the go-to person. The only thing she would ever tell me of my birth is that I was born at the time when Saran was murdered in Saclepea. That was a big scary story that gripped Saclepea and its environs in the later part of the 60s and early 70s. It is said that two persons with cutlasses and an ax broke into her house in the middle of the night when all her neighbors were asleep. They axed her to death, split her head, and drained her blood. The killers fled but were caught several days later in Bahn. According to my mother and other people, the killers were Ivorian Krahns and some said they were sent by President Tubman of Liberia or Houphouet Boigny of Ivory Coast. That's why everyone said that no one knew if anything happened to Saran's killers. No one could tell if they were ever put on trial for the murder or duly punished for it.

Saran's death was a mysterious and frightening situation in Saclepea. People were scared and were asking all kinds of questions about why it happened. The news traveled far and near but since my parents couldn't read and write, they couldn't remember the exact date as they told me later on. So, over the years, I have chosen my own birthdates. When I was playing the diversity visa lottery that brought me to the United States in 1995, I used several birthdates. It was my application with 10/24/1968 that won. As a result I came to the US with 1968 in my passport as my birth date.

When I was joining the US Navy in 1996, I was sensitive to being regarded as an old man in the mix of 17 and 18 years old recruits. I decided to push my birth date up two years to 1970. 26 years of age gave me a more comfortable feeling rather than 28 years among the teen recruits. Since then, I have stuck with 10/24/1970 as my birth date because that's the information on most of my official records such as my driver's license and US military service records.

My grandfather, that is, my father's father, was called Nvakaifa Konneh and since he was a kamoh the Manos and Gios used to call him Mollie Kaifa or Bolie Kaifa. Even today, those Manos and Gios who remember him call us Mollie Kaifa or Bolie Kaifa's children or grandchildren. Grandpa Nvakaifa was born in the 1850s in Beyla which is in present day Guinea. He was more than 100 years old when he died in 1962 in Saclepea. Back in those days when grandpa was born there was no country called Guinea. Beyla is one of the five towns in the "Mandingo country" that had Mesiadou as the capital which Benjamin JK Anderson visited in 1869 and 1874. The narrative of Mr. Anderson's visit was published as a book titled **Narrative of a Journey to Mesiadou, the Capital of the Western Mandingoes.**

As I have just mentioned above, when Liberia became independent in 1847, it was just limited to the settlements along the coast and did not extend to the 43,000 square miles territorial limit we know today. It would take more than 50 years after independence for the boundary of the nation to reach to the present square miles of 43,000. Citizenship of the emerging nation Liberia was limited to the settlers while the areas where the natives lived were considered different countries.

The coastal territories that became Liberia in 1847 needed to expand. In furtherance of this objective, there was a series of expeditions into the interior. The most famous of those expeditions was led by Benjamin J. K. Anderson to Mesiadou which was then called the capital of the Western Mandingo country. To the settlers, Mesiadou held great promise for the emerging Liberian nation because of what was perceived as its natural resources and vibrant political base with routes that extended all the way to the Niger River. The concept of nation as we know today did not exist back then. Countries were defined by tribes or alliances of tribes. So when Benjamin JK Anderson traveled from Monrovia to Mesiadou in 1868 through 1869, he was traveling from Boatswain country, Gola country, Kpelleh country, Lorma country, Vai country, and several other countries before he reached Mesiadou. The king who the settlers called Chief Boatswain was King Sao Bosso Kamara who was the head of the Condo Confederacy which controlled the trade route between the coast and the interior. It took Anderson more than six months to walk from place to place until he reached to Mesiadou in 1869. Anderson's trip to Mesiadou was proposed by Mr. Henry M. Schieffelin in New York. This proposal was done through President Daniel B. Warner of Liberia. During his visit to Mesiadou, Anderson visited other towns, including Beyla, Grandpa Nvakaifa's birth place which is about 8 miles from Mesiadou.

When Benjamin J. K. Anderson left Mesiadou to go back to Monrovia, King Vafin Dulleh gave him a letter written in Arabic addressed to the president of Liberia, James S. Payne. In the letter, King Vafin Dulleh talked about how Ibrahima Sesay, the king of Medina destroyed Mesiadou during the 1860s. King Dulleh assured the Liberian leader that everything in Mesiadou was at his disposal. Mesiadou wanted arms in exchange for Liberia's desire of a trade route through the interior. Anderson made a second trip to Mesiadou in 1874 and was embarrassed when he could not give any reply to the king's letter to the Liberian government four years earlier. By this time, Mesiadou was in decline. King Ibrahima Sesay, who Vafin Dulleh had complained about to Anderson during his first visit, was now the most powerful leader in the region with his headquarters in Medina. In 1879, King Ibrahima Sesay sent his son Fomba Sesay to Monrovia to meet with the President of Liberia. As it was reported in the local newspaper, Fumba Sesay's visit was considered as the most important event of 1879. On August 13th of that same year, he met with President Anthony Gardner at the Executive Mansion, delivering a message from his father, King Ibrahima Sesay. After several months of stay in Monrovia, Fumba Sesay left to take the message back to his father who would have finalized the discussion of Mesiadou as well as surrounding towns and villages to be part of Liberia. Unfortunately, Fumba Sesay could not make it back to Medina as his father was fighting against Almamy Samory Toure. The war between King Ibrahima Sesay and Samory Toure continued until 1881 when he was defeated by Samory Toure. Toure saved King Ibrahima's life but he executed all of his leading supporters including King Vafin Dulleh of Mesiadou, who Anderson had met in 1869 and 1874.

While Samory Toure's defeat of King Ibrahima Sesay might have been a set-back for the expansion project of Liberia all the way to Mesiadou and beyond, another reason was the lack of funding. The government of Liberia had applied for a $50,000.00 loan from the US government to facilitate the expansion project. However, the Representative of the United States in Liberia, John Smyth recommended that the US reject the Liberian government's request. According to him, Liberia was heavily indebted and was not in a position to pay her debtors. When the government of Liberia could not come up with the $50,000.00 that would have financed the expansion project, Benjamin Anderson as director of the Liberia Interior Association made some efforts to raise the money through private initiatives.

Grandpa Nvakaifa Konneh was a lone child, having lost both his parents at a young age. He was raised by his uncles. In his early 20s, he became one of those long distant travelers between the Savannah and the coast, following the same route Benjamin JK Anderson used those days to travel to Mesiadou. He was a trader as well as an Islamic cleric. He ended up in Saclepea in Central Liberia which many years later became part of Nimba County in 1964 as a result of President Tubman's unification policy. There is no written record as to when Grandpa arrived in Saclepea. Before he settled there, he made si-tikala, a special Islamic prayer made by kamohs to know what the future may hold. According to that sitikala, it was revealed to him that Saclepea would grow to become a very important town in years to come. He made some sacrifices. Over the years, the town grew bigger and bigger, fulfilling grandpa's prayer. Any place you go, you can tell people's pioneering status by developments in the center of town. It is in the center of town where our houses are located. Family sources even say that the present day Commissioner Compound in the center of Saclepea was Grandpa's peanut farm. This is supported by the fact that only the main street separates the compound from our houses. One could be standing on one side of the street which is our land looking at the Commissioner Compound on the other side. Grandpa is credited for introducing some farm and garden products in the area.

In 1922, Grandpa Nvakaifa was appointed by President Charles DB King as Marketing Coordinator for Saclepea and its surrounding towns and villages. That was one of the strategies used by the government to bring native people under its control. Grandpa was charged with the responsibility of making sure that various towns and villages brought a variety of items to the market; those who failed were fined. Grandpa's power and influence was mainly due to his work as ka-moh for people who wanted political power. Local political legends such as Johnny Voker of Yah Sonoh, Dahn Gbonwin of Saclepea, and Yenegan from Kanwee sought his help in their quests for prominence and political power. So behind the power and influence of these powerful Mano leaders were really powerful men like my grandfather.

My maternal grandfather, Alhaji Foday Donzo, was born in Jakodu, another of the five towns of Koninya, the Mandingo country. Just like my paternal grandfather, he too was involved in trading between the Savannah, forest and coastal regions. His brother Famod Donzo lived in Saclepea. It is he who raised my mother in Saclepea. At some point, Grandpa Foday decided to move back to Jakodu where he lived until his death in 1974. When her father returned to Jokodu, my mother stayed in Saclepea with her uncle, Famod Donzo. It was there in Saclepea that she got married to Uncle Vasayou and then later on to my father, Ngoamilleh.

When Grandpa Foday moved back to Jakodou, he took several Manos who used to work for him. One of the Mano persons that stayed with grandpa until his death was Lamine. He did not go back to his people. He became part of my grandfather's family. He died several years after grandpa had passed away. The several times I visited Jakodou, I did not ask Lamine to tell me of his family. I really did not know he was a Mano until years later when he was long dead. I was too small when Lamine was alive and there was no way I could think of any such question to ask him. I saw him as just any member of grandpa's family.

Another interesting thing about grandpa is that he was one of those people who walked through the vast expanse of the Sahara Desert to perform pilgrimage in Mecca. They walked through Western Sudan, now Mali, the Sahara Desert, Egypt and then to Arabia. Those days they could not fly or ride a car to cover that distance. The only alternative that they had was to walk in order to fulfill their religious obligation. When grandpa was departing for the long distant journey, he gathered his wives and children to pray for his safe return and if they didn't see him they would meet in the hereafter. Imagine walking from present day Liberia or Guinea all the way to Mecca in Saudi Arabia. Too much sacrifice for one's belief. That's how committed people used to be in whatever they believed.

I am named after my mother's grandfather from her mother's side. His name was Nvasekie Kamara, a powerful chief of Muandou, a town located in the Simandou region not far from Mesiadou. The Kamaras of Simandou share the same blood line with the Kamaras in Quardou Gbonie Mandingo District in Lofa County and those of King Sao Bosso Kamara in Bopolu. They are all descendants of Fonigaman Kamara, a powerful Kamara warrior who once ruled Mesiadou. The Kamaras are leaders and warriors in the Mandingo tradition. Another name for the Kamaras is Jomuanun or Jomandy.

As a little boy in the early 70s when I visited my grandmother Haja Mama Saran Kamara in Jakodou, she took me along with my cousins Ousman Sidibe and his sister Fanta to Muandou. Cousins Ousman and Fanta were visiting her at the same time from Abidjan, Ivory Coast. Their mother Makangbe Donzo was my mother's younger sister who lived there with her husband, Morry Sidibe. Grandma Mama Saran took the three of us to Muandou to see her people. That was my first introduction to the Kamara side of my family. Since I am named after the chief of the town, the people of Muandou used to call me, Doutee, the town owner. My childhood remembrance of Muandou is going to the rice and yam farms of grandma's younger brother Brahima Kamara. I also went, on several occasions, behind the big boys of the town to tend to the cows. In that part of the world, a man's wealth is determined not only by the size of his farm lands but also the number of cows he owns. Grandma's brother, Brahima had more than 100 cows. That made him a very wealthy man and powerful leader within the town, commanding the same level of respect his father, my namesake used to command in Simandou. One night there was a program in front of Grandpa Brahima's house. While everyone was sitting and listening to the kamoh who was preaching in his big yard, I fell asleep on the veranda. It Looked like everyone had forgotten about me or nobody knew that I was sleeping there. It was not until 5 am morning prayer when people came out and saw me sleeping very soundly on the veranda. Grandpa Brahima woke me up and said I should not sleep outside again before the witches eat me. The stories of the witches were very prevalent in the town. I was very scared when they told me how the witches would eat the soul of a person while his physical body would be lying in the room asleep. I was very thankful that the witches did not eat my soul while I was sleeping on the veranda that night.

Another remembrance of that visit was the weekly soirées which brought together the young men and women of the town. Such soirées consisted of someone beating the drums, one or two persons singing and everyone dancing to the beats. At other times in the night, there used to be camp fires around which people would tell tales. Even though I was a little boy, I never wanted to miss those events. For as long I live, I keep those memories alive.

When my paternal grandfather Nvakaifa was born in Beyla sometime around the 1850s, the border we know today separating Liberia and Guinea did not exist. Liberia as a nation was limited to the coastal areas of Monrovia and other settlements. There was no nation called Guinea. The Mandingoes being the long distant travelers and traders they have always been were traveling and trading between the Savannah, forest and coastal regions. Kola nuts which is an important commodity in the African tradition grows in the forest region and was needed everywhere. Mandingoes would travel to the forest region which in the Mandingo language is known as "toukour." They called the coastal area "kougee dahlla." They would buy the kola nuts and other forest products and carry them to the Savannah region. As they came and went, they also brought products from the Savannah region to the forest and the coast. The Condo Confederacy is said to have been formed to facilitate and protect such interactions between the various tribes long before there was a country called Liberia. It was some years later when the French came to claim territories in this part of Africa.

When the border lines were drawn many decades later, between 1911 and 1925 with the French dictating where the border posts should be and powerless Liberia often forced to accept whatever it was dealt with by the French or risk being swallowed by the greedy imperial power, it separated people that had known and interacted with each other into different nations. Where the old concept of country was based on tribes or alliance of tribes, the new concept divided tribes into different nations. Even if that might have been considered noble, the borderlines divided people of the same families. Places like Beyla, Nzérékoré, Dieke, and Macenta that could have formed parts of Liberia fell on the other side of the dividing lines. For instance, in 1892, the agreement between the French and the Liberian government placed Nyosomoridou in Liberia. Anderson passed through there in 1868 on his way to Mesiadou. Today, Nyosomoridou is in Guinea just like Mesiadou and the other five towns of Koninya.

The border line of approximately 350 square miles did not put an abrupt end to the relationship between the people who had dealt with each other through the ages. Manos, Mandingoes, Kpellehs, Lormas and other tribes did not cease to be families. In the case of my grandfather, Nvakaifa Konneh, who was appointed as marketing coordinator by President Charles DB King in 1922, his connection to his kin folks in Beyla did not end. One example of this enduring relationship between tribes across the borders was the series of conferences held between the Manos and Lormas of both Liberia and Guinea during Charles Taylor's regime. Our people in Guinea, Ivory Coast and Sierra Leone are no different from us. It is possible we could have all been citizens of one country. In fact we were the same nation with the Manos, Kpellehs, Lormas and Gissis until the imperial France came and drew the lines. We were the same nation with the Krahns, Gios, and Krus of today's Ivory Coast until the same imperial France came and drew the lines. In light of these facts, it does not make any sense that we will reject and harass these, our own people when they cross those lines to our side. Today in the various European countries that came to divide us into separate nations, one can travel from one country to another without knowing you have entered another country. So why should it be the other way around here?

I am very proud of the fact that I share the multiple heritages of Beyla, Jakodou, Simandou, Saclepea, Tengbene and Kpaytuo. I have romantically referred to these places in poems to show how proud I am of the multiple heritages that connect my past and present. It gives me a great sense of value, knowing where I am coming from and where I am going. It gives me the feeling that I belong to something that goes way back to hundreds of years in African history. For what is a man when he can't trace his heritage through generations? When he can't go any further than his father and mother? It makes me feel genuinely African to know my past and present; a past that can be traced all the way to Ancient Mali.

2

Traditional Quranic School

I SPENT THE JULY VACATION of 1981 helping my mother in the shop in Kpaytuo. Our school in Saclepea, Liberia Molsem Union School, was to reopen on Monday. My mother agreed that I leave on Saturday. She washed my clothes in preparation for school. She had bought me some new clothes and shoes during her last trip to Ganta which she also packed along with the old ones in my suit case. She gave me $10.00, out of which $7.50 was my school tuition, 50 cents for the car fare, and $2.00 for pocket change which was expected to last for a week. Since I didn't have to worry about food, the $2.00 was just enough for a week. Every morning I would buy 10 cents to 20 cents worth of kala or donut. Bread with butter used to cost 15 cents in the tea shop. Or sometimes during recess I would buy milk dust or cooked snails. It was feeling great going back to school.

"Make sure you hold tight to the money for your school fee," she had warned me. I promised to do so.

Our shop was on the main road that ran from Monrovia to Harper, Maryland County. Monrovia to Harper road is the longest road in Liberia. Kpaytuo is one of those towns the road passes through. Depending on where you were travelling, you would stand on the road to wave your hands for the cars to stop. On such a busy road one could wait for cars for as long as 15 to 30 minutes. I waved for the first car; it did not stop because it was full. The second car did not stop. It was the third car that stopped. I said goodbye to my mother and my little sister, Madagbeh. In the next 30 minutes I was in Saclepea at about 4:15pm. I went straight home and deposited my suit case in my mother's room in our big house. Since it was 4pm prayer time, I took my ablution and went to the mosque which was right there in our yard. I greeted everyone after the prayer. As usual, they all inquired about my mother and little sister and I said they were doing very well when I left them in Kpaytuo.

In our big house in Saclepea, all my father's four wives had one room each, but my mother spent most of her time in Kpaytuo managing her business. For my mother, business was good in Kpaytuo more than in Saclepea because she faced less competition there. As a result, my mother would only come to Saclepea when she had to. Since she spent most of the time in Kpaytuo, my father used to share his time between his three wives in Saclepea and my mother in Kpaytuo.

When I went with my brothers and friends to Weh River to swim on Sunday, I had $9.50 in my pocket. I took off my trouser, shirt and shoes and put them on the concrete floor of the bridge under which we used to swim in the river. This bridge was used by cars going to Tappita or Ganta. We used to swim as we looked at the cars passing on the bridge over us. For us living in Saclepea, we would walk for 30 to 45 minutes to reach there. Sometimes we would arrive by 10 in the morning and stay until 4pm. So when we got ready to go home, I checked in my trouser's pocket only to realize that someone had stolen the money. I raised the alarm to get everyone's attention. I told them that I had my school fee of $7.50 plus $2.00 in my pocket. Everyone was concerned, but whoever stole the money was not identified. I had to wait until my mother came to Saclepea market on Tuesday to let her know that my tuition had been stolen. She gave me the replacement for the tuition but not without some spanking for not acting wise by taking the money to Weh River. She asked me all kinds of questions, why didn't I leave the money at home, why didn't I give the money to one of her mates to keep it for me.

My mother was a very hard working woman. Not only did she have the shop in Kpaytuo, she used to make donuts to sell in the morning in front of her shop. She would travel to Ganta to buy goods in the Lebanese stores for her shop in Kpaytuo. On the lumber company's pay days, she would carry goods there for the workers to buy. My mother's motto was "work or do anything to get money but don't cheat, steal, or kill anyone." Even though she could not read or write, she valued education very much. Both she and my father were serious about my education, but they had different agendas. While my mother favored the traditional Quranic School, my father favored the western school. My father was one of the first in Saclepea to send his children to western school. All along in Liberia the Mandingoes had rejected regular western schools for fear their children would be indoctrinated against their culture and tradition. The schools either ran by the government or the missionaries were seen to be negative influences for their children. Some people went to the extent of saying that if you sent your child to these "schools of the infidels" you would burn in hell because it was against Islam and its teaching. Despite all that fear of defiling the tradition or burning in hell, my father sent my brothers to western schools. When my father sent his children to the "infidel" schools, he was criticized by some people. All schools that were not traditional Quranic schools were either an infidel school, Jewish school or Christian school.

While my father favored these "infidel schools," my mother favored the Traditional Quranic schools. She didn't like the fact that my father had sent my brothers to such schools. When she told my father her plan for me, he did not like it, but somehow he went along with her. It's because of that, Quranic School became my first learning experience. After one year of Traditional Quranic study in Saclepea, my mother sent me to Beyla where she thought I could get the best education to be a kamoh. It was in Beyla I developed a strong reading habit. With my golden voice, people would admire me and come from places far and near just to listen to me read the Quran and Kitab. As one of the bright students at the Traditional Quranic School, I used to write my lesson on wah, a wooden slate with homemade ink called duba. I used to have one of the longest wahs among the students and would on daily basis write on both sides passages from the Holy Quran. I had very good penmanship.

While I was going to the traditional Quranic School, and doing very well, my mother was so proud of me. It was her hope that I would master the Holy Quran to become a Kamoh, a well learned scholar of Islam, who would one day pray over her body and preach to thousands of people. Being sent away to Beyla was a source of constant quarrel between my mother and my father. When I came home in 1977, my father sat me down in the shop in Kpaytuo and said that he didn't want me to go back to Beyla and that I should stay and go to the kind of schools my brothers were attending. He said to me, "Think about it seriously because your mother will make you a stranger in your own country and I don't want that to happen." By that he meant that if I remained in Beyla and grew to be a man, I would definitely be called a "foreigner" in Liberia. He went further to say, "I want you to go to school, so you will be able to fulfill your citizenship obligation as a Liberian." It was because of that conversation with my father that I left the traditional Quranic School to start the Madrassa and English study at the Moslem Union School in Saclepea in 1978. One would have thought that my father had won the battle over my mother, but my mother could not give up so easily. When school closed in 1978, she sent me back to Beyla again. It was at the end of 1979 that I returned back to Saclepea. Over the years I have come to appreciate both my father and mother because they both meant well for me. Both made their decisions based on their understandings and limitations. Limitation in this sense applied more to my mother because she was thinking along the lines considered by the culture and tradition that nurtured her, while my father was thinking outside the box. Moslem Union School or madrassa which became my next learning experience combined both the Quranic study and the Western education.

Speaking of "madrassa" as mentioned above, the idea or concept of it for us has evolved over the years and the way we define and understand it is different from the ideological madrassas promoted today in some Moslem countries. For us, madrassa simply means school, nothing more, and nothing less. In the traditional Quranic School, we were only taught how to read the Quran. Students were not divided into classes as was done in madrassa. You could find 20 to 50 students each one reading different verses and chapters of the Quran. Each morning, each student would go to the kamoh (teacher) and read the lesson of the previous day. When the kamoh was satisfied, he would let the student repeat after him his lesson for the day. The students would come one after the other to meet with the kamoh. For the Quranic schools, session would start early in the morning, immediately after the morning prayer and lasted until 8 to 9'O clock.

The goal of the Quranic School was to teach the fundamental knowledge of Islam. For instance, knowing how to read and recite the verses and chapters of the Holy Quran, kitabs and how to conduct prayer. For the vast majority of the Traditional Quranic students, this was just enough. Some of them ended up being traders, tailors, farmers, drivers, carpenters, mechanics, etc. Others would go all the way to become kamohs, teaching, preaching and propagating Islam through evangelism. They would travel from place to place preaching to crowds in front of the mosques in the night. Some highly educated ones would end up being kamohs who would pray for people who came to them with various issues. Some clients want to be rich and some want promotions at their jobs. Others want to obtain important government positions. All these people who come with all these concerns and issues have to pay the kamoh for his service. Some kamohs receive enough money through this to provide a good living for themselves and their families.

Even though everyone is encouraged to go to the mosque, people can pray by themselves in the privacy of their own homes. For the women, the goal of traditional education was to only learn how to conduct prayer. They were not expected to be evangelizing or to be kamohs. Women were prepared to be educated in being obedient housewives. They could also be traders traveling from place to place with goods or they could be market women selling objects in the markets. They could also be shopkeepers like my mother.

Madrassa on the other hand, runs like regular school except that the main courses were the Quranic study, kitabs, and Islamic knowledge all taught in Arabic. Students were divided into classes based on their competence. The first year I ever attended madrassa was the year English learning was introduced into the system. That year was 1978. While the Arabic classes ran in the traditional manners, English classes taught courses as they were within the Liberian school system.

Our madrassa became part of the schools within the School District of Saclepea. Our Arabic teacher was Austaz Aleo Sanoe and our first English teacher was Mr. Lincoln G. Nya. He taught us ABC, S-O So and other lessons designed for primary school students in the Liberian school system. In those early days when English was introduced in our madrassa, I could not speak a word of it. My only language of communication was my native tongue, Mandingo.

One of the first English phrases I heard people saying was, "you joking." Even though I didn't know what it meant, I was nonetheless fascinated by the sound of the phrase. I said it to myself repeatedly, wondering what it meant. One day I said it to one of my cousins, Musa Konneh. When he repeated it back to me, I kicked him, thinking he had cussed me. When he was crying, he ran to one of our teachers, a Ghanaian by the name of Crown T. Gbetti Sapa, who enquired about what had happened. Musa reported to the teacher that I kicked him after he repeated my newfound phrase. Without telling any one of us the meaning, the teacher told me to show my hand. He gave me five lashes, told me not to bother my cousin Musa anymore and sent us back to class. Another teacher that left an indelible mark on me at the Moslem Union School in Saclepea was Richmond Konneh, my cousin. When he graduated from the Sanniquellie Central High in 1981, he took up a teaching job at our madrassa. One of the first lessons he gave us was about the Egyptian Civilization from the book, "Ancient Africa." That book is responsible for my fascination with history. It is because of the lessons in this book that History became my favorite subject.

For most students attending the madrassa, the goal was to obtain scholarships for further studies in the various Arab countries such as Saudi Arabia, Kuwait, Egypt or Syria. The madrassa had few options for its graduates most of whom used to end up being teachers or imams in the mosques. The administrators of the various madrassa school systems realized the shortcomings of that policy. That's why they introduced English learning. This gave students many options. They could branch off to regular Liberian schools or even if they went to Saudi Arabia, they had the advantage of learning other subjects in English. Many of those who only studied Arabic and went to Saudi

Arabia found themselves today at a disadvantage because it's hard for them to find any meaningful employment outside of madrassa or the mosque in Liberia. Some of their counterparts who studied both Arabic and English have earned degrees from the University of Liberia. Others have gone on to obtain advanced degrees from universities in Europe and America. One example of this is Mohammed Bility, who is a teacher in New York. In Liberia today, prominent Liberian Mandingoes such as Associate Justice Kabineh Janneh, and Varfley Dulleh, a University of Liberia student activist turned politician are products of the Moslem Congress High School where Arabic and English are taught. The Holland based Liberian writer, Vamba Sherif, who has written several books in Dutch, is a product of madrassa from Liberia as well.

One of the lasting memories I have of the Liberian Moslem School in Saclepea is the last visit of President Tolbert. He visited the school several months before his death in the April 12, 1980 coup. The president was on a tour and our madrassa happened to be on his schedule. We dressed in our crisp blue and white uniforms and lined up at the entrance of the school from the main road going to Bahn. We waited so patiently long for the president to show up. Soon the motorcade appeared and it came to a stop. The president got down from the car dressed in his famous white suit with a broad smile, waving to us, the happy students. He proceeded to the structure built of palm thatches where seating arrangement was made for the president and other dignitaries with him. Walking along side the president as he waved to the cheering young students was Mariam Foday, my cousin and one of the female students of the madrassa. She looked beautiful in her school uniform as she walked alongside the President of Liberia. While seated, the president and his entourage were serenaded with beautiful Arabic and English songs. Only some of the wordings of the English songs had stayed with me all these year. "O Mr. President, you are welcome here today, O Mr. President, you are welcome here today. O you are welcome O welcome; O you are welcome here today." That day was a great day in the history of our madrassa. Not too long after this visit, the president was assassinated.

3

Under the Bright Moonlight

IT WAS AROUND 8pm, Tuesday night. I was sitting in my mother's shop interacting with customers coming in and going out. My mother had gone to the mosque to pray. Earlier in the day, some friends and I had argued for hours about whether I was going to join the new organization they were forming and I had told them I would not. Now sitting in my mother's shop this night taking care of the customers, I saw my friend Kalu Donzo walking in with a broad smile on his face. I suspected that something might be going on and whatever it was it had to be a happy occasion. When he got close to me, he told me he had brought a "special message" to me from Sumaila Toure. Sumaila Toure was one of our big brothers in the town of Saclepea. He and my brothers were equal and I was kind of surprised as to what kind of "special message" should come from that man to me. I used to see him but except to say good morning or good evening when we passed each other on the streets, there was no conversation between the brother and myself.

I told Kalu to wait until my mother came back from the mosque. While we waited, I asked Kalu to tell me why Sumaila wanted to see me. When he wouldn't tell me why, I told him to go ahead and I would follow him when my mother had returned from the mosque.

When my mother returned from the mosque, I told her that my friend and I were going out. Once she agreed Kalu and I were on our way. I could still see excitement in Kalu's face as we walked from the shop in the center of town to the area around Saclepea Market where Mr. Toure lived. Still he wouldn't tell me why. As we approached the bright light emanating from the florescent lamp with a crowd sitting around, I was not sure of what this was all about. To my utmost surprise, the crowd started chanting, "Presso! Presso! Presso!" They had made me president without getting my approval. Sumaila showed me the special seat they had set for me. From now on, he told me, I was the president of The Golden Boys, a youth football club. Even though I didn't want to be the president, the respect shown to me this night was too magnanimous to reject.

I was not one of the star players of the team but for some reason the overwhelming majority of the members wanted me to be the president. All of this started a year before with another team, Hafia 80, for which I was the president for more than a year. As I was serving as the president of Hafia 80, some fellows suggested a name change from Hafia 80 to Golden Boys. I was opposed to this. The truth is that it really didn't matter to me what they called the team. I was not a player that the team was depending on and I could care less. I had threatened to stay away from the new organization because as far I was concerned, the end of Hafia 80 was the end of it for me.

So despite my threat not to be part of the new organization, they went ahead anyway to make me their president, thinking that once the vehicle got on the road, I would be there to get on board. With me being cheered up by the crowd of boys and girls, with every one of them singing my praise and telling me to sit in the specially arranged seat with big brother Sumaila Toure beside me, this was a respect and honor I could not reject. That night, other officials were named, with Layee Kaifa Bility becoming vice president, Meh Chemoh Kamara, the speaker and the least title went to Musa Bility, the youngest person among us. He was named the jersey boy. Musa used to be with his own crowd of boys, our junior brothers who had their own team called Young IE, headed by one of my younger brothers, Kafumba Konneh. His friends said that Musa's only interest in accepting the jersey boy position in Golden Boys was because he wanted to get close to the girls. The truth is, Musa had his way with the girls and he liked to be around them.

Our team went places and we hosted other teams from out of town. We went to Ganta, Bahn, Tappita, and Zontuo, all towns in Nimba County. The only place we visited outside of Nimba County was Palala, Bong County. On these occasions, all I did was cheer for my boys on the field and gave self-important speeches at the dinner receptions after the games. Before such programs, we would consult the dictionary for the big words that would make us sound bookish. Sometimes we used the wrong words but because it was a big word, no one cared about the meaning and usage. The fact that you could use several 'big words' was enough to solidify your reputation among your friends. They would cheer you on as the man who knew book.

One of the leaders among the Golden Girls was my sister, Makanibua. The girls were the backbone of the Golden Boys. When we had visitors from other places, we would go from house to house collecting cups of rice and 25 cents or 50 cents from each of the boys and the girls would buy ingredients for the soup and cook the food for our guests. The girls would serve our guests with food and drinks during the receptions. During the play on the field, they would stand behind the goal posts cheering the team. With the girls singing behind them, the players would become highly motivated in playing the ball on the field. We were always at a disadvantage when we went to other places, because our girls would not be there to cheer us on. The girls of our competitors would be there supporting their teams. That's called home advantage because no one in any town would want other people coming out of town to beat them. So you have to cheer your home town boys when they are playing.

On those occasions, our sponsor, Sumaila Toure made his bus available to take us places. Team members would hustle and put their nickels and dimes together and wherever we stopped, Mr. Toure as the sponsor would balance the amounts and buy the team jersey and sponsor our out of town trips. This was the same if we were hosting out of town teams in Saclepea.

So, when I was introduced that night as the president, Mr. Toure called me aside and told me he heard that I was reluctant to accept the position as president. He advised that I accept it because my friends had put their trust in me. He said the support of the boys and girls meant that not only did they trust me but they loved me as well. He explained that it was part of God's blessing for my brothers and sisters to cheer me on as their leader. With all the advice, I promised my commitment to the Golden Boys. The morning after the meeting, the Golden Boys was the topic of discussion among the boys and girls of our madrassa. During the recess, I was still being mobbed by friends with congratulatory messages and hugs and the chant: "Presso! Presso! Presso!" Up until I transferred to Buchanan in early 1984, I was the president of Golden Boys and Girls.

One of the consequences of my becoming president for Golden Boys is that it stopped me from driving wheelbarrow on Saclepea market days. As a wheelbarrow boy, I used to take people's goods and loads from one point to another. That's how I generated pocket change so I could be able to buy bread, cups of sardine, condensed milk, butter, or go to the tea shops and cook shops. Even when I moved to Kpaytuo with my mother, I used to come to Saclepea market to drive my wheelbarrow around on market day. One day my wheelbarrow driving career came to an abrupt end when one of the Golden Girls saw me and said, "Mr. President, you are the one driving wheelbarrow in town?" The way she said it meant as if to say driving wheelbarrow was beneath my status as president for the club. That was the last time I ever drove wheelbarrows to earn money. I was probably between 14 and 15 years of age. Even though I depended on my mother for everything, I liked to earn and have my own pocket change so I didn't have to run to her asking for 10 cents to buy kala (a kind of bread made out of rice and plantain). But now this girl thought that I was too good to be driving wheelbarrows in town.

For any member of my generation, Mandingo or Mano, no accounts of our experience of growing up in Saclepea would be complete without mentioning Aleo Donzo. Aleo Donzo touched our lives in so many ways. He was the man behind most activities in town that involved the young people. Talk about our biggest football club, the Black Star, Aleo Donzo was the man. Talk about the weekly social dances either on Johnny Voker High School campus or at the Commissioner Compound, Aleo Donzo was the man. Talk about our cultural performance group, Lanaya Club, Aleo Donzo was the man. Talk about the first TV and Video club in town, he was the man. Besides all these aforementioned, Aleo Donzo directly or indirectly sponsored many students, both Manos and Mandingoes. For the most part, Mano youths coming from outlaying villages and towns to attend schools in Saclepea, depended partially or wholly on the generosity of Aleo Donzo. Not only did he provide notebooks, pens and uniforms; he also provided money and food. He was a philanthropist.

Aleo Donzo was the store manager for the biggest store in Saclepea. The Donzo Store's only competitors were the Lebanese stores that used to be in town. By 1976 all the Lebanese were gone, leaving the Donzo Store as the biggest store in town. His senior brother, Alhaji Amara Donzo owned the store. From the time I was a little boy, going to Donzo Store to buy Kool Aids was my favorite pastime. Way back in the late 70s, the ice cube kool aids were sold for 2 Cents. Every time I had 2 Cents I would run to the store to buy kool aids. All kinds of flavors used to be there. As we grew up, we went beyond buying kool aids. We started buying Fanta, Coca Cola, chocolate milk, sardines, and condensed milk. Since the Donzos are my maternal uncles, many times if I didn't have money, I would go to get some items for free. It was not easy to approach Old man Donzo but it was easy to ask a favor from his little brother, Aleo Donzo. As one of his nephews, he did not disappoint me any time.

Back then we used to sing a song called "Aleo is a rich man, Amara is a poor man." The real meaning of this song was that the old man who owned the store and arguably the richest man in town used to love being simple and ordinary. It was Aleo Donzo who was living large. You would walk by and if you didn't know the old man before, you would not think of him as being the rich man. On the other hand, Aleo was young and involved in many social activities. He had a big sound system at the store that played the latest records from Nigeria, Guinea, Ivory Coast and Congo. Sometimes just for the music alone, the Donzo Store used to be a popular hangout spot in Saclepea. The store was the main attraction in town and it was difficult for anyone to spend a day without going through there. It functioned both as a retail and wholesale store. People who operated shops in villages outside of Saclepea used to come buy goods in the Donzo Store for their shops in their villages. Aleo Donzo and his brother were children of the late old man Funcia Donzo of Ganta, one of the brothers of my grandpa, Foday Donzo of Jakodou.

The Black Star Soccer Team was the major team in town. It could boast of many good players such as Joseph Marshall, Richmond Konneh, Solomon Donzo, Musa Koisiah, and one of my uncles, Mohammed Konneh (Siami Muadee). Every time Black Stars played out of town teams, it was a happy occasion. Aleo would take the sound system out to celebrate the victories. At some point, Lassana Kenneh popularly called Jomo Kenyata formed a rival team called Saclepea Special Sports Association (Triple S). When Jomo Kenyata had several cars running for him, he thought he could compete with Aleo Donzo. That's why he formed the Triple S but the team did not go too far. When he became broke, that was the end of Triple S. It was the Black Star that remained in action until the war.

The first time I saw TV was in 1983 when I went to Butuo, a border town along the Ivorian border. I had gone there with one of my aunts to sell goods in the market. The children in Butuo used to go to the compound of a Lebanese man, Dakah, to watch programs on RTI, Radio Television of Ivory Coast. My second encounter with TV was when Aleo Donzo brought one in town. In the evenings, we would go to Aleo Donzo's house to watch sports, music, and other activities going on in Ivory Coast. Even though we lived in Liberia, when it came to TV, only Ivory Coast we could depend on. If there was a television station in Liberia, that was limited to people in Monrovia and its environs. Then one day Old man Donzo went on his first visit to the United States in the mid 80s, he brought back a big screen TV and video deck for his brother, Aleo. With that, Aleo started a nightly show of the latest Indian, American and Chinese movies. The video show took the place of the traveling movie projectors other people used to bring to town.

During the Ramadan and Sacrifice of Abraham celebrations as well as welcoming ceremonies for important government officials coming to town, our gbombay club, Lanaya used to entertain. The performance consisted of the big drum and several smaller drums. The best drummer of our time was Bakali Sesay and the best dancer was my own brother Vasayou Konneh. Later on we had Solomane Kromah. Over the years in Lanaya Club, there were several female singing sensations. Among them were Mawata, her sister Yayea Kamara, children of my mother's uncle Alhaji Moli Kamara and one of my own cousins, Musu Konneh. These girls had the sweetest voices. They could sing our traditional Mandingo songs very well. The women, our aunts and sisters were heavily involved in Lanaya more than the soccer club. When Black Star played, the women would cheer the players on the field but it was the Lanaya program that the women dominated. Even though we the men danced, most of the dancing was done by the women. Every major town in Nimba, Bong or Grand Gedeh counties had its own gbombay club as well.

The president for Lanaya Club was Amara Fofana who we used to call Amara K. Doe. Yes, his name was Amara Fofana but since he was very popular with the members of Lanaya Club, the members thought he was our own version of President Samuel K Doe who was at that time a very popular president of Liberia. Amara K. Doe was in the height of his immense popularity when he died in a tragic car accident. Everyone in our community was sad because of K. Doe's death.

It was one or two years later in 1986 that our big brothers decided to "retire" from the leadership of Lanaya Club. We the younger brothers were to take over the club. There were two contenders for the leadership; myself and Losene Kromah. I had the supports of the boys and Losene had the support of the girls. The difference between the two of us was that I was in the 11th Grade and Losene was a 6th grade dropout. He was a driver driving for Saye Gblee who was a staff member of the Nimba County Rural Development Project (NCRDP). My supporters were Musa Bility, my cousin Ayouba Konneh and Ismail Fofana among others. They were against the fact that an "illiterate fool" like Losene would be our president. The girls did not see it that way. To them Losene was the best candidate. The voices of the girls were important in this decision making for the fact that when it came to paying money to support the club, they carried the lion share. The young girls and our aunts favored Losene and urged me to be the vice president. There was an impasse for more than a month with everyone standing his or her grounds. In order to break that impasse,

I called a meeting with my supporters and told them I was willing to accept the vice president position if that would bring peace among us. My men didn't want to hear that. How could a 6th grade dropout be the president for those of us going to school in grades between 7th and 11th grades? The girls who supported him were not going to school. Another factor to Losene's popularity was that he was dating Musu Konneh, the singer for the club. I was able to convince my supporters that Losene should be the president but the rest of the positions would be occupied by us. We settled for that and peace returned in the community. On one occasion when the Eagle Club visited us from Gbarnga, the president, Losene Kromah, was called to speak. He was so clueless with the broken English that I was called to rescue the situation. He was so embarrassed and every one of us felt embarrassed in front of our visitors because our president could not express himself. When we had the queen contest closed to the end of 1987, it was the same. I had to rescue the president to save the town from embarrassment.

4

Kpaytuo

ONE DAY IN 1984 IN KPAYTUO when my mother had traveled to Ganta to buy some goods, I was eating with one of my Gio friends in the shop. While we were eating, one of the elderly Mandingoes in the town happened to come in. He stood for a long time looking at us suspiciously as if to say we were guilty of something. Without saying a word, he left. I knew what I was guilty of. I am a Moslem, and my Gio friend was not. Most of the time, I used to go to the old man's house to eat. His wife would bring his food, and I would bring with me what my mother had cooked. As Mandingoes, it is part of our culture and tradition to eat together. There is nothing more proud to a Mandingo man, especially an elderly person than to have many people eating together from the same pan. That establishes his authority, his sense of value. Since the old man was always eating by himself, he thought it would be a good idea for me to join him whenever I could.

What separated me and my Gio friends of Kpaytuo is the fact that I am a Moslem and they were not. Because of my religious faith, drinking liquor or eating dog and pork are strictly forbidden. The worst act of moral transgression in the Liberian Moslem community is to be found drinking alcohol or eating pork. That can lead to being ostracized by the community. That is the worst shame you can bring upon your family. And when you are noted for drinking liquor, it would be ruled that you can no longer eat with your brothers and sisters from the same pan.

My Gio friends on the other hand had no such moral restriction. Many of them didn't belong to any religion. Not even Christianity, which is the dominant religion of Liberia. For them drinking liquor and eating dog or pork was normal. So in the eyes of the Mandingoes who are Moslems, one should not eat in the same pan with those who can drink liquor, eat dog or taste pork. That's why the old man was surprised, or I should say offended, when he saw me and my Gio friend eating together. Without saying a word, I could tell from the expression on his face that he was disappointed.

Even though I understood and respected the old man's reaction and the reason behind it, I would feel very uncomfortable to apply that rule with friends who were with me every day. I justified my action with the view that at the moment we were eating, I had not seen them drinking any liquor, eating dog or tasting pork. In the eyes of the Gios, this is discrimination. In the eyes of the Mandingoes, they are living and acting according to the dictate of their religion, Islam. This is a religious and cultural difference which is at times the source of misunderstanding between the Mandingoes and their neighbors here and in different parts of Liberia. Sometimes some may choose to overlook those differences in order to maintain harmonious relationships with their neighbors. That's why it didn't trouble me when I ate with my Gio friends in Kpaytuo. Having lived in America now for some years, I have come to understand that the best justification on the part of the Mandingoes should be sanitary concern. A Gio man living here in America will not want to drink from the same cup I have just drunk from. He will want that cup to be thoroughly washed before he can drink from it. Even in the so called civilized homes in Liberia, people eat from their own plates and drink from their own cups. Hygienically, that's the right thing to do. When this is based on hygienic reasons, it will be considered normal rather than when it's based on ethnicity and religion. Any other way it's considered discriminatory.

While Saclepea is my home in Liberia, I also consider Kpaytuo a home because I partially grew up there. We have houses there as we do in Saclepea. Many Mandingoes living in big towns and cities maintained residence in neighboring small towns and villages. During kola and produce seasons, they would go to those small towns and villages. Kpaytuo has been such a place for my family for a very long time. But unlike some Mandingoes who would only go to those small towns and villages during produce and kola buying seasons, we were permanent in Kpyatuo. It was where Uncle Vasayou, my father's big brother used to live. We have been there for generations. We had houses and businesses there up until the war broke out. The difference between Saclepea and Kpaytuo is that Saclepea was a mixed Mano and Mandingo town. On the other hand, Kpaytuo was a Gio town with few Mandingo residents. In Saclepea, most of my friends were Mandingoes. In Kpaytuo, my friends were Gios. As a young Mandingo boy growing up in Kpaytuo, I had no choice. Among my Gio friends were Solomon Yormie and his brother Mathew Yormie, Charles Kpanga, John Pulor and another John whose last name I can't remember now. There I had only two Mandingo friends between 15 to 16 years of age. They were Brahima Kamara and Sekou Kamara. At some point, Brahima passed away and Sekou went to Monrovia to live with his biological father.

I attended Kpaytuo Public School (KPS) on two different occasions, 3rd and 9th grade in 1980 and 1984. I was the class secretary in my 3rd grade class at KPS. The fellow who was the class president met me one day in my mother's shop and requested a favor from me. Having rendered that favor, he appointed me a secretary as a way of payback for my kind gesture. My job as a secretary was to write the names of noise makers and turn them in to our class sponsor. In the Liberian school system, a class sponsor is equivalent to a home room teacher. Noise makers would be required to come back on campus after school to cut grass. I had to be there to assign each one his or her portion of grass to cut. One day I wrote the name of a fellow and when I came later on to assign his portion of grass to cut, he decided to beat me up. He was bigger than me and I am sure he would have beaten me severely. I was scared of him but I had to write his name because he was becoming an outlaw in the class. By the time this fellow was ready to put his hands on me, our class sponsor, Peter Beah was there. He warned the fellow that if he beat me he would cut three times the size of the portion of the grass I had assigned him. After the school year of 1980, I briefly went back to Liberia Moslem Union

School in 1981 but later on transferred to Johnny Voker Elementary School. At JVS, I received a double promotion from 4th to 6th grade.

When I came back to KPS in 1984, I was in the 9th grade. I had completed 7th grade in JVS the previous year and was promoted to 8th grade. In 1984, I moved to Buchanan, Grand Bassa County to live with my big brother, Bankalie Konneh who was working at the government hospital as a physician assistant. I started the 1984 school year at St. John Episcopal School in Lower Buchanan. I liked Buchanan, one of the largest cities of Liberia, but I was not used to the restricted life at my brother's house. I didn't like it and I told my brother I wanted to go back to Saclepea. In Saclepea or Kpaytuo, I enjoyed freedom which I didn't have in Buchanan. Here my brother and his wife wanted me to be home at a certain time. They didn't want any friends to visit me. Particularly for his wife Anita, any friend that visited me was supposedly a rogue and I should not be bringing rogues in the house. She would want me to wash dishes, do their dirty cloths and the floor. All of these things made me to hate Buchanan and I didn't want to live there. Whenever I went out, I used to breathe freedom but when I returned home, I would feel depressed. The moment I saw the house, my heart would pound. I felt so uncomfortable in such an environment, it made me feel like a prisoner.

In Buchanan, my brother and his wife were living a typical middle class life compared to what life was like in the interior. They lived in a well furnished house close to the Atlantic Ocean. I always used to enjoy the sound of the ocean waves in the night. The house was a few blocks away from the Atlantic Avenue and the Grand Odeon Cinema in Lower Buchanan. There were 24 hours light, running water, a nice bathroom with a bath tub, TV and book shelves filled with books of all kinds. Anita, my brother's wife, was a teacher and was a voracious reader. Buchanan was the first place where I was introduced to the modern way of life. The house was a paradise compared to what our house looked like in Saclepea. In Buchanan, I used a commode. In Saclepea, it was a pit latrine. In the house in Saclepea, we had more than 20 people living under one roof. In Buchanan, it was just me, my brother and his wife, and her two sisters. The fact that I had to share the task of dish washing, floor cleaning, and washing clothes with these two girls felt insulting to me. In Saclepea, I had my sister Makanibua or girlfriends to wash my clothes. Sometimes my mother would. Compared to that, Buchanan was a different environment and I could not feel comfortable with that. That's why I told my brother that I would prefer to go back to Saclepea. I preferred my freedom in the darkness in Saclepea than servitude and restriction in the light in Buchanan. That was the thought on my mind when I met my brother and his wife sitting on the porch overlooking the street and I did not hesitate to tell them. They were surprised that I would reject the "quee" life of Buchanan to return to Saclepea where there was no light, or commode in the bathroom.

They asked me why and I told them that I felt like I was in prison and wanted my freedom. I was going to rebel, refuse to do all that my brother's wife wanted me to do and I didn't want my refusal to create problems between him and his wife. I didn't want it to be explained that because of me he and his wife were having problems. To avoid all that, I advised them to send me back to Saclepea. As a reaction to my action, my brother said that he didn't want me to stay in Saclepea. He demanded that I go to stay with my mother in Kpaytuo. Was he thinking that by sending me to Kpaytuo, he would make me change my mind? Kpaytuo was a small town compared to Saclepea. To people living in Kpaytuo Saclepea was a city. Some people in Saclepea considered Kpaytuo a bush. At that moment, I preferred to live in total freedom in Kpaytuo than the big city of Buchanan.

When I got to Kpaytuo, instead of continuing in 8th grade, I decided to take 9th grade. Taking 8th grade would mean two consecutive years in the "bush," something I didn't want. I could tolerate one year, not two. As I said before, this was my second time at KPS. I knew all the teachers except for a few who were new to the school. Two of my favorite teachers were Peter Beah and Joseph Lablah. I learnt that Mr. Lablah was a Mano from Guinea but nobody cared because he was very good at his subject, English. Peter Beah was jovial. When he used to give out test papers, he would divide them into billie goats, nanny goats, and sheep. Failing grades were classified as either billie goats or nanny goats. Teacher Beah would start with the billie and nanny goats. He would call the students name and ask the class what kind of goat. The students would say it based on the sex of the student whose name was called.

I was much involved in extra-curricular activities at KPS. I was one of the newscasters for the school, working with my friends Chris Zogbay, James Bleetan, and Satia Tallaford. I participated in dramas and performed poetic recitations. At the end of the 1984 school year, I passed with flying colors, doing very well in both the school and national exams. Upon my graduation, Satia Tallaford, Chris Zogbay, and I continued at JVS in Saclepea.

I remember one incidence in Kpaytuo that put me in a kind of embarrassing situation. One day I was in the shop when a Gio friend came to ask me for the meaning of some Mandingo words, "nyafuan mini," meaning someone with crossed eyes. I told him the meaning. I didn't ask him why but what I learnt later was that a Mandingo woman had said this to him. He decided to find out the meaning. That's why he came to me, his friend. I was told that he planned to sue the woman and expected me to be his witness. The woman was a relative of mine and my only relationship with the Gio fellow was that we were school mates. Where should my loyalty be, to family or to friend? I would be a traitor if I testified against this relative of mine. And my Gio friend would say I sided with her because we were of the same tribe.

I told my relative she was wrong and I apologized to my Gio friend. Other relatives got involved to calm the situation down. I even had to bribe the fellow with something to let it go.

5 | The Day Quiwonkpa Died

I STILL REMEMBER EXACTLY where I was when, the former Commanding General of the Armed Forces of Liberia, Gen. Thomas Quiwonkpa announced on November 12, 1985 that he had overthrown President Samuel Doe and taken over the government. It was Tuesday, Saclepea's market day. I had left our house early in the morning to go to the market. When I reached in front of the Donzo Store opposite the gas station next to the commissioner compound, I saw a group of people huddled around a radio. Out of curiosity, I stopped to see what was going on. Then I heard the general who was also known as The Strong Man speaking. According to him, he had come to liberate us from the dictatorial regime of Samuel Doe. He called on the "men and women of the armed forces, the police and the security agencies to join with us in the liberation of our people from fear, brutality, and blood tyranny. I call on the students, the workers, and all patriotic citizens to stand with us as we do battle against the forces of injustice and corruption."

I liked what I heard and was excited about the change. I could see the same excitement in the eyes of other people who were around the radio. From there all the way to the market, I could see the same level of excitement in the air. Somehow, things seem normal to me. It felt to me the real coup had taken place after so many years when Doe manufactured many coups as a way of getting rid of his perceived enemies who he would grab, put in jail, and then grant them executive clemency. Now he had finally gotten what a long time was coming for him. In my view, he had gotten the taste of his own bitter medicine, pure and simple. Coups in my eyes were Africa's version of democracy because that was the only means by which change could occur in leadership of a given country. African leaders can't give up so easily. The hope is to stay in power forever. So in the absence of transparent process by which a leader can be elected, the only way we can have change is if either a leader dies through natural death or he's overthrown. And since the civilians have proven powerless to effect change, it's the soldiers with the guns who have stepped in. This is the democracy of the strong crushing the weak. Doe overthrew Tolbert, and now Quiwonkpa had overthrown Doe. That's normal to me except when it involves the life of ordinary people who may not be president or ministers.

Between the place where people were huddled around the radio and to the market where I was heading, I was thinking, Doe, your time is over; it's now Quiwonkpa's time to rule. Case closed; let's move on as if life has always been normal.

When Samuel Doe and his group of 17 men overthrew President Tolbert, cut his throat, dumped his body in an unmarked grave and followed that with the execution of 13 former ministers, life went back to normal. Why should anything be different now? I looked at the same old sky and it was still the same as it had been thousands of years before I was born. Let the world be normal, presidents come and presidents go. That's how we do things in Africa. Instead of electing presidents for some years and allowing a different president to take over, we have to chase or kill one leader before another one can get to power.

At the market, I saw a fellow who was overzealously excited like he was part of what was going on in Monrovia. He sounded as if to say he had just talked to Gen. Quiwonkpa. This guy was talking to everyone that had time to listen to him and he sounded serious, demonstrating his own self-importance. Did he go to Quiwonkpa in Monrovia and Quiwonkpa told him the coup was already successful and that he should come to Saclepea and be his mouthpiece, I wondered. Did Quiwonkpa even know him? I doubt it. What was it that gave this guy the self-confidence to go around the market telling people what they would do in the night? I could not fathom what this guy was saying. Whatever plan he had gave him the audacity to say, with definite surety, that when the night time came they would drive the Mandingoes from town and "send them to Guinea." If everything about the coup had sounded normal to me, what I was hearing from this guy didn't sound normal. Doe was supposed to have been killed or hiding; and Quiwonkpa was supposed to be the president and what did all that have to do with being Mandingo? He made it sound like Quiwonkpa was president for only the Manos and Gios and not for Mandingoes; hence the threat to expel them like Idi Amin did to the Ugandans of Indian origin in Uganda. I could not believe what this man was saying. Is it because he was drunk with excitement that he would go around making these kinds of threatening statements as if to say he was the spokesman for the new regime? Was this threat to expel the Mandingoes part of Quiwonkpa's agenda? How could that be when he even named Capt. Mamadee Finneh, a Mandingo, as one of his appointees?

As he talked, he turned around to look this way and that way as if to say he was talking to a wider audience of people everywhere around him. And then our eyes met. I did not hesitate to show that I had heard what he was saying. We were happy that a change had taken place and a son of Nimba County was at the helm and we all should be celebrating and at the same time praying and hoping for better days to come for all of us. When he realized that I had heard what he was saying, he tried to assure and reassure me that when they say the Mandingoes would be driven out of town, he's not talking about my grandfather, "Moley Kaifa's children" who he considered as true sons and daughters of the soil. He said they all recognized that my grandfather was one of the pioneers in the making of Saclepea. He said no Mano of Saclepea would ever harm us in any way be- cause we are their nephews and nieces, my father and some of his brothers and sisters being the children of Mano women. He said we were different from other Mandingo people. As I saw it, he was try- ing to separate the sheep from the goats, when at the end of the day they are all animals. He kind of reminded me of my teacher Peter Beah in Kpaytuo who separated his class into billie goats, nanny goats and sheep. So in this case, we the children, grand children and great grandchildren of old man Nvaskaifa and his Mano women were the sheep and the rest of the Mandingoes were the billie and nanny goats. Were we to join the Manos, our uncles and aunts when they were to drive our fellow Mandingoes out of town? How were we to feel when our fellow Mandingoes were being driven out of town and their houses and properties seized? Were we to stand on the side and look and not share any sympathy for them? Could I take the threat issued by this self-proclaimed Quiwonkpa's spokesman in Saclepea very seriously? How widespread was this view among other Mano people and was it planned or spontaneous with some overzealous supporters of the coup taking law into their own hands? Whatever the case, I couldn't allow this fellow to spoil my day. I didn't go around telling my fellow Mandingoes, "watch out, they will round you up and take you to concentration camps tonight just like Hitler did to the Jews." Since I didn't hear this from Gen. Thomas Quiwonkpa himself on his radio announcement, I could not go around spreading any alarm among the Mandingoes simply based on what I was hearing from this man at the market. I couldn't help but wonder how many people like him were going around in other places saying the same thing.

As I learned later, there was mad jubilation in Bahn, a town in Gbelly Geh district. A group of excited Gio folks were going around issuing actual threats to Mandingoes. According to some eye witness accounts, they tied rope around a mouse and as the mouse struggled with the heavy weight, they were telling the Mandingoes to look at the mouse and expect their fates to be the same in the night. Some of them put their fingers around their necks to show that the Mandingoes should expect to be slaughtered like goats or sheeps. In Ganta, some lawless elements went around harassing the Mandingoes and issuing the same threat. Some of them went to desecrate the Mosque. In Yekepa, it was reported that some people went to the home of the director of Plant Protection Force, Charles Julu and killed his adopted daughter. Were these perpetrators carrying out these orders from Gen. Quiwonkpa? I don't think so. And were they representing the views of All Gio and Mano people? I don't think so either because I have met and befriended so many good Manos and Gios and based on that I could not pass judgment on all of them. What the fellow was saying in Saclepea and whatever others were doing in other places did not represent the reality to me. The only reality was what was going on in Monrovia, the capital. I did not think the man in the center of that reality shared the view of these vindictive folks on the streets.

As far as I was concerned, Quiwonkpa was my hero. Among the PRC members, Quiwonkpa was my number one. Despite his legendary status for the role he played in the coup that toppled President Tolbert, Quiwonkpa was a humble man. I saw him on several occasions in Saclepea. I saw him the first time he came to Saclepea after the coup. He was given a massive welcome by all of us. I was among the big crowd at the Palaver Hut in the Commissioner Compound listening to him as he spoke. We applauded his every word. We all were proud of him as the son of Nimba County. It was a beautiful moment.

After that first visit, he made other trips to Saclepea but those were low key compared to the first one. He would come in town with a few bodyguards. One time when he was walking on the street in front of our yard, one of his men saw my uncle Mohammed Konneh whose hands he excitedly shook. It happened that the tailor shop Uncle Mohammed Konneh used to work at in Monrovia was adjacent to Frank Tolbert's house on Clay Street. Since this soldier was among those that used to guard the house of the president's brother, they used to come in the tailor shop. That's where he and Uncle Mohammed knew each other. Then Uncle Mohammed moved back to Saclepea where he continued his tailoring job. I don't know how long their separation was but when they saw each other in Saclepea, they were both excited to meet and greet each other. He was telling the general about Mohammed and the general shook hands with him. That moved me very dearly about Quiwonkpa. Here was the man with the lion-sized image in the country but could walk humbly on the street, shaking hands with ordinary folks. The next day, old people from our community went to speak to him at his lodging place. They had come straight from the mosques after Morning Prayer. They prayed for him and the revolution. He told them he appreciated their coming to speak to him. He said they had carried on the revolution for all the Liberian people regardless of tribe or religion. He said we all needed to do our parts in advancing the cause of the revolution.

This solidified his image in my mind as a man of the people. A man of all people, not only of the Gios or the Manos. That's why when his problem started with Doe, I was on his side. In my eyes, he was right, Doe was wrong. That was my own verdict of their dispute. That's why I was excited to hear the voice of the general announcing the takeover, "Down with Doe." Even though I didn't get on the streets dancing and acting crazy, I was indeed excited for my hero to be in power. So whatever this self-proclaimed spokesman was doing in Saclepea, it did not diminish my love, support and enthusiasm for this prodigal son of Nimba County. What I heard the general say before and what I heard him saying now on the radio were completely different from what this guy was saying in Saclepea. So his foolish talk was not going to spoil my excitement for Quiwonkpa being the president.

A Coup, when successful and popular can be celebrated with jubilation on the streets. On the other hand when it fails, the aftermath is a reprisal. So a coup in any way is no ordinary walk in the ball park. Whether successful or failure, one thing is certain, some people will suffer and some people will be relieved. When it's violent, properties will be destroyed. More importantly, some people will take the law into their own hands and do their own things. Quiwonkpa's coup was no exception. When things seemed to be in Quiwonkpa's favor, those considered as Doe supporters had to hide or risk being mal-handled. Some of them were caught and paraded on the streets naked-. They were tamed by the seemingly victorious coup supporters. When Doe announced that he was still in charge and that Quiwonkpa was on the run, his supporters who were in hiding came out like wounded lions devouring everything in their path. They were the last laughers while those of us that supported the coup were crying, but we could not let anyone see our tears. We had to cry behind closed doors and when we came outside we pretended to be laughing with people who were celebrating the reverse of the situation. Just the same way the self-proclaimed Quiwonkpa's spokesman in Saclepea and other places were planning to execute their own orders; there were lots of Doe supporters and sympathizers doing the same thing when the table turned. Some Krahn members of the AFL passing through Saclepea from or to Grand Gedeh on many occasions after the coup would round up young Mano men on the streets and order them to pump tire. That is to cross hands with the right fingers holding the left ears and the left fingers holding right ears. They would order them to fall like trees or roll in the dirt. Sometimes these young Mano men would be dressed in their finest wears. These insensitive Krahn soldiers would still order them to roll in the dirt when they were wearing their Sunday best. When I saw these things happening my heart cried, but who was I to stop the Krahn soldiers from humiliating these young Mano men? If they knew I was one of those who were happy about the overthrowing of the Doe regime, they would have treated me the same way or worst. So I had to hide my feelings when I was witnessing those scenes. I was among those who pretended to be laughing while the Krahn soldiers harassed the Manos, but deep down I felt otherwise. When I could manage it, I didn't like to be in such places because I could not feel good standing there when my neighbors were being humiliated in such a way. But we had to pretend to keep our lives.   One thing I always thought about during those sad occasions was the way the self-proclaimed Quiwonkpa's spokesman and his friends might have treated the Mandingoes if the change was not reversed. How different would they have been from what I was witnessing? These questions were going through my mind when I saw this same fellow one day when another session of Krahn soldiers' harassment of Mano was going on. He was standing there feeling sorry for his fellow Manos being humiliated. Is this what you were going to do to my people, if things had remained as it was that day? I know someone that wanted to point him out but I advised the person not to do so. I told this guy that no matter what, the Manos were our neighbors and the Krahn soldiers will go and leave us together in the same neighborhood. That even though this guy might have planned something negative for us, we must leave him with his conscience.

When the coup failed, I prayed that no harm should happen to Quiwonkpa. I prayed and hoped that he would escape to safety. Bob Marley said that, "he who fights and runs away, lives to fight another day." When they were saying that Quiwonkpa was on the run, I was saying run Quiwonkpa run and come back another day. I prayed and hoped that Doe would never catch Quiwonkpa and humiliate him any further. That's why I was so disappointed when I heard days later that he was captured and killed. That was a sad day for me, the day I heard that Gen. Quiwonkpa had been killed. It felt so dark. I cried with tears in my eyes for Thomas Quiwonkpa. Except for my relatives and close friends, I have rarely cried for the death of any political leader. I have done so for only two persons, Quiwonkpa and Capt. Thomas Sankara of Burkina Faso. Even up to now I still find it difficult to remove the love I have for these two sons of Africa from my heart. The day I saw Quiwonkpa walking on the streets of Saclepea, no big entourage, shaking the hands of some ordinary people was the day my spirit took him. That love for this son of the soil is still burning many years after his death. Even though I have not been to Burkina Faso nor did I see Thomas Sankara, I loved him the same way I loved Quiwonkpa. I have not forgiven Blaise Compaore for Sankara's death as I could not forgive Doe for the death of Quiwonkpa.

Around this time I used to be the interpreter in our mosque, interpreting the Imam's sermon for those who could not understand Mandingo. The imam would read his sermon in Arabic, interpret it in Mandingo and I would interpret the Mandingo into English for the non Mandingo Moslems. On this Friday when I was supposed to interpret in the mosque, I was still grieving over the death of Quiwonkpa. I was enraged. I felt pain and powerlessness. I was dazed with frustration and confusion. Because of all these, I could not go stand up there to do a better job with my interpretation. I didn't want people to know what I was feeling deep inside of me. The level of sadness and confusion I experienced around this time inspired the poem, "The Darkest Days in Liberia."

The Sun of brotherly and sisterly love
    Ceased to shine, shine, shine
The win of brotherly and sisterly love
    Ceased to blow, blow, blow
The rain of brotherly and sisterly love

Ceased to fall, fall, fall
Blinding sheets of darkness
Enveloped the whole nation
Everyone became terribly sightless
In rolling and Bubbling Ocean of madness
All the scorching menacing hell broke loose,
As million-headed monsters came upon town.
Everyone raised up guns
Gunning down another brother and sister
Everyone raised up nasty swords
Slaughtering another brother and sister
Everyone raised up deadly axes
Axing another brother and sister
At day's end, everyone was weeping
And sorry for killing their own brothers
and sisters.

Part II
Revelation Time

6

One Fine Day

LIBERIA IN THE EARLY 1990s-Though it is more than 15 years, I can still remember exactly where I was when I first heard Charles Taylor speaking on BBC announcing the plan to remove President Samuel Doe from power. I was sitting on the porch of the middle house in our yard on Jamaica Road. As usual, I had my small shortwave radio on. Like many others, I was very excited. I wanted change and I was convinced that there was a need for it in Liberia at that time. I considered myself to be a proponent of true democracy which we didn't have in Liberia under President Doe. While this was the idea that informed my decision to support Charles Taylor, little did I know that my people, the Mandingoes, would be targeted as well.

My friend Foday Donzo listened to the radio while he was visiting his Mano relatives in Stephen Tolbert Estate around Double Bridge. Knowing how excited I could be about politics, Foday took a taxi to Jamaica Road to inquire if I had heard the Charles Taylor announcement on BBC. I told him I had heard and that I was very excited about it. It was on Christmas Eve in 1989, just a week for us to be in the New Year, 1990; and there were many pro-democracy activities going on in different parts of Africa. I was of the view that our pro-democracy activities in Liberia may be different from what were taking place in other parts of Africa. While Foday and I were high-fiving each other about the change that was on the national horizon, we didn't know that the war would lead to a kind of tribal and religious hatred we did not think existed in Liberia. When we met at Musa's mother's house the next day, Musa, his brother Sekou, Foday Donzo, Losene Bamba and I talked about the issues and the war Charles Taylor had announced. We all welcomed it just like many other Liberians. We had no connection to the power that existed. Therefore we had nothing to lose.

A week or two later, we started hearing news of how people we knew were being selectively targeted and killed. There were two relatives who had just arrived at our Jamaica Road residence. They both had come from different towns in Nimba County. Arafan Kenneh had been in Bahn and Mohammed Konneh, one of my paternal uncles, was in Saclepea. They had very interesting stories to share with us.

Our yard on Jamaica Road comprised of three complexes. Two were occupied by our family members of more than 20 people. The yard owner was our brother Musa Konneh and the family members were his children, his three wives, and the rest of us cousins. The other complex was a rental property occupied by some renters.

So this evening, we all gathered in Brother Musa's spacious living room to hear the firsthand accounts of what was obtaining in Nimba County. First to speak was Arafan, who was our nephew. He opened up by saying, "The war in Nimba is dangerous and a threat to the survival of our people." By that he meant the Mandingoes.

That was a surprise to me, being one of those sympathetic to the war to remove Dictator Samuel Doe. As he talked, you could see seriousness in his voice. He continued, "In Karnplay, they killed one of our brothers, Bangalie Kamara, the Police Commander." Almost all of us knew Bankalie Kamara and when Arafan dramatized the way he was killed, we all felt sorry for him.

"When the rebels entered Karnplay," Arafan continued in a high pitch voice loud enough for everyone to hear, "those of them that knew him went to his house where he was hiding in the attic. When Bangalie saw them trying to rape his wife and knowing some of the rebels, he came down to plead for her. That's when the rebels slaughtered him with knives and burnt his body. They poured gasoline on him and lit his body with matches and he burnt to ashes." Hearing this gruesome murder story of someone we all knew was emotionally challenging.

Having listened to Arafan telling us this gruesome murder story of Bangalie Kamara, Uncle Mohammed from Saclepea gave us his take on what was obtaining in Nimba County. "Right now," he said, "Mosiamana Koisiah and Amara Kamara have not been seen for more than a week and there is rumor they have been killed by the rebels somewhere behind Loyee. The two had left on a motorbike for a quick trip to Brevally. They were supposed to return the same evening but more than a week had passed with no news of them. It is strongly believed they might have fallen into the rebels hands." Mosiamana who was popularly known as "Small Man" was married to Uncle Mohammed's sister, Mafata. So as he explained about the disappearance of his brother-in-law, Uncle Mohammed almost cried. His explanation and that of Arafan filled the living room with fear, anxiety, and hopelessness.

Mohammed went on to say that as a result of these developments, some of our people in Saclepea had organized themselves to do nightly security patrol of the town alongside the government security forces. When we began to get this information, I began to have second thoughts about the war. One night when we were sitting down on Jamaica Road functioning as security for flee of used cars that were imported by our brother Musa Konneh, two other brothers and I got into some discussion about what was going on in Saclepea. While my brothers Kafumba and Losene were supporting the idea that our people in Saclepea and other places in Nimba County should leave and seek refuge in Guinea or Ivory Coast, my position was that our people should not leave their land for any reason.

When I talked about the current development during our next meeting at Musa Bility's mother's place, our friend Losene Bamba said we could expect things like that in the war but once the war reached to Monrovia and President Doe was removed, everything would be fine. He likened it to the waves of the ocean which rises and falls.

Months later around Iron Factory in Gardnersville, I saw large numbers of Mandingoes boarding cars and trucks bound for Guinea and Sierra Leone. The scene was more chaotic and you could see confusion written in the faces of the people climbing those trucks as if to say take me anywhere. There were people who could not afford the trip but they were there seeking help from friends or relatives. What was happening in Nimba County was being repeated in Monrovia. While this became a cause for alarm in our community, I could see that to many of our fellow Liberians, it wasn't a big deal. From Iron Factory, I got in the van heading for Central Monrovia. I was a silent witness to a shouting exchange between the two carboys and some passengers in the van. I don't know how it started as I got in the van, but the tone of the exchange was very acrimonious. One of the passengers said derisively, "The Mandingo people are running away from the country." Another one said, "They better leave before Charles Taylor gets here." With about 12 people packed like sardines in the van, everyone was anxious to say something about the Mandingoes fleeing. In those voices, I could not hear anything sympathetic. Instead of sympathy, the Mandingoes were ridiculed. On that particular day, the number of us Mandingoes in the van was few and no matter what we said, our voices were drowned out by others. Another one said, "Let the dingoes leave, we don't need them here. They are foreigners; let them go to their home."

The two carboys were the mouthpiece for the Mandingoes in that van. The tall slim one said, "I don't blame you ungrateful people, you sitting in the Mandingo man's car and talking nonsense." The chubby looking one with light skin jumped into it, "When the rebels get here, that not Mandingoes alone they will look for. They will kill some of y'all." Then there was a question from one of the passengers, "Why will they kill Liberians?" He went on to say, "No, they are not coming for Liberians. They coming for the dingoes who are foreigners." For some of these people, the departure of the Mandingoes felt like their burdens were being lifted. To some of them, the exodus of the Mandingoes was something to be excited about. It seemed as if the departure of the Mandingoes would create more free space for these folks. What I was hearing on this bus was no different from what was being said in the taxis as well as on the streets.

Having had the earful of these talks on the bus from Iron Factory to Waterside, I saw a newspaper with the headline, "The Mandingoes Are Leaving." There were several newspaper headlines on the same subject. What seemed bizarre and disheartening to me was the over sensationalization of the fact that the Mandingoes were fleeing. The stories in the papers were not expressing any sympathy for the fleeing Mandingoes. At the same time, Manos and Gios, who by this time were equally targeted by the government soldiers, were treated with sympathy. The media outlets were careful with the Krahns since the president was one of them. Indeed, public sympathy or public opinion leaned only towards the Manos and Gios; the Krahns were feared. And because the Mandingoes were powerless, we became the joke of the town. There was the notion of the Mandingoes being foreigners everywhere and for some people that justified whatever was happening to us.

At the campus of the Monrovia Institute of Technology in Sinkor, I was the only man among six women in one of my classes. During the break, one of the students asked me, "Are you going to Guinea or you staying here?" I told her I was staying and that I was not a Guinean. Another one asked, "Are you not afraid to die because the rebels are looking for your people?" When I said that the rebels were coming for Doe and his government officials, she said, "Don't be a fool, all the foreigners get to leave our country."

It felt like the darkest moment for me as a Mandingo. For all my life in different parts of Liberia, I had not felt this deep sentiment of hatred before. It seemed to be everywhere, day and night. I was afraid that someone might harm me. It plunged me into deep confusion, fear and anxiety.

When I came home that evening, I listened to other people telling similar stories of their experiences of the day. Now there were more talk of the entire family leaving for Guinea but I would not want to hear of it. I said, "I will not leave to go anywhere. I will stay here to the end."

Then our brother Musa Konneh, the yard owner said, "We have to leave. First, all the women and the children should leave as quickly as possible, then later on, we the men should leave." As he spoke, I could see that Brother Musa Konneh was very much afraid of what was to come and he didn't want to be here. He instructed that three vans be ready to take the women and children out of the country to Guinea.

The war was going on between the Krahn-dominated military and the Gio- and Mano- dominated rebel group. It was said that these three groups had their age-old differences. That age old difference had become a fully fledged war between the two groups and we were being caught in the middle of this tribal rivalry over political power. Our representation in the government was negligible as compared to those of Manos and Gios. The number of Mandingoes in the government could not be the justification for the tribal hatred directed towards us. Yet, there were many instances where ordinary Mandingoes were harassed long before the war. At immigration or security checkpoints in the country, Mandingoes were used to being harassed and now, because of the war we were being killed. To be going through all that with little or no sympathy from people we expected to sympathize with us was mind-boggling for me to say the least. Why was there this much hatred? This question has haunted me throughout since the war started.

Every day as we went out and came home in the evening, the news of the situation in Nimba County was getting worse and worse. We would talk about whatever we were hearing from the taxis, buses and on the streets. One disturbing piece of news was about the government soldiers also harassing our people. They were extorting money from the Mandingoes in the name of "saving them from the rebels." They would say, "You know the rebels are after you and we are here to protect you." And so the Mandingoes were dispossessed of whatever money they had. Aleo Foday was a victim of this harassment by a government soldier. He was the muezzin of our mosque in Saclepea. The soldier had grabbed his goat and when Aleo protested, he was shot.

On the other hand, the rebels saw us as "collaborators with the government forces." The government soldiers needed to be paid for "protecting us" and the rebels were killing us for "collaborating" with the government forces. So we were caught in the mix.

It was against this atmosphere of tribal discrimination and the war that it was announced that President Doe would meet with the Mandingoes at the Monrovia City Hall. I did not go to the City Hall for this meeting with the president. I followed the event on the TV and radio. The president spoke of the need to put an end to the rebellion. As he went along, the president reminded fellow Liberians that the Mandingoes "were Liberian citizens just like any other group of Liberians." If the president meant to teach history, his lesson of history was not well received. His statement was twisted by those whose minds were already made up against the Mandingoes. The critics' interpretations were that the president had conferred Liberian citizenship on the Mandingoes. From then on we were being called the "1990 citizens."

At checkpoints throughout the country even before the war, it was the Mamadees, Fantas or Sekous who were questioned by immigration, police or army officers to verify their Liberian citizenship. Some of these harassments might have been motivated by the desire for money. If they needed that extra income beyond their salaries which were always late, they harassed us. Sometimes it was $5.00, $10.00 or more. This had seemingly and shamelessly gone on forever.

Before and during the war, some drivers would not take Mandingo passengers because of the rigid screening at check points. National ID cards were no protection. Some of us had to speak other local dialects to authenticate our Liberian citizenship.

Every Mandingo in Liberia can tell some stories about discrimination at immigration and other security checkpoints throughout Liberia. I have mine to tell as well. Most of my travel in Liberia, when I had to deal with immigration officers at immigration checkpoints, happened between Ganta and Sanniquellie or Ganta and Monrovia. I also experienced this discrimination when I traveled to Ivory Coast or Guinea. There was an immigration checkpoint at the entrance of Sanniquellie from Ganta. Between Ganta and Monrovia there were several immigration checkpoints. At all these immigration checkpoints, one thing that was constant was ethnic profiling; and almost always those affected were the Mandingoes and anyone suspected of being a foreigner.

While I can't remember my first experience at an immigration checkpoint, I can recount so many experiences. I know many people who can recount their own experiences at immigration checkpoints somewhere in Liberia. One time I was traveling with my mother when we got to a checkpoint. The immigration officer came and told everyone to follow him to the office. At the office he was asking for IDs from some, but not all of the passengers. I can't remember how old I was by then, but I remember following my mother. I only could make sense of the whole situation later in life when I became more conscious and mature. Years later I would come to know that the immigration officers at checkpoints targeted the Mandingoes and anyone they suspected of being from other countries. I would find out later that if your name is George, Saye or Moses, you don't have to worry about these immigration checkpoints. If you were Mamadee or Konneh, you would face tougher questionings. The immigration officers won't be satisfied with you saying you were born in Saclepea or Ganta or anywhere else in Liberia. He would want to know where your grandfather was born, where your grandmother was born, and maybe where your great grandfathers and great grandmothers were born; even though none of those questions were suppose to be your business or his business. Why should I care where my grandfather was born to verify my citizenship as a Liberian? When I became aware years later, I wish I had known why those immigration officers told my mother to follow them to the office.

As I grew up and started traveling on my own, I would have many confrontations with immigration officers at checkpoints. On one of my travels to Monrovia, I was told to follow an immigration officer to the office. It was the same routine, but this time around I was ready for a showdown. Two immigration officers came to the car and were asking for names. If your name was Manmadee, you were told to go to the office. Several persons were asked their names but were not told to go to the office. I and four other passengers were told to follow them to the office. I asked questions, "why only we, the Mandingoes were being asked to follow you and others were left alone?" One of them asked who I was and I said I was a student. He told me to stay. Then I told them they had no right to ask the four other Mandingo passengers to follow them to the office. One of them said, "Young man, look like you know plenty, mind your business before you get in trouble."

I responded sharply, "If I didn't do anything wrong I couldn't see why I would be in trouble."

The four Mandingoes being asked to go to the office were two women, an elderly man and a young lady of somewhere between 15 and 21 years of age. I followed the immigration officers and the four Mandingo persons to the office. While I followed them, the immigration officers kept warning that I stay behind, but I told them I could not stay behind and see them doing injustice to other people. The officers and I had a back and forward argument about the illegality of their act of ethnic profiling. At the end of the whole illegal exercise, the four Mandingoes were told to give some money the amount of which I can't remember now. According to the four Mandingo passengers, they had businesses to attend and all of the talking at the checkpoint was wasting their time. They were saying to each other, "Let's find something for them." This was against my advice for them not to give anything to the immigration officers. Since they had decided to give money to the immigration officers against my advice, I left them and went back to the car. Since they didn't care about standing up and fighting for their rights, I thought there was no point of me talking any more to the officers. These Mandingoes prioritized profit making over standing up for their own rights.

Other passengers in the car who felt their time was being wasted would not blame the immigration officers but their fellow passengers who were being harassed. I heard one of them saying, "That's why it's not good to be traveling in the same car with those foreigners." Some of them blamed the driver for taking those "foreigners" in the first place. While they were talking all of this, I managed to control my temper. I was angry with the immigration officers but I was very disappointed with the four Mandingo passengers. The fact that they were willing to bribe the immigration officers for their own rights insulted me and infuriated my sensibility. Left with me, they shouldn't have to pay a penny. And what could I say to these passengers who were impatient and thought "foreigners" were wasting their time and therefore the drivers shouldn't have taken them? I felt they were too lazy to make any inquiry about the status of these people because they assumed that once the immigration officers called you in the office you must not be a Liberian. This is what I felt, but at the same time I felt that arguing with them would not produce any result. As a matter of fact I could not see what was there to talk about after these Mandingoes had agreed to bribe the immigration officers against my advice.

In psychoanalyzing the people involved in the incident, I came to several conclusions. Were the immigration officers motivated by the easy money they were collecting from these Mandingo passengers or ethnic hatred? Were they ignorant to think of the Mandingoes as foreigners and was this the reason why they picked on them all the time? For the Mandingoes, what dominates their minds is profit-making and as a result they are always in a rush to make profits and don't have any concept of the social injustice being done them. What their inaction was telling the immigration officers, not only at this check point but checkpoints across the country, is "harass me as much as you can but I will bribe you as many times as I can so that I can't miss my markets." In simple term, they were saying, "do anything to me I will take it kindly, but don't stop my hustle." As for their fellow passengers, it did not bother their conscience that injustice was being done. These immigration officers were nothing less than thieves preying on these passengers who were very ignorant of their very own rights.

At other times, I saw immigrant officers chasing people in towns and cities. There was an immigration officer called Eugene Keedor that made a name for himself in Ganta. I did not see him one day, but I heard that he used to go around on Ganta market days arresting the Mandingoes and releasing them when they gave him money. There was an immigration officer from Saclepea called John Vaye. He was assigned somewhere else, but always used to come home on Saclepea market days and arrest more than ten people at a time. All would pay him some money before he would let them go. He never missed the market day. I always used to wonder whether this was part of the training John Vaye and Eugene Keedor received when they went for the immigration training. Is it part of their training to go after people and collect money from them and let them go?

When I moved to Monrovia in 1988, I escorted a business partner of my brother Musa Konneh. My brother had encountered this Malian lady in Happer, Maryland County. She had come to buy goods in Monrovia to carry to Ivory Coast. While on Water Street, an immigration officer met us and asked the lady for her traveling documents. She had a Malian passport which she presented to him. Having seen the passport, he still wanted us to go with him to the Justice Ministry. I told him that since the lady had her passport which was stamped, he had no right to harass her on the street. When he said to follow him, I grabbed the lady's passport from him and told him to kiss my behind. He and I were getting into some commotion when the lady gave him some money to leave her alone. She gave the immigration officer this amount against my advice. She said that time was valuable and we should not be wasting it when we could be attending to her business. While I understood what she was saying, this particular incidence frustrated me to the point that I wanted to beat this common thief wearing a government uniform. Right after receiving money from the Malian lady, the fellow vanished into thin air. Maybe he went on the hustle to his next targets.

Admittedly, there is no official policy that considered us foreigners, but there is that implicit public attitude of resentment. History is there to settle all the matters regarding the Mandingoes' presence and citizenship in Liberia, but where ignorance and prejudice abound history does not matter.

President Doe's meeting with us at the City Hall did not mitigate our problem. We were now the "1990 citizens." Whenever someone said "1990 citizens," it was followed by "En you say you citizen? Sit down there and fool yourself. You will see. Doe fooled you, you not citizen." Many times I heard this being said on the streets, in the taxis and buses; and every time I heard such, it broke my heart and I felt powerless to do anything about it.

Sometimes, things taken for jokes can come to pass. For more than ten years, at some point or another, we heard from some of our neighbors the all too familiar expression, "Sit down there. You will see one fine day." We never thought that "one-fine-day" would come. Now it had arrived. Maybe if we had taken this serious enough, we could have formulated contingency plans. However, we had seemingly been complacent and for obvious reasons. We had co-existed with our Mano and Gio neighbors for years. Some of us share Mano and Gio heritage as already mentioned. Despite our cultural differences, we all grew up enjoying peace and harmony in Saclepea, Ganta, Tappita and Bahn. We respected each other's cultural practices. Whenever it was time for the Manos and Gios to commune with their sacred masked dancers, loosely referred to as "putting out their devils," we retreated to our houses early. We often felt obliged to comply until it was time for our early morning prayers. In Saclepea there was the Saclepea Youth Association with members from both the Mano and Mandingo sides. During Christmas and New Year, we used to come together and celebrate. When we were celebrating with the gbombay drums in the Commissioner Compound or elsewhere in town, the Manos and Gios would come to share in the joy. With all this going on, we did not see any threat in the expressions like "damn Mandingo man" or "you will see one fine day." For so long we have coexisted. Now there were talks of chasing us out of Liberia.

Many times I sat down with my friends Musa, Foday and Losene Bamba to make some sense out of what was going on. Every time we met, our discussions were dominated by what was happening. Couldn't we sit down as a people to talk about the differences that resulted into this war? We pondered over this question many times, trying to make sense of the prevailing situation. Foday's mother is Mano. Musa's maternal grandmother was Mano. I have a Mano background as well. Losene Bamba had brothers whose mothers were Mano. And here as we were sitting in Monrovia baffled by the war and its consequences, we couldn't stop asking, couldn't we talk this over as family? Maybe we could have reached a point where someone would have said to the other, "I am sorry" or "Please forgive me." But once blood flows between groups of people, it becomes difficult, if not impossible, to cool down the passion. That was what was happening between us and our neighbors in Nimba County. We felt like Jews in Hitler's Germany.

In all these ups and downs, we probably seemed to have had the wrong notion that Doe would stay in power forever and that as long as he ruled we would be safe. On that wrong notion, we went through April 12th and then November 12th. We still could not realize that the threat against us was real. We did not take any precaution. We lived believing that nothing would happen until the rude awakening on

December 24th, 1989, when Charles Taylor launched his war, recruiting many young Manos and Gios to form his fighting forces. The day was far away but it was surely coming. Given all that had passed, we should not have been surprised with what was unfolding.

7 | On the Run for My Life

THE FEW WEEKS PRIOR to making the decision to leave the country, I was really living large. I was sleeping in the big bed in Brother Abdullah Konneh's room. He had gone on a business trip to Nigeria. He was still away when our big brother Musa Konneh took the decision to send the women and the children away. When Brother Abdullah's wife Madiafin was leaving, she gave me the key to take care of their room until their return. The absence of she and her husband put me in charge of the room. It was well furnished. The bed was a king size made of wood, beautifully designed in Liberia. The sheets were embroidered very fashionably with mixed colors. There was a big sound system that had a loud sound. I had all my favorite cassettes. When I lied down in the bed and put the music on, it felt like paradise.

This room was a far cry from the room I shared with more than ten persons. Our room was what might be called the boys' quarters in the typical big yards and we lied down on the first come first serve basis. No one had any special place. Whenever the big fat bed was full, the rest of the guys would have to make room for themselves on the floor. I had shared this room with the nine other occupants since I moved to Monrovia in 1988 until transferring to Brother Abdulla's room. But this was supposed to be temporary until he came back or his wife returned to Monrovia. Their return was contingent on the expected outcome of the war which was slowly progressing towards Monrovia.

Until then, I was living large in their room. I had hoped to stay there until the whole thing was over. The comfort of that room was one of the reasons I didn't want to leave Monrovia. Some days, I would stay indoor just playing music, only coming outside to find food to eat. Sometimes the comfort of the room would make me forget about the war that was advancing towards Monrovia.

At the same time, more bad news was coming in. Among the news I got that scared the hell out of me was that a cousin of mine, Samuka Sherif was killed in Buchanan. It was said that when the rebels took Buchanan, my cousin went to hide in the home of some friends who reported him to the rebels as Mandingo. We heard, when the rebels found him they killed him in a very gruesome fashion. That news and others made me decide to join the exodus of people that were fleeing the country to safety either in Guinea or Sierra Leone.

With this horrible news coming in, we had another family meeting in Brother Musa's living room with those of us still in the yard on Jamaica Road. Brother Musa advised that we all leave to go to Guinea. He said, "The situation is getting bad by the minutes. We all want to live. Even if we have to die, we can't allow ourselves to die in the hands of the rebels. I will rather die a natural death in peace than a violent death in the hands of these rebels." As he spoke, he sounded like a preacher rather than the business man he was. Brother Musa was a successful business man with businesses in Zwedru, Grand Gedeh County, as well as Cape Palmas, Maryland County. He had stores in all those places including the one that used to be in Monrovia. Then he got into the used car business. He would bring ten to twenty cars at a time. So this night when the brother spoke, we all could tell that he was hopelessly scared. The room was silent after he spoke.

That night I did not sleep. The news of cousin Samuka's death and the short sermon given by Brother Musa that night interfered with my sleep. Though I was seriously thinking about leaving the country, some part of me was telling me to stay on and ride the waves of the unfolding developments. So in a sense, I was torn between leaving and staying. That night the king size bed and the music were not enough to get my mind off the war and its consequence when it reached to Monrovia.

There was a lot going through my mind the whole night. It occurred to me to write down what I was feeling. I found the courage to take a pen and started writing whatever was going through my mind. The date was May 26, 1990 and I wrote as followed:

I am at the moment of this writing in a pit of accusation, confusion, and frustration. I am the man with the restless heart, a man on the run, just like Michael Jackson sings in one of his songs. All this can be more or less attributed to what's going on now in the country. Some call it "Nimba Crisis," some call it "national crisis," and still others call it "the people's uprising," or "rebel invasion." Whatever it is or represents for each person depends on where he or she stands. Whatever it may be I cannot figure out what color it is.

I was excited when I heard the first trumpet. I was excited that someone could stand up to the dictator Doe had become. I had all along been with the impression that this is a "people rising up" to overturn an ugly situation or condition. But now I am disillusioned with the whole thing. I am afraid the flood may sweep me away; not because of anything other than the fact that someone will not want to see me beyond the stereotype of ethnicity and religion. None of my parents have been in government; they have been part of the struggling masses of the people. For them or me to be targeted right now is something I can't understand in this land of my birth, indeed, this land of my father's birth.

Sincerely, I am opposed to any killing of the poor and the innocent in this on-going crisis, be it that of the Gios, Manos, or even the Krahns. Killing people based on tribal or religious identity is uncivilized as monster showdown in Rambo movies.

A while ago I wrote a poem, which was entitled, "I Yama Rebel." In that poem, I sanctioned rebellion not only against the Doe regime, but any other oppressive regime in Africa and anywhere else. This is why I was more excited than surprised when I first heard about the current uprising. What will I say now when the very uprising I have welcomed is coming after me as well? I can't get over the fact that simply because I am a Mandingo I am wanted dead. Now I must run as far as the blue sky or anywhere else to save my life. Seeking refuge now is the only option, hoping to come back when the crisis, or whatever it is, is over. Liberia is my home as it is the home of any other Liberian. No other place can give me the comfort of a home than Liberia. Despite all the attempts to run me out, I love Liberia because it's the land of my birth and I hope my fellow Liberians who are hunting me now know this. I feel deep love for this country, a love I cannot share with any other country. While I must run now for my life before I am counted among the dead, I will carry that love for Liberia wherever I go. At this moment, I am feeling like Gen. Thomas Wehsen (one of the original seventeen who staged the April 1980 coup) when he said, "If I die I die for nothing." What crime have I committed that I must be killed? I am not convinced that being Gio, Mano, or Krahn should cause anyone his or her life. If God created every one of us in his own image, who are we to condemn what God has created? God did not commit a crime when some of us saw ourselves as members of any ethnic group, for He said He created all of us in diverse groups so that we may know each other. That is what Islam has taught me and I respect that. Can my would-be executioners tell me otherwise?

I have been thinking about seeking refuge at the homes of some close friends but I am not sure of my safety if I do so. I am afraid that gunmen running wild to kill may overpower those friends and take me away. The other thing is what if those friends are on the run for their lives, just like me?

In the past three days my life has not known any peace. I have been having nightmares, smelling violent death right next to my fragile door wanting to fall on me. Can I really convince Mr. Big O Ugly Death to leave me alone 'cause I get nothing to do with him?' I used to feel like I could convince these rebels that we are all the same and we are all part of this uprising. From what I have been hearing from people round town, I am not sure if any attempt to convince them will make them think otherwise. This is all the more so when I received the sad news few days ago that Samuka Sheriff, a cousin of mine in Buchanan, was identified by some friends as Mandingo and was killed. Hearing that my cousin was killed by some friends who knew him over the years has made me very scared to the extent that I want to leave now to save my own life. I can only imagine how cousin Sheriff's mother will feel when she hears that her last child has died in this war on the account of his ethnic identity. His mother is my mother's elder sister. I can imagine how devastated they both will be. Me added to that casualty list will be very terrible for our mothers.

If I could die from stray bullets, or become one of the collateral casualties of the war, I could accept that and for such reason, my decision to leave or not to leave would be easy to make. The fact that I could die not for any of the above reasons but simply be-cause of my ethnic identity or religious affiliation was very much unfortunate.

The only thing I have been doing these days is constant praying to the ever-living God for the oneness of the Liberian nation, pray-ing that God will save us from each other. Just a week ago, to be exact, May 19, I celebrated Malcolm X's birthday. Malcolm is my hero and I love him so dearly as a true revolutionary leader. I was alone celebrating my leader's birthday with God watching over me. I prayed that God would bless Africa, which Malcolm loved so much. I read some verses of the Holy Quran in both Arabic and English. I also read some passages from the biography of Langston Hughes. I listened to some lyrical poetry of Public Enemy, KRS One, Bob Marley, Gregory Isaac and Alpha Blondy.

As the day draws to a close, I have finally made up my mind to leave for Guinea the next day in one of my brother's cars. While away, I am sure to keep abreast of developments as they unfold. I may also be interested in keeping a diary about my refugee experience. While I am leaving, I am praying strongly that whichever side has Liberia's best interest at heart should have the final victory in this war.

8

The Road Is Bumpy

I LEFT MONROVIA ON MAY 27, 1990 along with my friends, Junior Parker and Samuel Kamara. The decision for Parker, Sam and I to travel together was made abruptly. Our final destination was Ivory Coast, Guinea being only a transit point. While thousands of others on the road were in great worry about their lives, we three were imagining what big show we would put up when we reached Ivory Coast. Both Parker and Sam were my partners in the Black Messenger group, an artistic collaboration. We had earlier planned to travel to Nigeria on a music recording project. Our original departure schedule was June 14, 1990. The three of us were to put some money together to facilitate our journey to Nigeria. Due to the escalating situation, we decided to leave before that time. We had 15 people squeezed in our van. There were many other vans and trucks full of people escaping the war that was advancing towards Monrovia by the minutes. It was a long convoy.

It was raining heavily and the road was terribly bad because of that. But the paramount concern to everyone was certainly not the rain or the bad road. What was on my mind, and I am sure on the minds of all these people in these cars, was the fear of falling into the ambush of the advancing rebels.

That day was full of drama for me. During the previous night we had another family meeting in preparation for our departure in the morning. While making the preparation for the trip, Parker came to see me and proposed that we travel to the Ivory Coast. His proposal was against the fact that I had dropped some notes at his place informing him that I was traveling with my family to Guinea and would be back as soon as the crisis was over. By that, I meant the war would be over either when Doe had defeated the rebels or the other way around. When I returned, we would make our planned trip to Nigeria.

I was surprised to see Parker and Sam in the morning on Jamaica Road telling me, "You know you can't go and leave us like this. You are the leader of the group. When you leave us like this, how sure can you be that you will meet us alive when you return?" That was a very hard question for me and I didn't have any answer for it.

About a week or two earlier, I had borrowed two books from the American Cultural Center which I had to return this morning. The two books were The Biography of Langston Hughes by Faith Berry, and Who Speaks for the Negroes? Being a lover of literature, especially poetry, I have developed a strong interest in Langston Hughes. Through reading his books and this biography, I am appreciating his contribution to the global black arts and culture.

After returning the books, I ran to the tailor shop on Carey Street, Crown Hill. Unfortunately my tailor had not finished sewing my trousers. He told me that by the time I return back from Guinea they would be ready. I wasn't satisfied with that assurance from the tailor. With that disappointed feeling, I headed back to Jamaica Road. I got off the taxi and started walking from the Jamaica Road and UN Drive Junction towards home at the other end of Jamaica Road. After passing Boatswain campus, I saw one of my cousins telling me that Sam and Parker were waiting for me in the house. I was wondering why they were there since I was not expecting them.

When I met them in the yard, I could not believe my eyes. They were dressed too shabby and sweating like hell as if to say they had been engaged in some hard physical labor. They looked anxious as well. They expressed their desire to travel with me to wherever. They pleaded that since we had already planned to travel, we needed to make use of the time immediately. Wherever I went they would, even if my destinations were to Mecca or to Jerusalem. All of this based on the artistic partnership we developed which had made us like brothers. When I agreed with their plan for travelling to the Ivory Coast, they left to go get their traveling bags. With the scarcity of taxis or buses, it took forever for them to come back. It took them so long that the driver and other passengers were grumbling, saying that if my friends were not coming, I would either get in the car or they would go without us. With the time stretching out into hours, I decided to go find out what was holding them. What I did not know when I decided to go to Jacob's Town looking for my friends was that I would find myself trapped. I went first to Parker's house where his aunt told me she had not seen him for over a week. My next destination was to Sam's house. When I met his little brother, he told me, "Sam left this morning without brushing his teeth." I was terribly mad, thinking that the driver and the other passengers would become more impatient the longer we kept delaying them.

When Sam's brother asked for my name, I did not see the trouble coming. He looked suspiciously in my angry face and went in to tell his mother that someone was there to see Sam. The Old Ma came out screaming, "You tricky boy! My son left from here saying that he going Africo. Three days ago, you left a note that you are going to Guinea. Since then Sammy never sit down in this house." I could see the red fire burning in her eyes as if to say I had committed the worst crime. She was cursing and threatening to take me to the police station with the charge that I was taking her son to the rebel-training base in "Africo." I lied that I didn't know if her son was traveling to the Ivory Coast, that I had only come to inform him that I was traveling to Guinea with my family. Regardless of what I told her she won't listen to me. She kept saying, "my son or you." I started walking ahead of her with the hope of finding a taxi that would take me to Jamaica Road. When she discovered my plan, she started yelling "Ro'! Ro!..." As she yelled, four gentlemen formed a thick circle around me, blocking my escape route. She told them I was eloping with her son and they should help her to take me to the police station. She continued to say, "My son or the police station!" I had no intention of showing her where Sam was and I didn't want to go to the police station for fear that I could be in deep trouble if she told them what she was charging me with. With that concern and the odds being against me, I cooperated with her and we took a taxi to Jamaica Road.

It was Parker who first saw us, me and Sam's mother. He hid. Unsuspectingly, we entered the living room where Sam was sitting with my family. After a barrage of protest mixed with insults, she grabbed her son and out they went. What took place with Sam and his mother at the intersection of Jamaica Road and Somalia Drive is anybody's guess. In no time, Sam came back to join us. He and Johnson who lived with his parents had tricked his mother. As a result he was able to join us again. We went to Vai Town at the truck parking, afraid that Sam's mother or some family member would see him.

After the dramatic showdown with Sam's mother, we were now on the way, praying that we should not fall into the rebel trap or ambush. The scene was maddening. There were too many cars, too many passengers, most of them Mandingoes, all running for their lives. Life is so good, so dear, very much worth running for. The only thing that bothered me in all this was the jeering chants of "1990 citizens go home." We were running away from physical calamity, and all these folks could do was to cheer us in such a derogatory manner. I could not see any sympathy from these chants of "1990 citizens go home." Some were even saying "don't come back again." Different kinds of nasty phrases rose in unison. I'd known that Mandingoes were so hated in this country until then. I could not imagine that people would jump so joyously for the systematic killing of fellow human beings.

As I heard those voices cheering, it felt like I was being forced to leave against my will. I was not only running away because I didn't want to die from stray bullets, I was being chased by hate to leave the country. It became a very painful experience for me.

While we were running for our lives from the rebels, we still had to deal with some government soldiers at the checkpoints. Some of them demanded money as usual. Hundreds running to thousands of dollars were forcibly taken from us by the government security agents, such as the police and the soldiers. They were really taking advantage of our predicament to enrich themselves. That meant we were catching hell on both sides of the fence. While I could understand the harassment from the rebels, I could not understand why those government agents would harass us. At one checkpoint, we were put under a gunpoint by a lone soldier. He was shouting at the top of his voice, "Wana hell, you fucku' I blow you." For a government soldier who had taken the oath to protect and defend the nation and its citizens to act like this was a violation of the very oath he took. He advised that we sleep there until in the morning. The roads were literally rocky, full of potholes as big as swimming pools. The cars went in and out of these potholes. All around us were lush green forests, beautiful natural scenes. There were tall mountain ranges and steep hills with cars travelling on narrow roads climbing. Sometimes the passengers would disembark to push the cars. Sometimes we went for hours before seeing villages. Here and there we passed through these little villages where you couldn't see anything but sheeps, goats, chickens or dogs. Sometimes we saw one, two, three persons or small groups to and from farms. Some of them carried hunting guns on their shoulders, fishing nets, or hoes and cutlasses. The day would be hot and humid and the night would be cold. Even though these were parts of Liberia, there was a great difference between these environments and the urban centers of Monrovia, Buchanan or Gbarnga. And so we had a bumpy ride. Anyway, these rocky and bumpy roads were better than any death from bullets in Monrovia. It was now better than being killed by some confused lunatic who did not have any clue as to why they killed; except to say that you, a victim, belonged to this or that ethnic group.

When we approached the border crossing from Liberia to Guinea, I couldn't count the number of cars and the people. Processing all these people through the immigration checkpoints of both countries went on forever. However, I must admit, the rules were somehow relaxed on both sides because of the extra-ordinary magnitude of the situation. But still, the immigration officers couldn't just abandon their posts for people to flood in. While waiting in that long line in the car, I wrote a poem, "Political Crisis."

What to do
And what to say
Where to go
And where to hide

Where to walk
And where to run
That's the question
Every body asking now
That's the question
Every body wants the answer
Political crisis
Blowing in the air
Political crisis
Blowing in the air
In the north and south
In the west and east
Political crisis is everywhere.

This poem was inspired by the fact that what was going on in Liberia was not an isolated incident. It was the period of pro-democracy movements that were shaking the foundations of One Party Systems that were the norm in many parts of Africa. While in most of these countries such as Ivory Coast, Togo and Benin, there were street demonstrations where pro-democracy activists clashed with the soldiers and police, Liberians might have thought that such street demonstrations could not work in Liberia with the entrenched military regime of Samuel Doe. So for us in Liberia, war was what we had.

After three days of rough journey on these rocky and bumpy roads, we finally arrived one dark and cold night in Nzérékoré, Guinea. Since we had other passengers outside of our family, it was advised that it was too risky to let anyone out of the car. We agreed to sleep in the car until day break.

9

Born Here, Die Here

NZEREKORE IS THE LARGEST CITY in the Guinea Forest Region and capital of Nzérékoré Prefecture. It's the third largest city in Guinea after Conakry, the country's capital and Kankan, the capital of Upper Guinea. Though it's originally a Kpelleh town, Nzérékoré's commercial activities are dominated by the Mandingoes and Fulas. There was a saw mill which was very vital to the local economy. Even as the third largest city of the country, Nzérékoré did not have running water. There was no electricity and no public transportation. All distances were covered by foot except those with their own cars and motorbikes. When walking about in the night, beside the car or motorbikes' headlight, you may see dull light emanating from the lanterns, candles or flashlights. Despite all this, Nzérékoré is a lively city. The city now had an influx of people escaping the Liberian civil war.

It had been more than 10 years since the last time I had been in Nzérékoré. I had no clue where I was supposed to go. The driver took us to Dorota, thinking that we might find some people there we might know. When we got there, guess who I saw? It was my father, his friend Kalifala Kenneh and others. The last time I saw my father was in November 1989, a little over a month before Taylor's declaration of war. When my father and the rest of the family members in Saclepea left for Guinea, I was in Monrovia. They were excited to see me in Nzérékoré. His friend, Kalifala Kenneh teased me, "Since you came, no one will stay in Monrovia now." He said that because they had heard from relatives that had come before me that I said I was not going to leave Liberia. So no one was expecting me in Nzérékoré. I was stubborn and didn't have any intention of leaving Monrovia. The next question my father and his friends wanted an answer for was, "How was the situation when I left from Monrovia and whether Doe would beat the rebels?"

I knew that what I was going to tell them would not make them happy, but I had to tell them the truth. Bluntly, I said, "If Doe does not run away, the rebels will grab him and cut his throat." My father and his friends were not amused by my blunt analyses, but I thought I had told them the truth. My father supported Doe. During the 1985 General Elections in Liberia, my father did not like the fact that I was supporting and campaigning for Dr. Edward Kesselley. Some of his friends told him that I was very stubborn in my support for Kesselley. One day he told me, "My yard is Samuel Doe yard, if you don't like that, you can pack up and leave my yard." Thinking of that I knew my father could not have been amused with what I said to them about President Doe but it was the truth and I could not sugarcoat it for them.

In Monrovia, we heard the chants of "1990 citizens go home." In Nzérékoré, we were greeted with "Born here die here." In Liberia, the Liberian Mandingoes distinguished themselves from their kinsmen from Guinea by calling themselves "Born here, die here." Meaning they were born in Liberia and they would die there. Such phrase was offensive to the Guinean Mandingoes who felt insulted and discriminated against by their fellow Mandingoes in Liberia. Guinean Mandingoes that took this to heart saw the perfect opportunity to tell us, "You said you were born there and you would die there in Liberia, what make you come to Guinea now?" They were mocking and telling us to go to where we were born and supposed to have died. Some of them would say, "You never thought today would come; now you are here." There even was a crazy man in Nzérékoré called Abu Face who was among those welcoming us with the "born here die here" slogan. For those Guinean Mandingoes calling us "Born here, die here", it was like a sweet revenge for them. Besides the Mandingoes in Nzérékoré, the Kpellehs too were somehow resentful of our presence. Already they had their issues with their own Guinean Mandingo population. Now there was an influx of Mandingoes from Liberia.

We stayed in the car to where my father was lodging, at a relative's residence. Uncle Kalifala Konneh was my father's cousin from Beyla, but residing in Nzérékoré. After we had deposited our bags to the room given to me and my friends, we set about surveying the town. From one place to another, the newly arrived Liberians running away from war were everywhere hoping that the war would soon end so they could go back to Liberia. You could hear more English spoken on the streets of Nzérékoré than Mandingo or French. The general estimation at the time was that the war would end either when Doe captured Taylor or vice-versa. The refugees were busy wrestling with the Guineans over the relief food sent by the humanitarian organizations. Claiming to be refugees, some Guineans were receiving relief supplies and selling them with high prices while the poor penniless refugees went hungry. After about three weeks in Nzérékoré, we could not see any convincing reason to stay there. We decided it would be better for hungry goats to find greener pasture somewhere else. Abidjan, as we thought, wouldn't be less than that greener pasture. It was actually our destination, Nzérékoré only being a transit point. We had heard of so many big stars that were flying in the world, crediting Abidjan as their starting point. Abidjan, to our estimation, looked more like the entertainment capital of West Africa.

Part of the reason we didn't spend much time in Nzérékoré was because some members of my family, who were themselves refugees from Liberia, were not comfortable with the fact that I was traveling with friends whose "people were killing our people in Liberia." Parker is a Bassa. Sam is a half and half, a mixed Mandingo and Lorma. His Mandingo identity was not so pronounced as mine and so he could not be easily identified as a Mandingo. Those family members could not see any difference between him and Parker. So I was in trouble for bringing these guys whose "people were killing our people" in Liberia. Since they were not Moslem, they could not eat with us. They were served food but they had to eat separate from the rest of the people. I did not feel comfortable with that, but I could not force my relatives to do something against their will. One morning my father called and told me that the presence of these "people whose people were killing our people" was causing embarrassment for him. "We flee our homes to seek refuge with our distant relatives over here. You cannot abuse their sympathy and generosity by bringing people whose people are killing our people in Liberia." With that said, my father told me to leave with my strangers and go anywhere I wanted to go. Since it was never a plan for us to stay in Nzérékoré, what my father said was not a big deal to me. Regardless, we didn't have any intention of staying in Nzérékoré. Three days after that conversation with my father, we left for Ivory Coast. The only problem was that we were running out of money. We had left Monrovia thinking that the money we had was enough to take us to Abidjan. However, with that little amount we had, we continued our journey. My brother Funcia who had brought his car with him from Ganta, Liberia and was operating it in Guinea took us to the border with Ivory Coast. We prayed for each other. From there we continued our journey into Ivory Coast.

If the Liberian Mandingoes thought they had escaped the tribal hunting in Liberia and were now in safe haven, that myth would be shattered sometime in 1991. In Nzérékoré, there was a mayoral election in which there were two Mandingo candidates and a Kpelleh candidate. It was the Kpelleh candidate that won the election to become the mayor of Nzérékoré. Maybe out of sheer joy and excitement over their victory, some supporters of the victorious Kpelleh candidate attacked some Mandingoes which touched off ethnic conflict in the city. There were running street battles between the Kpellehs and the Mandingoes in Nzérékoré and the Kpellehs could not distinguish between the Liberian and the Guinean Mandingoes. They mobilized their people to break down the big mosque in Dorota, a section of Nzérékoré heavily populated by the members of the Mandingo ethnic groups. The Mandingoes went on top of the mosque calling on people to come and defend the mosque. Two crowds met and results were the violent street battles. Homes belonging to both the Kpellehs and Mandingoes were burnt and people were killed. Since the Kpellehs could not win the battle in town, they went to the little towns and villages around Nzérékoré and started attacking the Mandingoes. In one instance they went to a town on a market day and started killing every Mandingo they could see. My mother's eldest brother, Vafuebue Donzo was one of the casualties of such attacks.

The fact that they had run away from the war in Liberia became the main reason for the Liberian Mandingoes to stand firm in Nzérékoré. In that sense, Nzérékoré became the last stance. To most of them there was a conspiratorial feel to it between the Kpellehs in Guinea and their cousins in Liberia which might include the Manos because Nzérékoré also has a Mano population. It was like the Manos, Gios and Kpellehs had succeeded in chasing the Mandingoes out of Liberia and now they wanted to try the same thing in Guinea. So for the Mandingoes, it was like a do or die battle. One thing this incidence did was it increased the recruitment efforts of the United Liberation Movement for Democracy better known as ULIMO. The Liberian Mandingoes realized that they could never feel secure in Guinea and the best thing for them was to go back to Liberia; the only way was to fight their way back in. This realization significantly boosted the ULIMO recruitment among the young people.

10

Three on the Road to the Mountaintop

IF WE EVER thought of making it to Abidjan with the amount we had from Monrovia, we were misleading ourselves. We got stranded in Danané, an Ivorian town near the Liberian border. The situation was not too desperate, because I had some distant relatives in that town who welcomed us with open arms. Under their hospitable care, we spent a week. All the money we had was 500cfa, about one United States dollar. That could only buy us three bottles of Coca Cola. Being helpless and hopeless in Danané, we had to sell my typewriter. That typewriter was one item I could not leave Monrovia without. I was constantly writing on the way and would use the typewriter to type what I was writing. While I refused to leave the typewriter in Monrovia, I was constrained to sell it in Danané to finance our trip to Abidjan. Our calling price was 30,000cfa. The middleman told us the buyer could only pay 10,000cfa. We had no choice. My distant relatives were so kind, filling up that amount to something that could transport the three of us to Abidjan. They also gave us little pocket money to buy food on the way. All this happened after we had unsuccessfully sought assistance from the United Nations High Commission for Refugees (UNHCR). They took down our records without giving us the assistance we were seeking. We tried the police. We couldn't get any help.

While making all the efforts to get to Abidjan, we met a fellow who we thought meant well. He came to give us some advice. He warned that Abidjan was not a good place for penniless refugees like us. He said going to Abidjan without the proper traveling documents was dangerous. He thought we could be easily hunted down by brigands in the city. They would take all of our meager possessions. We thanked him for his advice and told him that we would not allow anything to stand in the way of our optimism. We boasted that we were not village dwellers in Liberia, that we lived in the city, and that there would be little surprise about what we would see in Abidjan. After all, Abidjan was simply another city, even if it meant a city bigger and fancier than Monrovia. And before this trip, I had been in Abidjan on two different occasions. I was not a total stranger going there this time. I knew what to do when we got there. So this man couldn't tell me anything about Abidjan I didn't already know. With such resolution, we boarded the bus for Abidjan. While pushing towards Abidjan, some romantic feelings about the city and what we hoped to accomplish there developed in my mind. And then came the poem, "Abidjan."

ABIDJAN

A great treasure house
Of lively soulful African arts,
A charming city full of
Beautiful attraction for the senses.
A beautiful garden where hope
Flourishes like flowers.
There we will jump for the million stars
In the cool evening sky.
We are not brigands.
We are not loubards.
We have truck load of creative talents
And mountain high of determination
To rise to the 7th sky of stardom.
Will you let us in, will you let us,
Even if we don't have papers?
Will you let us
Walk on the red carpet

So we may forget our worries
And be happy?
Youpougon, Cocody, Plateau,
Make way for your new guests.
We coming with positive vibration
From Liberia we know
Way before the sound of the guns
Started sounding on the horizon.

It was a clear morning when we arrived in Abidjan. Trying to show to Parker and Sam that I know my way around Abidjan, I told them to follow me as we entered the Gbaka, a mini bus. I made sure we entered the one going to Youpougon Sicogi, where my aunt lived with her children. This was not like my first visit to Abidjan in 1985 when a Good Samaritan I met on the bus took me to his house and escorted me in the morning to my aunt's place. Then I had only the address of the place written in a note book. When I showed it to this Ivorian fellow who was my seatmate, he told me not to worry, he knew the place. That was then. And now I was not a stranger in Abidjan.

When we got to my aunt's house, we found out she had traveled out of town but her children were there. They were very happy to receive us. Although our arrival added onto their burden, they were generous enough to share whatever they had until their mother returned.

Sicogi is a government real estate company in Abidjan. My aunt, Makangbeh Donzo, her mate, Ma Fanta and their children lived in this two bed room real estate house. Their grown children had already moved on their own, sleeping at different locations in the neighborhood. Their husband, Morri Sidibe had passed away some years before. With the two bed room occupied by my aunt and her mate, the only room for us was the living room. We spread mats on the concrete floor to sleep. This was nothing strange to us because in most African homes whether in Liberia or Ivory Coast, there are large numbers of people from the same extended families living together. People share beds and when anyone can't find space on the beds they would sleep on the mats spread on the floor. It was the same situation we had on Jamaica Road in Monrovia. We shared this public housing project of my aunt until Parker and Sam moved in with some Ivorian friends, Kadafi and his brother Dedier. It was there Parker met Virginie, Dedier's sister who fell in love with him.

Having seen the Liberian situation nightly on their TV screens, many Ivorians were fascinated with us in their community. We became instant celebrities who everyone wanted to talk to. Many of them were curious about the English we spoke. Some were just curious to see Liberians in flesh. They had seen lots of suffering faces on the TV. The clean cut images we presented was strikingly different from the suffering and hungry picture they had seen on TV. They told each other that there were some Liberians living in their neighborhood and many people came just to see us. Many of them were generous with money and food. These friends invited us to their homes to eat with them. They would introduce us to their families who treated us like they had known us forever. While we appreciated the generosity of these friends, we knew we had a mission and that was the music. We wanted to find somewhere where we could start our music project. From talking to one person or another, we were told about Mamadou Doumbia, a veteran Ivorian musician and band leader. I had known Mamadou Doumbia since I was a child in Saclepea when he toured Liberia. He was a pretty big name in Liberia among the Mandingoes. On several occasions in the past, he played in various parts of Liberia, including Saclepea, my home town. With that thought on my mind, we approached the old man. I told him how I had grown up in Saclepea listening to his music and how much of a fan I had been over the years. He was impressed with the fact that I had known him in Liberia. He and his players helped to arrange two of our songs. We carried that demo around with the hope of finding some producers. Every day we would wake up with the feeling that we needed to tighten our belts, keep hustling till we made it. For us, failure was not an option.

One of the many Ivorian friends I met was Zepheran Gbadobre. We were walking about one day when we came across his record store where he was playing Denis Brown, a Jamaican reggae singer. He thought we were there to buy cassettes. He asked in French what we wanted. When he knew we could not speak French, he started talking to us in English. He spoke perfect English even with the heavy French accent. After this first meeting, Gbadobre found me the next day at my aunt's place. I went with him to his house which he shared with his parents and siblings. They all greeted me and welcomed me into their family and said I was welcomed to come there any time. That first day, we ate foufou made out of plantain.

As time went by, Parker, Sam and I found different friends whose houses became our eating spots. If there was no food at my aunt's house, we would go visit these friends and we were never disappointed. Gbadobre's house was one of my regular spots. There was another one called Dramane Kone. Gbadobre introduced me to Paul, a strong supporter of the Ivorian opposition, Ivorian Popular Front(FPI). While Gbadobre and I visited Paul from time to time, I met Bintu Camara who also introduced me to her parents. When I told them my grandmother was a Camara, the old man told me I was their nephew and welcomed in their house any time. Besides these strangers whose homes became my eating spots, I had several other relatives residing in Abidjan. Uncle Ngafin and brother Kamuadee were in Adjame. With these relatives and friends, food was never a problem. We experienced abundance of Ivorian hospitality.

While we found many friends that were generous enough to share with us food and pocket changes, I thought that we could not sit forever depending on their generosity. Sometimes I felt guilty for these guys to be giving so much to us when they themselves needed it. I started to think of what we could do to earn some money. I called Parker and Sam and told them, "Gentlemen, while I appreciate the generosity of our friends, I think it would be better that we go around looking for any work to do so as to be able to earn some money."

"What kind of work can we do?" Parker said.

"I don't think that will work," Sam said.

Up to that point we had pinned our hopes on finding a producer for our songs. I told them that before we found the producer, it would be better for us to find something to do so we wouldn't be a liability on other people. I told them that I would feel more comfortable accepting money that I work for than the one just given to me free by other people, no matter how good their intentions were. I suggested that we leave our community and go to some affluent neighborhoods asking people to give us any job they had. Perhaps some well to do person, discovering that we were Liberians and were serious to make it would feel sorry for us and help us. I was able to convince them and we agreed to go the next morning.

We took the gbaka to Niagon. We got off and started walking about. We went to the first home and told them if they had any dirty clothes to wash. We didn't have any luck there. After about three failures, we saw some people making bricks for building houses. We approached them and they agreed. At the end of the day, we earned 6000cfa. We split the money with each of us taking 2000cfa. The next day when I told them for us to go again, Parker said he felt degraded to do these kinds of work for money. Sam said the same thing. I told them that I could not understand why they would gladly take free money from people but they were too good to work for money unless they were sitting down behind desks in fabulous offices.

I was inspired by the stories of Malians and Burkinabes who came to Abidjan to wash cloths for people in the neighborhoods. They would be going to houses and asking people if they had dirty clothes to wash. They would earn enough money through this menial job. They would work and save enough to open their own shops or stores. Some would return to their countries with lots of money. For those that opened stores, they would go on becoming rich while those whose dirty clothes they used to wash would be struggling to get money here and there. When they saw that the man who used to wash their clothes had surpassed them in their own country, then they would be envious and jealous of their success. No matter what I told Parker and Sam, they would not listen to me.

11

Houphouet versus Gbagbo

I HAD MANY IVORIAN FRIENDS during my one and a half year stay in Abidjan during the early 90s. Among my male friends, Gbadobre was my best friend. I accompanied him to many places, even on several occasions to his church. As a Moslem, I had not been to a church before except when I attended St. John Episcopal School in Buchanan. At that school, there were some mandatory school programs that were held in the church. So it was with Gbadobre that I went to the church. Not that I had any interest in converting to Christianity but just to demonstrate my own sense of tolerance when it comes to matter of religion. Gbadobre knew I was a Moslem but he did not question my religious belief. He was very kind and was one of those that made my stay in Abidjan a memorable experience.

This time was perhaps the most politically charged moment in Ivory Coast's recent history. There was what I would call Gbagbomania. Gbadobre was one of those for whom Gbagbo was a political messiah who had come to redeem the Ivorians from the corrupt leadership of the old man. He was a strong supporter of Gbagbo's Ivorian Popular Front (FPI). If you talked to Gbadobre, he would tell you that everything wrong in Ivory Coast was because of Houphouet Boigny's PDCI party. He called them robbers who were robbing the Ivorians of their resources. When I told him Gbagbo was just like any other politician who would demonize his opponent to achieve his political objective, he said, "My friend, Gbagbo is a good man. He will be better than these thieves." Sometimes he would want to say more about what qualified Gbagbo than Houphouet to rule Ivory Coast but could not say it perfectly in English to make me understand.

Politics was a routine each time Gbadobre and I met. One night we were at his place with some friends that had come to visit him. He introduced me to them as his Liberian friend. Of the three friends, two could speak English but they had a problem with the fact that those of us from Liberia could not speak French or were not making any effort to speak their national language. "How can you not speak French when you are next to two French speaking countries, Ivory Coast and Guinea?" I didn't have any answer for that. Seeing that I was feeling embarrassed, Gbadobre changed the subject back to politics. After listening to all the negative things they were saying about Houphouet, I said that the old man's more than 20 years in power had produced more tangible results than the more than 100 years with more than 10 presidents in Liberia. I said, "Look at the beautiful networks of roads all over the country, transportation and communication. Look at the beautiful buildings and skyscrapers." His response was like, "These are all good things but all we want now are employment and better wages and salaries. PDCI has failed to deliver these goods to every Ivorian." He went on to say that Ivorians were suffering because of Houphouet and PDCI. "Ivory Coast is a wealthy country," he said, "but the wealth is only benefiting PDCI and its supporters."

Another night, I accompanied Gbadobre to the FPI Youpougon's headquarter for a meeting. This meeting was to be attended by FPI supporters from Gagnoa where both Gbagbo and Gbadobre hailed from. But this meeting was a fundraiser for a candidate running to represent Gagnoa as a deputy in the Ivorian Parliament. The number of people attending the meeting was too small, only 29 people came. While we were already there, Gbadobre had another appointment that evening. He was struggling with the decision whether to keep that appointment or stay at the meeting. After sometime thinking about it he decided to go for that appointment. How could he leave without other people feeling negative about him? He devised a strategy by which we would leave without anyone noticing that he had left. We agreed that he would go out and after a few minutes I should follow him.

When I was about to leave as per the agreement between me and Gbadobre, a fellow called me and started asking all kinds of questions. The man had come late to the meeting. He had been eyeing me with suspicion since his arrival. When I went in the bathroom to urinate, he followed me. When I returned to my seat before Gbadobre devised a plan for us to leave, he was still eyeing me. Then when I was about to leave, he confronted me, asking for my name and what was my purpose of being there? I was speechless because I could not express myself in French. Gbadobre was not there to defend me and his friend who had come with us sat there looking at the man interrogating me without offering any word for me. In my broken French, I told him I was accompanying my friend who was an FPI member. After a few minutes of gesticulation, he let me go, but not without thoroughly searching me. He secretly followed me to my surprise. He was still following me when I joined Gbadobre some distance from the meeting place. After some serious argument between him and Gbadobre which lasted for more than five minutes, he shook both of our hands. Gbadobre later on explained to me they had experience with PDCI folks infiltrating their meetings pretending to be FPI supporters only to report their activity to the government.

I would expect to be in trouble with the government for attending the opposition meeting, but now it was the opposition that was suspecting me of being a government spy. Around this time there was a rumor that some Liberians were arrested for anti-government activities. I was wondering what could have happened to me if the government agents had seen me at this opposition meeting? With Liberia being a divided country between Amos Sawyer's interim government in Monrovia and Charles Taylor in Gbarnga, where could I be deported to for meddling in the Ivorian politic? But I was scared that even if they couldn't deport me, they could harm me without anybody knowing since I was not a known figure. Since the government was a strong supporter of Taylor, I was seriously scared that Taylor's secret agents could harm me. When I expressed these concerns to Gbadobre the next day, he told me not to worry because nothing would happen to me.

Days leading to the Ivorian national election in October 1990,

Laurent Gbagbo appeared on the National TV. According to Gbadobre, that was the first time their leader had appeared on TV. According to my friends, Gbagbo's appearance on TV was long overdue. Many people who never used to watch TV except for movies or music programs tuned in to watch this special program. Gbadobre never use to watch what he called, "False propaganda" by PDCI officials. "They have used TV to lie to people for more than 30 years to control our country. So with the appearance of Gbagbo tonight, every TV set was overcrowded with people eager to see Gbagbo talking.

One of the more explosive issues in the election was whether "foreigners" would be allowed to vote. There are many Ivorians with connection to Mali, Senegal, Burkina Faso or Guinea. Even though many of these people have only known Ivory Coast as their country, some other Ivorian continued to call them foreigners. That reminds me of my own situation in Liberia. While the ruling party was seen as inclusive, the opposition was more xenophobic and its supporters were threatening a backlash against the foreigners. Some threatened to kill any foreigner who would not keep out of the Ivorian affairs. Even my own friend Gbadobre was not immuned from this so called anti-foreigner outburst. One time he said any foreigner who failed to keep out of Ivorian politics was looking for death. Another time he said, "Any death of foreigners we are not responsible." He advised that I kept in door until the election was over. One time I visited Mohammed Sow at Cinema Dialogue and there was a man who was insanely drunk and shouting explicitly at foreigners. He shouted that if the foreigners didn't keep out of their politics what was happening in Liberia was small compared to what would happen in Ivory Coast.

12

Good Friend Losene Bamba...!

IT WAS FRIDAY and on most Fridays I would go to Adjame to my Uncle, Ngafin Konneh's place. Uncle Ngafin had moved to Abidjan since 1986. He would go to Liberia to buy truck loads of music cassettes and brought them here to sell. So while there were many of us who were here because of the war, Uncle Ngafin was already here. Many times he encouraged me to move to his place but I didn't want to go away from Parker and Sam. Even though they had many friends, I was the one that brought them to the Ivory Coast and I had to stay around them. Another reason for my Friday trip to Adjame was to attend the Friday Prayer at the Grand Mosque, the biggest mosque in Abidjan.

When I disembarked from the gbaka right opposite the mosque, I was walking to the place where Uncle and his friends usually met. I met him and many other people I had known in Liberia. Uncle told me he had several letters for me from my brothers and friends in Monrovia and Nzérékoré. We walked to his house five blocks from the Grand Mosque. The letter from my brother Kafumba Konneh in Nzérékoré was a reply to my previous letter I had written him inquiring about relatives and friends in Guinea and Liberia. He said that most of the people I had inquired about were alive the last time he heard about them. Mohammed Konneh, Abu Konneh, Musa Bility and Foday Donzo, according to Kafumba, were all at Gray Stone at the American Embassy's compound in Monrovia. The letter also said that Kalu Jah Boy was in detention in Conakry because he was caught with weapons. He was a member of the Liberian Army. When Doe was killed, Kalu came to Conakry, according to the letter. My little brother Ousman and his friend, Bangalie Donzo, escaped from their captors and made it to Guinea. They both had been in the Liberian army as well. They had sustained some injury while still being detained by the rebels. Hassan Bracewell and his family were seeking refuge at a church in Monrovia. According to Kafumba, they got the information from our brother Abdullah Konneh and Papa Foday who had just arrived in Nzérékoré from Monrovia. Papa Foday was a member of the AFL, the Liberian army.

After a while I got the news that my friend Losene Bamba was killed. I felt so terrible when I heard that news. It felt as if a red-hot iron had cut through my flesh. Losene Bamba was my homeboy. He was a good friend, a promising young man of our town, Saclepea. The way he carried himself had convinced us that one day he would be a leader not only of his persecuted Mandingo folks, but the whole nation. He was very intelligent and bright. He was a rising champion for all-inclusive democratic values in Liberia. The last time I talked to him was in Monrovia when we met at Musa's mother's place on Carey Street.

Losene's parents were not counted among the so-called prominent people in Liberia. They had not worked for the government. Just like my parents, his parents were illiterate but hardworking folks. This twin son of theirs had been very thirsty for knowledge and was determined to go to any length to seek it. His parents had been working to support him as he went from place to place in pursuit of education. First when I heard about Losene's death, I was not told the circumstances under which he died. It was another time that I met a fellow at the Liberian Embassy in Plateau who had come from Monrovia. He told me about what led to Losene's death. According to this guy, when the rebels hit Chicken Farm where Losene was staying, he was taken by them. Losene felt secure with a Mano friend who was an NPFL fighter. Accordingly, this friend protected him and took very good care of him. One day when the friend had gone to the war front, some other NPFL fighters came to where he was and when they found out he was a Mandingo, they killed him.

As I thought about Losene, I felt somehow guilty that I was alive and he was dead. During our last meeting in Monrovia before I left, we all had vowed to stay, that we were not running away from Liberia because some misguided people thought they could run us out. I wish I had met him one last time before I left. Maybe I could have convinced him that it would be better to live to see another day. I never had the opportunity to explain my change of heart to him. Only if I had met him one last time. I have thought so many times...

13

Nightmares

I DID NOT only get the death news of Losene Bamba, I also at another time heard about the death of Vamunya Sanoe. As I was told, he was at Graystone seeking refuge until one day he trusted someone he knew who promised to help him with some food. I heard that when Vamunya followed this friend of his to Westpoint, he met with other rebels who upon recognizing him as a Mandingo could not spare his life even when his friend pleaded on his behalf. What was surprising in the case of Vamunya is that his grandmother was a Mano and he could even pass for Mano by speaking the dialect and giving them a false Mano name.

Since hearing this sad news, I had a series of nightmares. The first of the bad dreams occurred on October 21, 1990. It was an encounter with the rebels in Monrovia. I slept in the room with some friends. In the morning we put the radio on BBC which was reporting the latest round of fighting in Monrovia. After the news, I found myself walking on the Old Bridge linking Bushrod Island to mainland Monrovia at Water Side. There was to and from foot traffic on the bridge. I saw a fellow coming opposite me. He was dressed in a grey coat suit, and black shoes. He was very dark in complexion. I instantly recognized his face. He had either been a schoolmate or classmate at Johnny Voker High School in Saclepea. He recognized me as well. He appeared very serious, looking straight in my face. I could smell the foul odor of his mouth. He pointed his index finger at me in a very unfriendly manner. He said loudly enough for everyone to hear, "You are a Dingo." Dingo is usually a derogatory way of calling someone who is Mandingo.

"No, I am not," I managed to say but the trembling in my voice and the contortion of my face betrayed my confidence.

"You think I don't know you are Mandingo?" he asked with 100% certainty of my ethnic identity, but I kept denying to his annoyance. At last he said I would have to pay with my life for lying to him. He took hold of my right hand with a firm grip. I could see people going to opposite directions of the bridge but no one showed any concern. They acted as if they considered their own survival far more important than another person's. At this point, it was not advisable to intervene on behalf of someone in rebel custody because you could be the next person. Realizing that no one would come to my rescue, I thought of the only alternative. If I was going to die, I didn't want to die lying down. I had to fight if need be. When I started fighting to free myself from his tight grip, another rebel came to his aid. The new guy who joined him was huge. He was also someone I knew. We had eaten together. When we had the Tribute to Peter Tosh program back in Saclepea in 1987, he was a partner. I had given him money to buy cigarettes. He once converted to Islam. My last time seeing him was during my last visit to Saclepea in November 1989, a month before the war was announced by Charles Taylor. I can't remember his real name but his popular name we all knew him by was Kou Gbay.

Kou Gbay lifted me like a baby. He tried to take me to the direction of the death camp. I was shaking my hands and feet fiercely as my voice was loudly pleading for mercy. I told him I was "half n half" a mixture of Mandingo and Mano. He said being half n half didn't make any difference once I had any Mandingo blood in me. I pleaded to Kou Gbay to think about our old time relationship. That didn't make any difference either. I talked until I had nothing more to say. I cried till I could cry no more. All my cries fell on deaf ears. I became so helpless and hopeless to the point that I resigned myself to my fate. I was convinced now about death. I started thinking about my father and mother as well as other members of my family and how I would not be able to see them again. I felt bad that they would not even see my body. I would be buried in some unknown grave or my body might rot on the streets with dogs, and flies feasting over it. The thought of such added to my helplessness and hopelessness.

I was awakened by someone in the house and it was time to pray my morning prayer. As I turned, there were beads of sweat all over my body. Now I knew it was just a dream. A bad dream indeed.

A week after this nightmare, I had another dream. This one was the opposite of the nightmare. I saw Foday Donzo, Musa Bility, Kalifala Koisiah, Sekou Bility, and Amara Donzo. Foday told me he had been in Kakata, a rebel controlled area. I kept thinking of asking how he survived in the rebel controlled area as a Mandingo. But he was in a hurry to go somewhere. We didn't have much time to talk. I had a conversation with the rest of the people just mentioned. When I woke up, I could not remember anything we had talked about.

As I thought about the first dream, and considering my would-be-executioners who happened to be people I knew personally, I thought about how Bamba's friends who he trusted with his life could not protect him. I also thought about Vamunya Sanoe who trusted a friend who could not protect him. Then one of the reasons that convinced me to leave Monrovia was the news of the death of my cousin Samuka Sherif in Buchanan. All of these are clear evidence that I might have had similar fate as these friends.

Before the war, some of my best friends among the Manos and Gios were Anthony Myer, Vincent Sahn, Betty Mehn, Sahn Bambia, Chris Zogbay, Doris Duo and Peter Saye. Every time I think about Bamba's situation my mind runs to these friends of mine. Every now and then I struggle with the fact that these guys could do any harm to me. Before the war we enjoyed each other's company. That's why it's very unbelievable for me to believe that any of these guys could have harmed me.

14

Platonic Relationship

PLATONIC LOVE IS defined as a non-sexual affectionate relationship between opposite sex. This may not conform to what is considered a Platonic Ideal of love; chaste but passionate, based on not the lack of romantic or erotic feeling. In accordance with its original definition, Platonic love is meant to enrich and strengthen relation with wisdom and the platonic form of Beauty. Plato's Phaedrus and Symposium make in depth analyses of Platonic love with an example being a love between a man and a boy. In the Phaedrus, Platonic love is considered to be a form of "divine madness" which is considered as a gift from God and the expression of it is rewarded in the hereafter. Symposium has a different take on the matter: "a situation by which love takes one to the form of beauty and wisdom is detailed."

What is stated above is how I will describe my relationship with Nicole Guei. Like I have already talked about Zepheran Gbadobre as being my best male Ivorian friend, Nicole was certainly my best female Ivorian friend. The circumstances under which we met and the extent our relationship reached is very unusual. I had gone to bed on Sunday night with the plan to visit the United States Cultural Center in Cocody, and the Liberian Embassy in Plateaux the next morning. Then on Monday morning when Parker, Sam and I had eaten breakfast, I boarded SOTRA bus #86. On this day, something kept telling me to pay the bus fare. I was glad I did because when we got to Adjamé, the inspectors boarded the bus. While they were inspecting, one person jumped through the window and they caught two persons for not paying their fares. Many times I used to ride the bus from one point to another without paying. But whenever I decided to pay the inspectors would get on board. Only on one occasion the inspectors got on board when I had not paid the fare. I thought of jumping through the window, but I weighed the consequences of that and being caught. Jumping through the bus window was very risky because there was a possibility of being knocked down by a passing car or having to fall down hard on the concrete pavement. According to information, there had been several fatalities reported of people that jumped through the bus window. For those who got caught, the penalty was to pay 10,000cfa or wash eight long buses. In any case, I would prefer washing the bus or paying the fine of 10,000cfa to risking my life by jumping through the window. While these were the choices I had on this day, fortunately, the inspectors left without asking me. On this particular day, I remained in the bus until Cocody. I got off at a point which was about a few blocks from the American Cultural Center. Every time I was in Cocody, I was reminded of "Cocody Rock", one of the famous songs of Alpha Blondy. As I walked from the bus stop to the American Cultural Center, I saw two girls who were coming from the opposite direction. I heard them talking and I thought they were Liberians. Feeling as if I were on Broad or Carey Street in Monrovia, I spoke to them. To my surprise, they said they were Nigerians, but they were curious to know which part of Liberia I was from. Ironically, they wouldn't tell me where they came from with their familiar Liberian accent. This encounter came just after a few days when another young Liberian male told me he was a Ghanaian born in Liberia. Maybe I should believe they were not Liberians. Maybe the situation in Liberia at the time made them feel uncomfortable to call themselves Liberians. Whatever their case might be, anyone hearing them talking would assume they were Liberians because the Liberian accent is a unique one among the different variations of English spoken in Africa.

Around that time some Liberians were afraid to disclose their identity for fear of harassment by the Ivorian security forces in Abidjan. It was no secret that Houphouet Boigny's government was pro-Taylor.

Based on this it was alleged that those Liberians who were not Taylor supporters were viewed by the Ivorian security forces as a threat to peace in Ivory Coast. This was especially so within the Liberian Krahn community. I came across two Krahn girls from Liberia who confirmed this information. They were some of the Liberian girls I used to hang out with. The two girls told me they were afraid for their lives. So based on this I could not be surprised that people with typical Liberian accents would pretend to be Nigerians or Ghanaians. It might have also been because of the tribal sentiment that one way or the other defined the Liberian civil war.

After exchanging a few words with these "Nigerian" girls, I continued to walk towards the American Cultural Center's library. When I got there people were standing in line for security checks. Among them there were some students from the University of Abidjan. While these people spoke French to the security guards, I spoke English when they got to me which caught the attention of everyone. I went in the library and left after 30 minutes to go to the Liberian Embassy in Plateaux, the administrative district of Abidjan. Outside the library I heard someone calling my attention. Apparently she had walked after me when I left the library and as I learned, she had taken interest in talking to me when we were standing in line.

When I turned to see who was calling me, it was this beautiful Ivorian girl. She said with a heavy French accent, "Are you a Liberian?"

"Yes, I am." From then she and I started talking. She introduced herself as Nicole Guei and told me she was a student of the University of Abidjan majoring in English. She said she wanted to improve her English and thought the best way to do so would be to engage in conversation with an English speaking person. On that note, she proposed a friendship and I gladly accepted. It was right then she told me to accompany her to see her place. I accepted that invitation thereby cancelling my trip to the Liberian Embassy in Plateaux. Whatever I was going to accomplish at the Liberian Embassy was minor compared to the opportunity of being a friend to such a gorgeous woman.

She told me that she lived at the university's dormitory but we were to visit her home before going there. She stopped a taxi which took us to Deaux Plateaux. When we got home, her dad was not there but the housekeeper was there. She had finished cooking plantain fufu and soup made of fish and beef. Nicole and I ate together. When we finished eating, we took another taxi that took us to Cite Mermoze, her university dormitory. When we got to her room, she told me to wait. I was all by myself in the room for about 15 minutes. She came in with some of her friends, Patric Manete as well as Lucy, all of them studying English at the university. We talked about the phonetics of the English language, different variations of the language in terms of accents representing different places. We also exchanged views on family, relationship, politics and so on. I found both of her friends, Patric Manete and Lucy very interesting. They were very well informed and intelligent. Lucy said she had travelled to several countries including Ghana, Burkina Fasso, and Niger.

After a while in the room, Nicole asked that we all go to what is called in Abidjan "Alokodrom." Such a place where fried plantain is sold with either atike or fish is all over Abidjan. There was one not too far from the dormitory. The four of us walked there and ordered fried plantains, fish and some soft drinks. As I bade them farewell, Nicole gave me 5,000cfa and told me to come the next weekend.

When I got home I told Parker and Sam about my time and experience with Nicole and her friends. I told them about the beauty queen I met and how hospitable she was to me. Parker said he would like to go with me for the next visit. When the weekend came, he and I went there. Nicole had invited the two friends the last time and there was another friend, Rachel who I did not see the last time I was there. The treatment was the same as my previous visit. When we were leaving, she gave me 10,000cfa which I shared with Parker 50/50. It was like that every time I visited her.

15 | Christmas/New Year 90-91

WHEN THE CHRISTMAS of 1990 and the New Year 1991 were approaching, we received many invitations from our Ivorian friends, both males and females inviting us for parties. Everywhere we went there was chicken, beef, drinks, music and lots of fun stuff. It was party all day long from one place to another and we wanted to be at all the places. At this time, some new comers had joined the three of us, and got to meet a few other Liberians. The new arrivals in the community were Joseph Natoe and my nephew Mohammed Sheriff. Others we met were TY and Nicole Blyden. It was a beautiful mix of Liberians in Sicogi. Joseph Natoe was a Gio, Parker was a Bassa, TY was a Kru, Blyden was a Congon and then me and my nephew Mohammed Sheriff. Joseph Natoe was the only person among us who was somehow working. He used to design and paint sign boards, banners and t-shirts. Back in Liberia, he had been working with a promotional agency, Afromedia, in Monrovia. Now in Abidjan, his professional work gave him some advantage. Even though he would have liked better compensation than what the few jobs were bringing in, he seemed to be doing well. We all agreed with him that something was better than nothing. One way or the other, we all used to hang around him. Whenever he got paid for doing some jobs, he would buy food and we would eat.

During the Christmas and the New Year, we were either invited to these parties as individuals or as a group. Even though we spoke

English and they spoke French, those invitations demonstrated Ivorian hospitality towards their fellow Africans. We might belong to different tribes, religions, or nations, but that did not erase the fact that we were all Africans. The fact that we were labeled as Anglophone and they were labeled as Francophone was just because of the colonial past. For us Liberians living in this community celebrating the holiday season, the tribal animosity playing in Liberia did not affect our shared camaraderie there in Abidjan. We all might have not known each other in Liberia, but circumstances there in Abidjan forced us to look out for each other, confirming the adage that when two quarreling compatriots meet in another country, they put aside their differences based on common interests. There in Abidjan, we needed each other.

Perhaps the main event of the holiday season was the Alpha Blondy Concert on New Year's Day 1991 at the Parc de Sports in Trechville. I went there with my friend Mohammed Sow and it was a great event that lasted for two hours. We got there sharp 1400 and waited in line for two straight hours. It seemed like the whole of Abidjan was there and the crowd was uncountable. We all looked like we were hungry for Alpha's African version of reggae beat. With everyone anxious to see Mr. Reggae d'Afrique, his I-Three came, moving on the stage rhythmically towards the three mics positioned. With qualified vibrancy, the three charming girls lighted the whole stadium full of people. At that moment, musical art was at its zenith and the crowd was ever going so wild in response to the I-Three performance. The beat was traveling in our bodies like electric current. When everyone was shouting joy and happiness, Alpha emerged on the stage, surrounded by his entourage. He was draped with his big red-yellow-green Rasta flag. As he unwrapped, the crowd went wild with everyone chanting "Alpha! Alpha! Alpha!" The show was on and everyone was dancing along with the music. Glory to the Almighty One and let the devil be dead. I was dancing out the reggae feeling. My friend Mohammed was doing the same. It was the spirits of the New Year and the music that was setting everyone on fire. "Brigadier Sabari," from Alpha Blondy's first album signaled the end of the two-hour show. It was money and time well spent. The bus fares and the entrants were paid for by Mohammed. Mohammed, though a Guinean, had lived in Liberia before the war. He was one of my good friends in Abidjan.

When I got back that night, I joined my friends to other parties in the neighborhood. The next day, Joseph Natoe told me to accompany him to Niangon to meet his friend Old Man Gondah. I was eager to see the funny man from Liberia. Years leading to the war, Old Man Gondah was one of the popular TV stars of the Malawala Balawala comedy troupe and every evening thousands of people would crowd around TV sets to see Old man Gonda and fellow cast members of the popular show. The last time I saw him was on the TV screen in Monrovia. Since I didn't know him then I was eager to see him in person in Abidjan. I could not think that one day I would meet him in less glamorous of a setting. When we met him, he was telling us about his experience in Ivory Coast compared to what it was in Liberia. On the surface, one could tell that life was good for the funny man in Abidjan. He was living in his brother's house. His brother was an Ivorian who he said was some kind of big man in Ivory Coast. Given that reality, Old Man Gondah might have not been suffering in Ivory Coast but he was surely missing the fact that he was a TV celebrity in Liberia. Here in Ivory Coast he was just an ordinary person. He told me that he and Alpha Blondy attended the same elementary school in Odiene, a town in the north of Ivory Coast. Down the line, Alpha Blondy became an international musical star, representing Ivory Coast while Old Man Gonda became a popular TV star in Liberia. It was the first time I learnt that his Ivorian name or real name was Jean. I'm not sure anyone in Liberia knew this about this Malawala Balawala funny man. That might be because everybody that came from somewhere else was afraid to talk about wherever they came from because of the stigma attached to the word "foreigner" in Liberia. Six months after the Alpha Blondy's show, Mohammed Sow and I attended another reggae concert. This time around it was Ismail Isaac. It was during the end of Ramadan 1991. Ismail had just arrived from France with his latest release, "Rahim." The crowd was huge but felt short of the number that showed up for Alpha's concert. We were in one section of Palais de Sport. While Alpha sings bilingual, Ismail sings mostly in Mandingo. According to people who understand and speak French, Ismail is not as fluent in that White man's language as Alpha is. Anyway, French or no French, he's got the voice that can shake the earth and he made the best of it for two solid hours while the crowd was jamming to his vibrant Mandingo reggae beat. I was soaked in sweat. Sow bought some cold water to cool our thirsts. Somehow, I began to envy Ismail for his sweet voice, which had such a magical feel to it. And those beautiful girls backing him made me wish one were mine to love and kiss.

16

Friendship and Betrayal

IT WAS ON OCTOBER 24, 1991 we completed three songs for our demo at Mamadou Doumbia's studio in Youpougon. There were only three songs instead of the six we wanted. We could not afford the amount the old man charged. The agreement was for us to take the three songs on the demo to look for a producer who might pay to complete the project. I had many relatives in Abidjan but I couldn't go to them to sponsor a music production. I come from a conservative Islamic background which frowns on such things as music. I am a grandson of a man who was a religious scholar and builder of a mosque. With that being the case, I could not go to any one, not even Uncle Ngafin, to say I needed his support for what I wanted to do. As such, the three of us Sam, Parker and I decided to search for help elsewhere.

After a while going up and down in Abidjan looking for producers, the only person we found that showed interest in our efforts was Virginie, a young Ivorian woman. The connection was through Parker. From my aunt's house, Parker and Sam had moved with Dadier and his brother Kadafi. We all were happy that Parker and Sam had found a place to live. I personally thanked Dadier and his brother Kadafi for their kind gesture. Virginie was their cousin who was spending time at their place and she was a woman who was highly connected in Abidjan. She was very resourceful. I understood she was in a relationship with a guy that lived somewhere in Marcory or Treichville but there was some problem in the relationship. While spending time with her cousins Dadier and Kadafi, she met Parker. When Parker explained to her that we had done a demo at the studio and we were looking for producers, she promised to take us to some people she knew and if not she might undertake the project herself. That assuring message sounded very much like music in our ears. The conversations between her and Parker developed into a full blown relationship and that even cemented her resolve to help us.

We called ourselves the Black Messengers. Parker and I were introduced by a mutual friend called Reggie Thompson on Jamaica Road back in Monrovia in 1988. I became to know later that Parker was a sensational performer at talent shows in Monrovia. He used to be out there with popular upcoming Liberian stars at those talent shows. I had the lyrical skill and he had the talent for singing and dancing. That was a great combination. Being a creative person with a lot of ideas, I was looking for some outlets to showcase my creative talents. When Alpha Blondy came out with the Brigadier Sabari album, I was so fired up with creative ideas and it set me on a mission. I saw music as the avenue for that. That's what drove me to it. For me, I had many alternatives; music was not a mean to an end. For Parker, music was his only hope of a better life. He invested all of his time and energy into it. So we both approached it with great passion. When it came to political or intellectual discussion, I had my usual friends like Musa, Losene or Foday. When it came to music, Parker was my buddy. We were seen together everywhere in the city. He introduced Sam to me and together we formed the Black Messengers, a named I coined. This has a political undertone and that was the difference between Parker and I. Parker was not about politics or social consciousness. For him, it was about fame, money and women. With our diversity of thoughts, we found the common ground. Because of me, he was able to hone his lyrical skill. For the trip to the Ivory Coast, Sam was the money man. I was the strategist and Parker was the main singer. That's how it was planned when we planned to travel even before the war. Only I had experienced life outside of Monrovia or Liberia.

Virginie's assistance would make it the first time that any opportunity had come to us through Parker. Virginie would give him money and sometimes he shared with us what he was getting. That put him in the driving seat of our operation because he had charmed the lady who was throwing us the lifeline so much she fell in love with him. He emerged as the king of the pack.

For some reasons, Virginie did not like me in that house. She was not comfortable with my presence. I came to realize that it was because of Alhassan, the son of my aunt's mate, Fanta. Alhassan was one of those thugs known in Abidjan as loubards and he was very much feared in the neighborhood. We had no blood relation except that he was a brother to my cousins from one father. Since I lived in their house, some people in the neighborhood took that against me. I had many unfriendly reactions because of Alhassan. That was the reason of Virginie's attitude towards me; Parker did not explain to her that he and I had come a long way together.

Yes, Alhassan had a bad reputation but never one day did he do anything to me or any of my friends. He was always cautious around us. We all got along with him fine. His mother, Mah Fanta was very kind to us as well.

One day Sam came to visit me at home. He was not happy with Parker. Apparently Parker had told him he was going solo, that he was the main man and that Sam and I were just hanging on his talents. I could not believe what Sam was telling me and I said I would have to hear from his own mouth.

Sam and I had met around 4pm. Around 11:30pm, Parker stopped by to break the news himself. We sat down watching a musical show on the TV. I did not tell him what Sam had told me but I could see that he had something on his mind. He was in a very pensive mood, perhaps calculating how he was going to break the news to me. He said he wanted us to go to the kiosque which was just around the corner. While there he bought two plates of spaghetti and meat with bread. I took a bottle of Fanta and he took a Coke. I still did not bother to ask him because I knew he would tell me eventually. When we got through eating with the clock ticking to 12:15am at which time we all had to go to bed, he told me what was on his mind. He went into a long talk about how we had been good friends all along but that now he had decided to go solo. He said he wished me and Sam good luck with our endeavors. I did not react in any emotional manner. I acted normal and I told him if that was how he felt, it didn't matter to me. I only said that members of groups can only decide to go solo when they are already known and that it was premature for him to break up the group when it was still an unknown entity. While I kept my cool, Parker was almost teared up as we parted. In the morning when I met Sam, I told him about last night with our man, Parker.

With us separated now, Virginie gave two options to Parker. By this time they had moved into a house which Virginie was renting. The two alternatives were whether to do a recording in Abidjan or Paris, France. Virginie was traveling to Paris to stay. So the question was whether Parker should join her in Paris to do the recording there or do it in Abidjan. Parker chose Paris over Abidjan. With that understanding, Virginie went to Paris, France with the plan to send for Parker at a later date. At the end of the day, Parker did not travel to Paris and he did not record in Abidjan. Though disappointed, Sam and I acted as if nothing had happened. We moved on back to Liberia.

17

My Last Days in Abidjan

TWO WEEKS BEFORE my last day in Abidjan, which was set for Friday, November 7, 1991, I was with my good friend, Nicole Guei. During my more than a year stay in the Ivorian capital, she had been my "something to fall back on." She showed me true Ivorian hospitality in so many ways that I won't forget.

It was during the morning hour on Saturday when I knocked on her dormitory door. When she knew it was me she said, "Entrez" and I entered. She had already prepared a nice morning meal. The main topic of discussion was my home going. She asked whether it was safe to go back to Monrovia or any part of Liberia. Since I was beyond all doubts that I must get back home, I told her yes.

Our schedule for the day was our last outing. From her Cite Mermoz Dormitory of Abidjan University we boarded a bus for Plateau where we hung about for several hours. After Plateau, we headed for Adjamé where she was to do some shopping for her pending visit to upcountry. In Adjamé, she bought some things for her brothers and sisters staying with her mother upcountry. The last thing she bought this day was a nice blue T-shirt for me, which she said was a souvenir by which I must remember her when I was back in Liberia.

We were in the shop around Cocody bus stop in Adjamé on De Gaulle Boulevard. She bought two bottles of soft drinks, a Fanta for me, a Coke for herself. Slowly and slowly we drank, both of us in a reflective mood. Perhaps we had talked about a whole lot of things except something else which both of us might have thought necessary to keep private. For in any situation, it's not too good to force people to bring out what they would rather keep inside. As such I didn't bother asking her as to what was rumbling and tumbling through her head. Maybe for the same reason, she might have thought to leave me with my private thoughts.

Our last moment together was at the bus stop, waiting for bus number 86 which would drop her off at the TV station. Then she would walk to her Mermoz dorm. After about ten minutes waiting, the bus came. A multitude of people started rushing in. She held me tightly close to her, gave me three friendly kisses on my cheeks. She released me, turned back towards the bus. Her departing words were, "Don't forget about me. *Il faut m'écrire.*"—Do write me.

I refused to look at her getting in the bus because my eyes were becoming teary. It was really an emotional moment for me. I am always tearful when I am leaving somebody for good after a long period of intimacy.

November 7, as I stated earlier, was the last day for me on the block in Youpougon Sicogi, a suburb of Abidjan. My friend, Mohammed Sow, whose room I had shared for the past four months, escorted me to my aunt's house. I told everybody that God willing I was leaving for good. While Sow and I sat in front of the house, my traveling companion, Sam, came and shook our hands. We picked up for Cinema Dialogue where Mohammed had his fledging business. He took us to a nearby Café for breakfast. The breakfast included tea with milk, spaghetti with fried beef and bread. We watered down every bit without much delay. Mohammed then walked us across the street to the bus stop by College William Ponty, opposite Cinema Dialogue. After saying goodbye to Mohammed, we boarded a *gbaka* (mini bus) and went to my uncle's house in Adjamé. After some minutes of chit-chat with him, we said goodbye and left. Before leaving, Sam and I were approached by a Nigerian fellow by the name of John, who was also returning to Liberia. He had resided in Liberia before the war. When the war broke out, he went to his native Nigeria where according to him things did not go well. As a result he decided to go back to Liberia. Like us, he too was returning with the hope of picking up where he had left off. So now it was the three of us that would partner on the return journey to Liberia. We walked around Adjamé doing little shopping. After the shopping we headed for Plateau.

We disembarked at the Hotel De Ville some minutes before noon. It was just about time for Friday prayer and I joined the multitude of fellow Moslems in a nearby fence. After the general prayer, I prayed Two more rakats. That was my own private time with the Creator, asking him to bless our journey back home. Thereafter, I joined my friends, Sam and John. We walked back and forth between Hotel De Ville and the Liberian Embassy until four o'clock when it was time for all the returning refugees to say our permanent goodbyes to Abidjan. It was about that time we met Mr. and Mrs. Denzel, who had paid for our returning tickets.

Denzel is a West Indian and his wife Laura is a Liberian. According to them, they met and got married in New York City. We met the couple through a mutual friend, Blyden Nicol who knew Laura from Harper, Maryland County, Liberia. Through Nicol, Sam and I, our friend, Joseph Natoe, had helped the couple prepare their African foodstuffs to be taken to America where they were operating a business center specializing in selling African food.

All the expected passengers were instructed to board a bus at the place where the ship to repatriate us was anchored. As we said goodbye, we were not only saying goodbye to Abidjan, we were saying goodbye to aloko, atcheke, banan futu or yam and all of the good friends, men, women, young and old, who had made our more than a year's stay in Abidjan a memorable feast.

At exactly 10 pm, the ship started its maneuvering to disembark. In the ship, what I had imagined to be a bread and butter experience turned out to be a very bitter one for me. Throughout the three day journey from Abidjan to Monrovia, I got seasick and became weak from constantly throwing up. Sam and John took care of me for the duration of the trip. On board the ship, we met some new friends, Bayor and Basoh. They all did their best for me. Bayor especially, was hustling tea, bread, medication and rice for me. They provided everything that was paid for. After having spent my last money in

Abidjan to buy a banana, few cups of sardines, and six loafs of bread for Sam and me, I was broke. I wanted to keep at least 1000cfa during the sea voyage. I couldn't do so because Sam wanted a bottle of wine. According to him, this would prevent him from vomiting. As a Moslem, it's forbidden to show someone where liquor is sold. Giving money to someone, knowing he or she is going to buy an alcoholic beverage is also wrong. After he pleaded with me that only wine would keep him from being seasick, I went against my religious ethic. Now all of us were poor like mosque rats. Only Bayor had some money and we depended on him.

Somewhere mid sea as we sailed, we saw some twinkle of light in the distance across the horizon. Many people said that it was Buchanan. At that moment, the feeling of being hijacked by Taylor's fighters, who in recent times had proven to be good sea pirates, gripped me. I dreaded the consequences of such misfortune. I prayed fervently to Allah to save the day for all the people on board the ship. Allah will not forsake his children on the high sea to be overcome by any sea pirate, I prayed and hoped. We sped through smoothly without encountering any danger. Allah, through the abled captain of the ship, led us safely. We neared Monrovia during the early hours of Monday, November 10, 1991. By 5:00 am, we were within the perimeter of the port. While we were some distance away, the ECOWA Monitoring Group (ECOMOG) patrol boat came to make assessment and give us the go ahead. We couldn't readily dock because other ships were anchored. They had to make way for us before we could move in to their space.

While dragging about on the ship, I met some other new friends. They were three charming Senegalese girls on their way to Senegal. We talked about a variety of subjects. At the end of our conversation, we all realized how much we had in common. At the time we talked, we could see a large crowd, which had come from various areas of the capital to greet their returnees. After we had jubilated about having more fun, time came for the last serious business. Every one of us returning with hundreds of suit cases was to be thoroughly searched by the ECOMOG soldiers to make sure we were not coming to disturb the peace they were sacrificing so much to maintain on this island in the sea of uncertainty. This process of rigorous searching kept on until 1:00pm., and then Sam and I, having parted from other friends, saw ourselves outside the port, wondering how to get home. He had to go to Jacob's Town and I was heading for Jamaica Road, not too far from the port.

In my eyes, Monrovia looked very dull, compared to the beautiful, vibrant Abidjan I had left behind. I took a clear view of some of the damages of the war. I couldn't see many beautiful cars plying the streets as before. The taxis and the buses looked over-used. While waiting for a car to take me home, I tried buying something, my first purchase of any item in Monrovia. That was a bag of cold water, which was going for 50 cents. The last time I purchased one it was going for 10 cents. At the Gardnersville parking, whereas before I would pay 25 cents to Jamaica Road junction, I had to pay $3.00 for me and my two traveling bags. Speeding on the Somalia Drive, I could see the marks of war everywhere. Electric wires were down. Projects were abandoned; houses that were once beautiful lay in ruins.

I got out of the taxi at the Jamaica Road junction. Walking into the family yard, I could still see many more marks of the war. Everywhere there were some ugly reminders of the war. I could imagine how rough and tough it was for those who lived and survived all the madness of the city reduced to dog-eat-dog factionalism. Our yard that used to be a lively Mecca for more than thirty members of an extended family was a complete ghost town as if to say it was thirty years ago when people used to live there. The few family members that had returned and those that had survived, I was told, had gone to town on their daily hustles. I shook my head with sadness. Noticing my reaction, someone standing by said, "But here is ten times better than any place Taylor's boys reached. We were blessed here because Prince Johnson was in control."

Being back on Jamaica Road was a joy for me. The last time I fled the city because I didn't want to be a statistic. I hoped to live to see another day ("he who fights and runs away lives long enough to fight for another day"—Bob Marley was up and about in my head). The presence of ECOMOG encouraged me to come back to Monrovia after more than a year in Abidjan. I prayed and thanked Allah. While

I was free now to go wherever I wanted to go, I couldn't be brave enough to venture outside of Monrovia where Taylor and his forces were in control.

After dropping my bags in the room, one of my brothers, Sekou, and I took taxis to Cary Street where he worked as a tailor and where I met a lot of friends and relatives. All along it was endless embrace, one after the other. We had been torn apart by the war, some staying here and some of us fleeing to safety elsewhere. It was a great thing to see all the emotions and tears of happiness. This moment of getting together again was so beautiful that its sparkling grandeur beautified the ugliness of the fratricidal war. As I looked across from my brother's tailor shop, my mind went back to 1984 when I used to sleep in an underground room of a building that was leveled by the war. Was anyone living in the house when it was destroyed during the heat of the war? That was the question on my mind but I didn't ask anyone.

18

Bloody Sunrise in Barkedu

NOW THAT I WAS BACK in Liberia, I had been meeting and talking to family members and friends. We told each other stories of our experiences. While I spent my time in Abidjan, Ivory Coast, others spent theirs in Guinea or Sierra Leone; and there were others who did not leave the country. They stayed in Liberia and survived the gun battles in Monrovia. They heard the various gun sounds—RPGs, bazookas, M16s and saw piles of lifeless bodies everywhere in the city. For those of us returning after the storm had calmed down, our stories were different from those of the survivors who witnessed and endured the pitch battles between rival warring factions. Of all the stories I heard from the survivals and the returnees, the story of Barkedu Massacre stands out. That's where my brother Bangalie Konneh and his newly wedded wife Mazetu Dorleh took refuge as they fled from Monrovia. My brother and his wife were among the escapees before the rebels entered the town. What they told me about the Barkedu Massacre is the story below.

When the war started in Butuo, Nimba County, little did the people of Barkedu know that it would reach their side of the country, because they were too far away from Monrovia, the seat of the government. Just like many others, they thought it was going to affect only those in government. However, they were sadly mistaking, because the war executed by the so-called "revolutionaries" led by Charles Taylor was as much about them as it was about those in government.

Barkedu and the chiefdom it falls under are unique in the geographic setting of Liberia. Barkedu is one of the many towns within the Quardu Gboni Mandingo District in Lofa County. The district has had shifting headquarters, depending on where the ruling Paramount Chief resided. The population of the chiefdom is 100% Mandingo. It is rich in legends of famous chiefs, warriors, Islamic scholars and artists. The oral history of the area tells of the legends of the Kamaras, beginning with Sifani Felay, whose son, the powerful Vaflay Kollie, fought fiercely against the French colonialists who wanted to take his land and annex it to the French colony of Guinea.

Long before then, Sifani Felay had been visited by the delegation from the settlers. A bilateral agreement was reached to make the territories under his control part of Liberia. A treaty was signed to that effect. So when the French came to take the land by force, Sifani Felay's son, Vaflay Kollie, posed a major challenge to them. Having failed to defeat him, the French agreed to sign a deal with him, forming the boundary between the French colony of Guinea and Liberia, fulfilling the agreement reached between his late father and the settlers. In 1908, there was an elaborate ceremony marking the observance of the boundary settlement between French Guinea and Liberia. This treaty also recognized Voinjama and the Zorzor District as part of Liberia. At the ceremony, another Kamara chief, Bongoh Moigbeh, served as the chief spokesman for the natives. Col. Robert E. Lee represented Liberia on the Franco-Liberian Boundary Delimitation Commission. On his way to Musadu in 1865, the famous Liberian explorer, Benjamin J.K Anderson passed through here.

Other towns within the Quardu Gbonie Mandingo Chiefdom are Jamuloh, Kennellah, Sanzano as well as Nyamahkamanu, the home of Dr. Edward Kesselly among others. However, Barkedu is much known to outsiders. During the onset of the war, a massacre that preceded most of the well-known cases of similar mass killings in Liberia changed the town forever. While most Liberians were quick to condemn the Lutheran Church massacre in Monrovia, there was complete silence in the entire nation about what took place in Barkedu on July 12, 1990. This is an account of this NPFL adventure in that part of Liberia. Perhaps in the flurry of activities occurring mainly in the heart of the nation's capital city, and the fact that travel links were cut off, the Barkedu incident got little or no coverage at the time.

When the NPFL started its deadly adventure, the citizens of Quardu Gbonie from other parts of Liberia, especially Nimba County, came home to escape trouble, hoping to return to their places of residence when the situation subsided. It was the largest gathering of the sons and daughters of the area in many years. Many of its sons and daughters who had not been there before came to seek refuge. As time went by, the threat of the war drew closer and closer. Rumors spread in town that the rebels were in Zorzor and the Mandingoes were being targeted. A Peace Corps volunteer, who had lived in the town of Barkedu for more than fifteen years studying the Mandingo culture and tradition, confirmed this. This caused serious panic in the whole chiefdom. He told them that it was true that the "liberators" were hunting and killing the Mandingoes as reported in Zorzor and other places and advised the town folks to cross the border into Guinea to safety. This warning happened on the 9th of July 1990. On the 10th, there was a mass meeting of Lofa citizens in Voinjama to discuss the rebel advances. At that meeting, all of the ethnic groups within Voinjama District, including the Mandingoes and the Lormas, were present. It was reported during the meeting that the rebels were capturing places, including Zorzor, with little or no resistance and the only people being sought by the rebels were government officials and the Mandingoes. The rebels succeeded in recruiting many able body Lormas and they were burning down Mandingo homes and other possessions.

After all of this information provided during the meeting in Voinjama, members of other tribal groups decided not to stay around for any additional meeting since they didn't have any problem with the rebels. They said that those being targeted should figure out a way to deal with the situation. To the Mandingo delegation, that was a plain betrayal on the part of fellow Lofans. The disappointed delegates went back with their reports to the anxious town. When the report was given, thousands were dumb-founded and became completely hopeless. In the midst of all this, some maintained the courage to find ways to deal with the situation.

Opinions in the town were divided, with some elders strongly pleading that everyone flee to avoid unnecessary bloodbaths, while others led by the town chief, Musa Ballo urged the citizens to stay. He told them they could not abandon their fatherland. He pleaded fiercely that everybody should stay and even at some point threatened to fine anyone wanting to desert the town. He started invoking the legends of Vafley Kollie and other past warriors of the area. He praised the past leaders for defending the fatherland against the powerful white colonial forces. He admonished them by saying that "If Sifani Felay and his sons could not desert their sacred heritage in fear of the white soldiers; it would be an act of betrayal to their memories if the sons and daughters of Quardu Gbonie fled their land." Chief Balloh called on his people to be proud, strong and tall like their forefathers who never retreated from nor surrendered to any enemy force.

Chief Ballo might have been right in alluding to the glorious past, but he didn't have a well-trained army, nor was he prepared to fight like what those in the past did. The chief romanticized the past glory in the face of the pending calamity when he couldn't boast of even five trained soldiers ready to fight against the advancing rebels.

Panic-stricken citizens started to leave the town, heading for the border of Guinea with the hope of returning when things quieted down. Among them were my brother and his wife.

On the 12th of July when the NPFL fighters got to town they made a public announcement through the town crier and asked everyone to assemble under the palaver hut. Chief Balloh mobilized his people to listen to the message the "liberators" had brought. On behalf of the town folks, the chief welcomed the rebels and lauded their efforts to remove dictatorship off the back of the Liberian people. He said he and his town folks were with the "liberators" in spirit and were even ready to provide manpower to strengthen their efforts. He presented $3000.00 (USD) and three cows as a token of appreciation to the fighters. After praising them it was now time for the "liberators" to respond to the kind gesture of their hosts. In a matter of seconds the kind hosts were turned into hostages.

The first thing the" liberators" inquired about was whether there were any Mandingoes from Nimba in the midst of those in Barkedu, making it sound as if only the Mandingoes from Nimba were being hunted. The scared people responded "no." So far that was the only question asked and having heard the answer the "liberators" declared that they were now in charge of the town and everything in it was theirs to take including the $3000.00 USD and the three cows. They demanded that every other thing such as jewelry, money and other valuable items be reported. They said they didn't care whether there was any Mandingo from Nimba or not, that all "dingoes" were the same and that the "only good ones are the dead ones." The commander gave orders to his fighters to "shoot them all." As the fighters started shooting, the situation became so frantic, so panicky, and at the end of the shooting spree, some died by bullets, others by knives and cutlasses; they were butchered into pieces. Some lucky ones managed to escape the scene of the terror whose estimated victims were anywhere between two and five hundred people. Some of the escapees, including the town chief Musa Balloh drowned in the Lofa River while some luckily made it to Guinea. They broke the sad news to their fellow citizens in Macenta, Guinea and other bordering towns. After crying and mourning, it was decided to retrieve the bodies of loved ones for Islamic burial. But all attempts to retrieve the bodies proved futile because of the rebels' presence. When the rebels had executed their plan of action, they retreated but kept coming in small numbers to check if the Mandingoes would come for the bodies, believing that the Mandingoes never leave their bodies unburied.

So was the situation in Barkedu at the onset of a war many thought would be a passing moment before life returned to normal. A terrible massacre of defenseless people had taken place for no other reason than the fact that they were Mandingoes. What was so annoying about it was the deafening silence of the whole nation about this massacre and similar ones that took place in the mosque in Tiaplay, Sanniquellie and elsewhere in Liberia. This shows the hypocrisy in the way some Liberians have reacted to various incidences of the war. Some were vehemently condemned while others were tacitly approved.

19

When Allies Turned Against Each Other

CEASEFIRE WAS BEING observed among the warring factions. The United Nations Mission in Liberia (UNMIL) was supposed to encamp the fighters and start disarmament and demobilization. There were lots of positions to fill out in support of the disarmament of the combatants. Those of us that wanted those jobs flocked to various encampment sites to fill out applications. I ended up in Bomi Hill, a ULIMO controlled area. We stood in long lines to get applications, filled them out and returned them for interviews. The prospect of making $30.00 to $50.00 a month was great and everyone was so excited to get those jobs.

That day when I was accepted, after being rejected twice, I was so excited. I jumped for joy. Even though I was already employed at the Muslim Clinic as a registrar, I was ready to take the new job for some personal reasons. While this would be a second job for me, for a lot of people it was the first job. So with the prospect of a new job, all the successful applicants were excited for the opportunity to work for UNMIL. Working for UNMIL was good for two reasons: helping to rehabilitate and return our brothers and sisters to normal civilian life and getting paid while doing it. Indeed, it was heartwarming to help out these young people who had been fighting in the bush.

But our joy of having jobs was short-lived as the ULIMO political disagreement over Dr. El Mohammed Sheriff and Thomas Zia blew into a military confrontation between forces loyal to both sides of the political divide. In the evening of our job interview, this split was visible. There were groups of fighters standing here and there discussing. When the firing started in the morning, I was at Gen. Mohammed Dumbuya's residence. I was his guest. I traveled in his car from Monrovia when I came the evening before. That morning at his residence, ULIMO soldiers loyal to him assembled and stood in line formation. They were discussing the intelligence they had been gathering overnight. As they discussed, someone came and reported that the ULIMO soldiers loyal to Roosevelt Johnson were advancing on them. The reaction to this information was swift. Every fighter was mobilized except for the civilians and the wounded soldiers. They left Dumbuya's house to go engage their "enemies." I was one of the civilians that stayed in the general's residence along with the wounded soldiers.

Throughout the whole time that the soldiers left to engage their "enemies," I was scared to death. I was not a fighter. I didn't even have a knife to defend myself. All the while I was thinking if the "enemies" prevailed and came to the general's house, they would kill everyone of us indiscriminately. We the civilians, who included the general's own family, could not depend on the wounded soldiers to defend us. They were already wounded from previous military encounters before the split in ULIMO. The friends and allies that were fighting against the common enemies were now enemies to each other; and I was in the midst of this new battle. All along I had been very fortunate to not be around any actual violence of the civil war except for the Octopus Operation which I survived in Monrovia. In this situation, I was praying for Gen. Dumbuya and his men because my life depended on their victory.

An hour or so later, Dumbuya and his men triumphantly returned. There were wild cheers and dance, celebrating their victory against their "enemies." They brought with them one of the wounded "enemies." This guy was bleeding so profusely and there was no sympathy or mercy for him from his allies turned enemies. I heard someones saying to cut his throat. I saw real pain in the face of the victim. He was crying for mercy but there was no sympathetic ears willing to listen to his pleading voice. I began to think about what soldiers do to their enemies on the battlefield. I truly felt sorry for him but I could not express my emotion because to have done so would have meant a betrayal of the cause my brothers and sisters were fighting on my behalf. I could not afford to look at this guy in the terrible condition he was in. I had to hide my feeling. So I left the soldiers to deal with the issue in their own way. I went back to the house. I had come to Bomi Hill looking for a job and look what I got.

Since the war started in the early '90s, that encounter was the second time I came close to danger. The first was the Octopus launched by Charles Taylor in 1992. During this time we had to flee from our various residences across the bridge to city center. While seeking refuge in central Monrovia from my residence on Jamaica Road, I was always thinking about what would happen if Taylor crossed the bridge to come to town. I dreaded such thing ever happening. The only alternative was the sea; either that or a mass killing of people that were already considered as enemies by the NPFL. In any case, we all survived the Octopus. Since then with all the peace talks and now the formation of the transitional government, one would think that the war was over. That was why we were in Bomi Hill seeking jobs with the demobilization and disarmament process. With the Octopus and this outbreak of war, I now understood that in a war-torn country such as ours, anything could happen. One moment you are celebrating peace, the next moment you are running helter-skelter.

While they were celebrating victory, there was a decision to take the civilians to Monrovia. They realized it was not good to keep their families in the battle zone. There were several cars available to take us back to Monrovia and I got into one of them. After passing through checkpoints here and there with the soldiers in battle gears, we finally made it to Monrovia. The newspaper headlines were that the Krahns and Mandingoes were fighting, something I disagreed with. To me it was more a political disagreement that had resulted into this military confrontation. I wrote a couple of articles to counter the negative press reports that were inflaming the situation. Of those articles one was, **"ULIMO Internal Conflict: Not Krahn Mandingo War."** Below is the article as it was published in local newspapers at the time.

ULIMO, by definition of its posture on the Liberian scene, is a liberation movement composed of the down-trodden Liberians who have been the major victims of the NPFL's tribal and religious cleansing that started in Butuo, Logatuo, Kamplay and other towns and villages along the Liberian-Ivorian borders. Having been humiliated, degraded, dehumanized and chased out of their motherland by the all advancing and winning NPFL, these down-trodden masses of Liberians were living as dispirited and destitute individuals in Guinea, Sierra Leone, Ivory Coast and many other countries in and out of West Africa. Those of them living in Sierra Leone became the victims for the second time when the NPFL launched its attack on that country, using its surrogate, Foday Sankoh.

Living in such a hopeless and desperate situation, there was a need to do something in order to restore their sense of human dignity, indeed their manhood. This served as a rallying call in mobilizing thousands of brave men and women, both young and old, to confront the mighty war machine of the NPFL. There was a readiness to measure face to face with the almighty NPFL. It was a show-down between good and evil.

In those early days, though it was declared as a broad based organization, ULIMO was predominantly a Krahn-Mandingo makeup. It was an alliance forced into being by the compelling reality of the day. Yes, an alliance forced into being as a result of the tribal and religious hypocrisy demonstrated by some Liberians as the war advanced. That ULIMO became a predominantly Krahn-Mandingo makeup only proves the fact that both ethnic groups were the hardest hit as victims of the mindless aggression of the NPFL and only they could have had the strong heart to face the murderous Taylor and his gangs of "killerators" (who else could volunteer in the fight against the NPFL besides the two victimized groups when in fact many other person was either its supporter or sympathizer?)

In the beginning there were many doubting Thomases who never thought that ULIMO could capture and control any inch of the Liberian soil, owing to the fact that only Gankay Taylor was the growling lion in town. No one thought anyone was capable of stopping Taylor's Mighty Empire. But the attitude of the doubting Thomases soon evaporated by the spirited move of the brave ULIMO warriors who were so thirsty for freedom, justice and equality. Inch by inch, they liberated some territories from the NPFL.

Little by little, when the movement started growing in strength, power struggle which is common to all organizations, especially military ones, became eminent. Unlike political or social organizations where disputes may be resolved through roundtable discussions, disputes in military organizations are usually settled with guns. Power, like riches, is something everybody wants. This power struggle continued from the formation of ULIMO in Sierra Leone. It became more controversial when Raleigh Seekie's leadership announced that it had relieved Alhaji Kromah of his function as the spokesman of the organization. The only reason shown by Seekie's leadership was that Alhaji Kromah was "trying to import an Islamic fundamentalism into Liberia through jihad," a charge Kromah has denied all along. Of all the millions of words, the Seekie and company have misused this word, "jihad," to poison the minds of Liberians and win their support since it seems the worst fear of many Christian Liberians is "jihad."

One of the first persons to fall victims to this power struggle was Major General Albert B.S. Karpeh. After Karpeh's death, the power struggle continued between Alhaji Kromah based in Conakry, Guinea and Raleigh Seekie based in Freetown, Sierra Leone. Alhaji Kromah emerged as the victor when he made the triumphant entry into the ULIMO controlled territories with headquarters in Tubmanburg. He was welcomed with the full backing of the ULIMO high command. For Seekie, going to Tubmanburg was too much of a gamble, which he couldn't afford to play. As a result, he faded out. This was the sad case for Seekie despite the fact that he reportedly enjoyed the moral and financial support of powerful influential persons in the former Interim Government of National Unity. They put at his disposal powerful public relation machinery. With all that, it was a losing battle for Seekie. He kept his cool until later when he resurfaced with Roosevelt Johnson. The battle Seekie lost was the same one being revived by Johnson who was now using the Thomas Zia issue as the pretext. Everyone needed to understand that the Thomas Zia issue was just a part of the grand design of Seekie and company with Johnson fronting as its military commander.

Another victim of the ULIMO leadership crisis or power struggle was Major Solomon Kamara, a youthful hero to most ULIMO sympathizers. He was cut down at the height of his popularity within the movement. He was considered a Kromah loyalist. It is speculated that his murder was masterminded by Gen. Roosevelt Johnson. Shortly after the assassination of Major Kamara, Johnson had to run for his life because of his alleged involvement. In the interest of maintaining unity in the organization, Johnson was welcomed back, but had all along been planning his present activity.

After months of verbal warfare, the fighting men and women of ULIMO finally declared Alhaji the legitimate leader of the organization. Apollo Jay Swen and Col. Bartee attempted to remove Alhaji Kromah with the full backing of Raleigh Seekie and his powerful backers. But the coup did not materialize. Jay Swen and Bartee were found guilty of the charges but were pardoned by Chairman Kromah. Interestingly indeed, it's Swen and Bartee today who are the front line commanders for Johnson. It's this same Jay Swen who allegedly murdered a Fula shopkeeper in New Kru Town and was wanted by IGNU.

The internal power struggle as described above was not characterized by Krahn-Mandingo rivalry. Krahns and Mandingo residents of Monrovia and elsewhere have had a cordial relationship. It was because of the Krahns that the Mandingoes were victimized, having been falsely accused as "Doe supporters." The collective suffering both groups have experienced at the hands of the NPFL gave birth to a strong bond of solidarity and friendship.

Unlike the past, the present power struggle within ULIMO became fiercely bloody between forces loyal to the ULIMO national chairman and those loyal to its chairman of the military wing. Also unlike the previous time, this time the power struggle became characterized by ethnicity. The enemies of the organization had succeeded in creating a split based on ethnicity, since that was the only way to advance their objectives. In this process, many fighters and the general public became misinformed. As a result, the best friends of yesterday became the worst enemies of present.

While the crafty politicians might have been working in the dark to create this split, many newspapers were used to spread lies and misinformation. It was the newspapers with their mind blowing headlines that turned ULIMO's long time power struggle into a Krahn-Mandingo war. In this process, they chose their own heroes and villains. Many times they came out with headlines that read as if to say the Mandingo elements of the organization were a bunch of heartless killers hunting and killing the Krahns. All these nerveracking headlines were deliberately intended to inflame the heart of every Krahn person against the Mandingoes. The headlines all along portrayed those loyal to Alhaji Kromah as only Mandingoes who were perpetrators of violence against the Krahns and other Liberians. To the Krahns and other Liberians who were badly misinformed by the unfair media propaganda, Johnson was portrayed as the good guy while Kromah was portrayed as the villain. These newspapers ceased to be a medium of information. In reverse of the role they profess to be performing, these papers became negative propaganda machines against anyone who did not think like them. Many of the journalists had not visited where actions were taking place; instead they sat comfortably in their offices in Monrovia and got whatever they considered to be information from secondary sources who they often referred to as "reliable sources."

In situations as such, no one from either side could pause to think as to what was right or wrong. Yet they were interested to be fed the wrong information that either this brother or that sister was killed by heartless and ruthless Mandingoes. In that process, this person or that person would obviously take sides with the man who was portrayed to be championing his cause. That was how the likes of Johnson have become heroes to some.

20

Their Liberia, My Liberia

ON AUGUST 3ᴿᴰ 1994, I responded to my first major intellectual challenge. At about 4:00 PM on Monday, I received a verbal invitation to serve as a guest lecturer at Zion Community College (ZCC) in the Social Science class of Professor Williamson. At first I was dumbfounded. I trembled with surprise. Why me? From 4:00 PM that evening to 9:00 AM the next morning, I could count only fifteen hours. Not enough time to prepare for a lecture of any kind. At best, a week or two would give you enough time to adequately prepare yourself.

Professor Williamson was a Social Science instructor at ZCC and he had assigned one of his classes to do a research project on the "Mandingoes in Liberia." The students' findings were supposed to incorporate everything about the Mandingoes, their culture, religion and their relationship with other Liberian tribes, as well as their principal occupation. Wasn't this a very controversial topic for anyone in Liberia when the speaker was a Mandingo and his audience did not believe that "he too built Liberia"? For the audience too, it was a controversial issue. They were told to find their guest lecturer to speak on the topic. That search for a guest lecturer spotted me somehow.

The students' assignment coincided with the publication of my article on the Mandingoes, a scholarly research that was a response to derogatory remarks made by Rev. Samuel Hill against the Mandingoes in Liberia. Many of those on this assignment might have read that article and thought I was the best person to handle the task at hand.

I did not intend on lecturing there due to the lateness of the invitation. Among reasons that prompted me to, I must cite: 1. My article propelled me, somehow, as an "authority" on the subject; 2. Should I fail to appear, it might raise some doubt as to whether I was the original author of the published article for which I claimed credit. The most elaborate recompense for having done something good is when people come to you to say they like what you have done or are doing. And many, except a few critics, had expressed an overwhelming endorsement for what I was doing. Because of this, I found it compelling enough to go serve as the guest lecturer at this particular occasion, and 3. Wasn't it so prestigious and intellectually rewarding for me to appear as a guest lecturer at an institution in which I was still one of the students? After all, my more than 100 poems published, and dozens of other published articles should at least qualify me to serve as a guest lecturer to share my limited knowledge on some important issues, for no one is omniscient but God.

With that in mind, I arrived at ZCC's AC Building some twenty minutes late. This was due to the difficulty of getting a car during the morning rush hour. I met the class being warmed up by Mr. Williamson, the professor himself. I lightly greeted the class and the fellow who had contacted me the previous day acknowledged my presence. This was followed by an introduction of the program and me by one of the students. Then everyone got ready for the "showdown." I could feel an immediate tension from some quarters of the class. Consumed by prejudice, a section of the group greeted me with discourtesy, while the other section greeted me respectfully and seemed to be pleased with my presence. But I think guest lecturers/speakers should be received with open minds by those that invite them. Rare is the case that those inviting the guest lecturer/speaker already have their own version of the matter, however perverted that may be, and are only interested in putting their invitee on "trial." In that sense I was like a lonely soldier in enemy territory. Nevertheless, I couldn't be that scared for I was armed with enough facts to firebomb the hall. I had the published article, as well as the masterpiece, *Christianity, Islam, and the African Race (1887) by* the renowned scholar, Dr. Wilmot Blyden. This book contained a lot about my Liberia whose existence had been ignored by many people more because of ignorance as well as tribal prejudice.

After someone had read the class work, which I listened to very keenly and took some notes, I began my lecture preceded by some comments on the assignment. I was told to be brief because of time factor (I would be allowed to speak for only fifteen minutes). That would be an inconvenience for someone who had much to say; however, I decided to make the best of the allotted time. In this brief lecture, I touched on three issues: 1. the inseparableness of the terms Mandingo, Moslem, and Islam in the minds of most Liberians; 2. Mandingoes' presence in what is now called Liberia hundreds of years before the coming of the settlers who claimed for themselves the title of "the founding fathers"; and 3. King Sao Bosso Kamara (Chief Boatswain) and his Condo Confederacy etc. All of these points were enough to emphasize that Liberia belonges to the Mandingoes as much it belonges to any other ethnic group. This fact could not be replaced by any invented fiction bordered on sheer prejudice.

My brief lecture was followed by questions from the inquisitive, unruly students who did everything they could to put me on the defensive. I had offended their sense of value by accusing the "Christian conquerors" for the "wrong education" they imparted to other Liberians that questioned the citizenship of the Mandingoes/Moslems. One of the questions was "Which county in Liberia do the Mandingoes originate from?" Though other questions were asked and answers accepted, this one was the most controversial and it consumed most of the question and answer period. Another important question was about the sources of my information about "Chief Boatswain being a Mandingo." To the first question I pointed out three counties: Bong, Nimba and Lofa. I said that though the Mandingoes could be found in most parts of Liberia, their presence in the three counties named above, their involvement in local politics to some extent, their relationship with other ethnic groups and the properties they own are enough proof that they are integral parts of those counties. In other words, Mandingoes and other natives in those counties are inseparable, except in religion, which the Mandingoes have all along kept to themselves with no serious effort to convert other tribes.

If the Mandingoes had skillfully promoted their religion as they skill-fully did with their trading towards and among others, many native Liberians would have been Moslems today and Christianity would not have had many followers and sympathizers among the natives as is the case today. The reason for this is that the Mandingoes have more in common with the natives than the strangers coming from across the ocean. The reluctance of the Mandingoes to carry on seri-ous evangelism among other natives must be interpreted as a respect for the others' religion of ancestral veneration.

Another question that was asked repeatedly during the program and has been asked at other forums is why the Mandingoes do not allow other Liberians to marry their daughters. This was indeed one of the most contentious areas defining the Mandingoes' relationship with other Liberians, particularly the male Liberians. This one has remained one of the factors of the vexing issues that have contin-ued to fuel anti-Mandingo sentiment in Liberia. Recently, a friend of mine told me, "While I support most of your positions regarding your people, I don't understand why you guys don't allow other people to marry your sisters." I told my friend, as I told these guys here on Zion campus, that the issue is more of a cultural difference than what most people think. I told them that it is more because Mandingoes regard marriage much more differently than the rest of the population. Both Islam and Christianity urge their female members to marry to their kinds. While Moslems observe this more rigidly, the Christians are more liberal. They don't seriously follow the teaching of their reli-gion when it comes to marriage. So in a sense, you can't tell the next person to be more liberal with his religion simply because you are with yours. I went on further to say that one thing that was being overlooked in this discussion was the fact that despite all the talk of intermarriage, most marriages occur within the group than the other way around. In other words, more of the same people from an ethnic or racial group marry to each other than outside of their group. To put it another way, marrying outside the group is an exception to the rule. For example, more Krus are married to other Krus as compared to those that are married to someone outside the group. This is the same for the Mandingoes and people all over the world. That is why ethnic, racial or cultural groups have existed intact for all these thousands of years.

If intermarriage was as widespread as some are suggesting, there would be no ethnicity. We all would be one mixed up ethnic group. So no matter how we feel about this, intermarriage is an exception but not the rule of male-female relationship. This makes it very irrational for anyone to target or kill another person because his sister or daughter could not be married into another ethnic group.

One of the most important religious obligations to observe in the Mandingo community is marriage. No male-female relationship is accepted as legal or moral except marriage. Just because I am a Mandingo does not mean I can be a boyfriend to a Mandingo girl and expect her family to accept that as a legitimate relationship. Nor can I take a girlfriend to show to my parents. To do so is against the ethical and moral values of our religious and cultural tradition. Islamically, I am not supposed to have any sexual intercourse with any woman that I am not married to. Even if I have to do so, I am fully aware that I am contravening the moral code of conduct of my religious and cultural upbringing.

Compared to the general Liberian society where it's normal for a man and woman to cohabitate for years before thinking and deciding about marriage, the difference is clear. For us, this is a "no no." This is because you don't go to the store and ask to wear a pair of shoes for weeks or years before thinking and deciding to buy it. Similarly, in the thinking of the Mandingoes, you cannot live with the woman you are not married to under the pretext that you are trying to understand her before making a serious commitment to take her as a wife.

According to the Mandingo tradition which is heavily influenced by Islam, to marry requires the man to be ready in so many ways. After reaching an agreement with the girl, you have to approach her parents through your parents. Your parents may designate someone to act on their behalf. This third party should inform the girl's parents of your desire to marry their daughter and convince them that you can take care of their daughter, that you will not abandon her in difficult times. When everything is said and done, it's not just between you and the girl; it is also between the two families. With the involvement of the family members on both sides, you cannot just walk out of the relationship without a concrete reason. As you can see, marriage for us is not an easy process. Without satisfying the condition, I cannot just marry a Mandingo woman simply because I am a Mandingo. All of these complex hurdles placed in the way are a test of the true intent of the man and his commitment to marriage. Anything that we find difficult to get, we place more values on it. Equally so, anything we get so easily we place less value on it.

If a poll is taken of marriage in the Mandingo community in particular and the Liberian society in general, the result will be very different. The numbers of women you will see in the general Liberian society reaching their old age without getting married are too many. There are also too many broken marriages, too many out of wedlock children and too many abandoned single mothers who are struggling with children of run-away fathers. In the Mandingo community, a woman giving birth to a child out of wedlock is still being frowned upon. This is normal for the general Liberian society. These are some of the issues one has to consider when trying to talk about intermarriage between the Mandingoes and other Liberians. For the Mandingoes, the question is, how can you want to marry my daughter when you don't believe in marriage? Look at all these women that are not married in your own community.

As clear cut as these answers to these questions were or seemed to be, the questioners were not satisfied. They still pressed me for the Mandingoes' original county ties. I told them there was no county in Liberia exclusively populated by any single tribe. There may be one or two predominant tribes as is the case with the Kpelles in Bong, Manos and Gio in Nimba and the Bassas in Grand Bassa Counties. In Lofa there are Lormas, Gissis, Golas, Mandingoes and others. Even Grand Bassa, which bares the name of the Bassa tribe, is not exclusively populated by the Bassas. Even Professor Williamson tried to enlighten his students on this, but to no avail. He said the division of the country into counties is political in nature and has nothing to do with ethnic factor. He cited Grand Kru, Rivercess, and Margibi Counties as typical examples. None of the facts would convince the diehard agitators so consumed by ignorance and prejudice.

As for the sources of my information, I told them about Dr. Abayomi Cassell's *Liberia, The First African Republic, (1970),* Dr. Blyden's *Christianity, Islam and The African Race* (1887) and Nathaniel Richardson's *Liberia's Past and Present* (1959). I told them that the history of Liberia was clear about the Mandingoes in Liberia and there are many books to prove it; but some Liberians, especially the students, are so lazy to read them. Or maybe they read but prejudice does not allow them to believe what they read.

After all this, I was pelted by those so blinded by prejudice. Nothing would convince them that, "I too built Liberia," and that "I too, am a Liberian" just like them. I told them that my forebears also suffered to make Liberia what it is today. They screamed out loudly, "We don't care what y'all do, you're not citizens!" They went on screaming some more, "And you see what Krahn people doing to y'all, we going to flush y'all out of our country. Y'all foreigners them; you want to take our country, our good Christian country from us."

It sounds unimaginable that those hateful words would come out of the mouths of young college social science students. What kind of social scientists are they going to be when in fact it is the social scientists that must help to answer the basic sociological questions of the society?

Their teacher urged them to free their minds of prejudice, but they wouldn't listen, accusing him of being on my side. One may not blame the students, for society teaches them to think so. Schools that should serve as banks of knowledge have given them very little or no chance at all to borrow. They graduate after twelve to fifteen years of schooling without any knowledge of their own history, while they will tell you how the white man met the Indians in America. They will tell you about Hollywood movie stars, Columbia musical stars, but will be dumb, blind and deaf about the history of their own country. What a shame! The whole thing was to me a rude awakening to reality.

After the experience two young ladies followed me, raining insults on me, similar to the ones during the lecture. I talked to them and tried to get them to reason, but they wouldn't listen to anything from me, be it factual, reasonable, or otherwise. Not getting their understanding, I too got mad and started throwing back at them. "Some of you with these diabolical plans will not live to see the result of your wicked plans," I said and meant it. I owe no one any apology for the remark, for I had been pushed enough and I couldn't take any more of it.

These are the realities of my Liberia, a Liberia that exists outside the consciousness of my fellow Liberians. These brought to my mind many scenes of the recent past. Scenes of terrible experience for people simply because they are of this group or that group and belong to this or that religion. The immigration checkpoints, false cases of police and criminal connivance, the negative media propaganda, all of which amount to national conspiracy backed by international forces to eliminate my kind? All amount to fifteen tribes versus one tribe. No matter how much contributions we have made to the creation and development of this nation, they ignore it, making it look like we are "Johnny Just Come (JJC)."

The war executed for my elimination has so far failed to eliminate me. Now the troubling question for my brothers is how come I am not dead, but still living, competing with them for the positions of director, minister, and even the presidency? They are surprised or amazed to see a trader-turned director, minister or president. To them that is unimaginable. But to the nature of human beings, it is imaginable.

The main message of the whole experience of August 3rd is that Liberia has got its Mandingo problem just like Germany had its Jewish problem, America its Black problem or Israel with its Palestinian problem. It will take the good in every one of us to solve this problem. Together as one people, we will be able to build a wholesome society. May Allah guide all of us as we strive to rebuild our country from the ravages of this brutal, ethnic-religious war. For no matter what we do, this is their Liberia, this is my Liberia and this is a Liberia for all of us. By living together and loving each other like brothers and sisters, we will be able to reach to the top, just as America has done significantly.

21

Meeting Clifford Flemister in Monrovia

TOWARDS THE END OF 1987, I visited Monrovia. I read an article in the Herald Newspaper about W E B Du Bois and the writer of the article was one Clifford Flemister. The article was very inspiring to the point that I was moved to write a letter to the writer expressing my appreciation for his well written article. I wrote and mailed the letter when I got back to Saclepea. Back then, NCRDP (Nimba County Rural Development Project) provided mail service to their employees and residents of the town. We used to mail and receive mail through this service. When I mailed the letter, I did not expect any reply. I did not think that a writer for any newspaper in Monrovia would have time to reply to someone all the way in the interior of Nimba County. I assumed that people in the big city had a lot of things to worry about and writing to someone in the interior may not be part of those worries. The truth is that up to the time I read that article, I didn't know who Flemister was. I had not heard about him from anywhere prior to reading that article.

I can't remember how long it took but after a while I received the reply to my letter from Clifford Flemister. It was a long letter. In it he said lots of things. Among them he said, not very often do people take their time to write thoughtful responses to articles published in the newspaper. He said he was pleased to have heard from me. He said that any time I visited Monrovia I should look for him. I was moved by the letter so much that I showed it to some of my friends and for a while it was one of my prized possessions, along with a diction-ary I got from the BBC Post Mark Africa program as a prize for Star Question on the program. From the way Flemister expressed himself in that letter, I got the feeling that he must be somebody important in Monrovia.

When I finally moved to Monrovia in the early months of 1988, meeting Flemister was one of the many things on my agenda, the number one being entering the University of Liberia but the only ob-stacle to that educational ambition was the fact that I had failed math and science on my WAEC exam.

In Johnny Voker High School in Saclepea, I was among the three top contenders for valedictorian of the 1987 school year. It was go-ing to be me, Wellington Suomie, or Vincent Sahn. Unfortunately, none of us passed the national exam and there was no graduation ceremony. We all were badly disappointed. Our friends and relatives were all disappointed. Some suggested that we wear the gowns and march since we passed the school's exams. The truth was, that made no sense because we would only be fooling ourselves. How could we wear the gowns and proudly march when we knew we had not passed the national exam which is one of the criteria for graduating from high school in Liberia? The national exam certificate is at the top of the requirement for entering the University of Liberia. Given this as it was, it would be pointless to wear those gowns and march as graduates.

With this being the case, moving to Monrovia in early 1988 meant I had to prepare and retake the math and science portion of the na-tional exam. My cousin Mariam Foday who was a classmate decided she was going to stay and re-sit the exam in Saclepea and graduate in front of her relatives and friends. She could not spend all those years going to school and not march proudly among her family and friends, especially when she was the first Mandingo girl to graduate from high school in Saclepea. As for me, whatever the case, I was moving on to Monrovia. So when I moved there in 1988, retaking the exam was a priority next to meeting Clifford Flemister. In my reply to him, I had informed him of when I was going to be in Monrovia.

It was on a Monday. I can't remember the specific date, when I went to the address on the letter Flemister sent me. It was a building on Carey Street close to the junction with Johnson Street. The building, which did not look too impressive to me, had three stories. It probably had not been painted for a while. It looked browner than the original color of white it had been painted with. When I found myself inside the building, I went to the receptionist and told her I was there to see Clifford Flemister. She told me that he was not in the office and she wasn't sure when he was going to be back that day. Feeling somewhat disappointed, I wrote a note and left it with the receptionist. I told him I was the one who had written him from Saclepea, Nimba County. When I was leaving, I saw it written somewhere that the job they did in that building was consulting. I didn't know what that meant.

The next day when I came back, the receptionist was friendlier. She had been instructed by Clifford Flemister to usher me in his office when I arrived. When she saw me, she escorted me straight to his office. Behind a brown desk, I saw this gigantic light skinned man taking my little hands into his big hands. He was huge. I had not imagined him being this big a man. He was very warm and asked me about my plans. I told him about my plans to retake the national exam and enter the University of Liberia. He wished me well, speaking with an American accent. I became hopeful that my relationship with this very important person could mean something good for me in Monrovia. That first meeting between Clifford Flemister and I went very well and it made me feel very important. It made my day. While talking, I saw him writing a note. When he finished writing it, he folded it and went outside, leaving me alone in his spacious office. When I was leaving, he gave me $10.00 and told me to get a note from the receptionist. When I opened the note, he had written that I had bad breath and that I should go see a dentist. The dentist he had recommended me to was Dr. Charles Jupiter who had his dental clinic on the corners of Broad and Johnson streets. Whatever the cost of seeing the dentist would be, it was on him, he said. Since I was not doing anything that day, I went straight to Dr. Jupiter's office. When I finally met Dr. Jupiter, he pulled my two bad teeth and made a denture for me to wear.

Over the next two years until the war, Flemister was a mentor and big influence. I understood him to have great interest and love for Liberia and Africa as a whole. He demonstrated the same kind of love Du Bois or Kwame N'krumah had for Africa. Every time spent with him was a lesson in Pan-Africanism. As our relationship developed, he encouraged me to attend meetings of an environmental organization called Save My Future. On several occasions, I attended their meetings. As time went by, Flemister asked if I had "friends that think" like me. As a follow up to that question, I introduced my friends Musa Bility, Foday Donzo, and Losene Bamba. It was Musa and I who warmed up to him, visiting him frequently at his office at Rovia Bank on Carey Street and at his home around Jamaica Road and UN Drive. We kept visiting him until the war which caused me to leave for the Ivory Coast.

Another important person we met at this time was Mrs. Massa Diomande who used to work at the Ministry of Education and Bill Frank Enoiyei, an old hand at the Ministry of Information. Foday met them both on separate occasions. He introduced me and Musa to Mrs. Massa Diomande and then me to Bill Frank Enoiey. From the interior, we had come to Monrovia to go to school and at the same time seeking for the opportunity that would help us in the process. At that point, visiting Flemister, Mrs. Diomande, and Bill Frank became parts of our regular routines in Monrovia. They were generous enough to welcome us into their offices and in the case of Flemister, Musa and I became regular visitors to his home as well.

At this time, Musa was living with his uncle Alhaji Samuka Dulleh in Chicken Farm, Jacob's Town. Foday who was supposed to be attending LTI in Salayea, Bong County, was spending time with me at my brother Musa Konneh's yard on Jamaica Road. Foday had left the school as a kind of rebellion against his father whose support was inadequate to keep him up with other students. His school mates were the children of the elites of the society. Operating two pharmacies in Ganta and Saclepea, Foday felt that his father had enough money to support him but because he was too stingy, he was not giving him the supports that would keep him on equal footing with his school mates. As a result of this, Foday thought that it would be better to attend some average school than looking pitiful among the children of the ministers, and directors. Our friend Losene Bamba on the other hand had hooked up with some good friends whose generosity enabled him to live some comfortable life in the city. We did not see him every day. Sometime we would bump into each other and then we would start talking about the ups and downs of life in the city. Musa's mother Muassia Dorleh lived on Carey Street and her house was our usual meeting point and she always used to make sure to keep food for us.

My relationship with Musa and Foday goes way back. I was like a mentor and big brother to both of them. First, it was Musa's brother Sekou that used to be my friend and still is today. One day Sekou and I were walking on the street and we met Musa at our gas station opposite the Commissioner Compound in Saclepea. Sekou started beating his brother because he had sent him on some errand and Musa had not come back to tell him the result. I told him it was not right to beat his brother on the street. I advised him to wait until they reached home. Sekou was not satisfied with my intervention. Instead of continuing with his brother, he directed his anger towards me. That was the beginning of my relationship with Musa. At the time, Musa and Foday were friends and I became a big brother to both of them. Foday was a tough guy, which earned him the nickname, Layee Grona," meaning he was street smart. Not that Foday was a street kid but because he was too hardheaded, too mouthy for his age. I was all about learning. You won't catch me anywhere without a book, magazine or radio listening to BBC, VOA or Radio France International. I was always serious and studious. That's one of the habits both Musa and Foday copied from me. Other friends used to say that I was acting small by being friendly with my small brothers but that did not bother me. I was comfortable with them.

For me, friendship should not be defined by age but by common interests. Today, I can count too many friends but if I have to make a list, two friends will top the list and that will certainly be Foday Donzo and Musa Bility.

Perhaps the most enduring symbol of my relationship with Musa is his son named after me. It was during one of our games in Bahn that Musa sealed the deal with his son's mother, Mariam Kamara. The baby was conceived on the bed Musa and I shared. When the pregnancy became visible, she had to leave Bahn to live with Musa's parents in Saclepea. That was 1987. Then there was a rumor that Mariam Kamara's father, Alhaji Mohammed Kamara, who was a member of the House of Representatives representing Zoe Geh District, would stop in Saclepea on his way to Monrovia, and while in Saclepea grab Musa to put him in jail. When Musa got wind of this rumor, he left and went to live with his uncle in Monrovia. In his absence it was my sister Makanebua and I that were looking after Mariam Kamara, his girlfriend. It was then decided that if the baby would be a girl, she would be named after my sister and if a boy he would be named after me. It was my luck and honor to have the child named after me. Ndoman, as we call namesake in Mandingo, is now a full grown man and has graduated from a university in the US with a BA degree. The last time I talked to him he expressed his interest in attending the London School of Economics.

In any case, the relationship between me and Musa is generational. His grandfather, Vamunyen Bility was a contemporary
of my grandfather. His father was a friend to my father's big brother, Vasayou. His brothers and sisters had similar relationships with my brothers and sisters. His big brother Lassana Bility was a mentor to me. He was one of our big brothers in Saclepea that I really admired and I was always around him when he was in Saclepea. We were next door neighbors and then his sister, Mariam Bility was married to my brother Abu Konneh. That's how far back we go as friends and family. Foday on the other was a Donzo, a son of one of my uncles.

We had our childhood vices as well. Together on several occasions, we grabbed chickens and ducks in the night and cooked them. We would go out in the night looking for chickens or ducks. One night we went out with my nephew Kalilu Koisiah to Nvabangalee's place. We checked in his chicken coop. What we found there were ducks. We grabbed one of them. As we grabbed the duck, it made some noise which woke the old man. We heard the sound of someone trying to open the door of the house to which the chicken coop was attached. We ran with the duck, cooked it that same night and ate it. The next morning I went to speak to the old man. His son Siaka

Sanoe who was a friend of mine had traveled somewhere and since I used to come to the house to speak to them from time to time, I pretended I had come to speak to him. Old man Nvabangalie told me about the "rogues" that visited him in the night and stole one of his ducks. He even mimicked the noise the duck made to demonstrate to me what transpired in the night when the "rogues" visited him. Deep inside, I knew I was one of the "rogues" but I could not say it. Neither in this particular situation nor in any other ones did I get caught. One night, Musa was not so lucky. He got caught with one of my brothers, Musa, his namesake. Besides the two of them there were three other boys, all accused of stealing chickens. When they were being beaten, my heart was pounding thinking that Musa may talk about what he and I did. Neither he nor anyone else called my name. It would have been a very big surprise to many people to know that I was involved in such an act. I had the image of being a good boy and no one would associate me with such childhood vices. I was a good guy to everyone but just like many boys of my age, I had my own dirty little secrets which I hid from everyone. Somehow, I felt guilty that others were getting beaten while I was walking free. As I stood there watching the two Musas and their friends being flogged, my mind went back to Uncle Kalilu in Beyla. As students of Traditional Quranic School, it was forbidden for us to go to the movie or dance but every now and then we used to sneak out. At some point our Kamoh found out. Everyone received 25 lashes. Uncle Kalilu came forward and said, "I too was there and I haven't gotten my 25 lashes." As he requested, he got his 25 lashes. Was that out of honesty or naivity? Come to think of it, Uncle Kalilu was just being naïve because no sound mind would have done what he did. As Uncle Kalilu might have felt guilty then, I was feeling guilty now seeing the two Musas and their friends being flogged while no one said a word to me. At the same time, I convinced myself that no one is perfect. At least I was not part of this particular one, which they were getting beaten for. That was part of our past in Saclepea. Now we were in Monrovia hustling our way through a difficult situation. It was at this juncture I met Flemister and introduced my friends to him.

Flemister was a patriot. Love of country was for him a devotion.

He cared not just about Liberia; he had a deep love for black people everywhere in the world. He was a pan-Africanist in the true sense of the word. You could see this in his conversations and his writings. Musa and I visited him from time to time, drinking from his fountain of knowledge. We visited him at home and at his office at Rovia Bank. Then the war came. I went to the Ivory Coast. When I came back in 1992, after a year and a half, I realized that Musa was still in touch with him. When Musa told him I was back in Monrovia, he was so eager to see me. At this time, he was an influential person in Amos Sawyer's Interim Government of National Unity (IGNU). When the power struggle was going on between Alhaji Kromah and Raleigh Seekie, it seemed as if the interim government felt more comfortable dealing with Seekie than Alhaji Kromah. One day at his home, Mr. Flemister made certain unflattering statements about Alhaji Kromah that did not sit well with me. At this time, just like thousands of Mandingoes, my love and support for Alhaji were very extreme. I was his fanatic and would have taken the bullets for him. So at this moment in Flemister's house, I did not hesitate to tell him what I felt about his unflattering statement about Alhaji Kromah. I responded to his statement by saying that, "whether somebody likes it or not, Alhaji is our leader." I could tell from his reaction that he didn't like me saying this. From then until his sudden death in 1994, my relationship with him never got back on track, though I continued to visit him. Though he did not tell me to stay away from him, I could tell that a distance had been placed between him and me. As I think of him today, I don't think of the disagreement I had with him which was political. I think of him as a Pan-Africanist who deeply loved Africa and Liberia in particular. I think of him as a kindhearted man who showed genuine interest and love to total strangers like me. Not too many of the elites of our society would open up like that to someone they don't know. Most of the time to even see them can be a war.

22

Alhaji Kromah and the ULIMO Struggle

I WAS STANDING AT THE JAMAICA ROAD and the UN Drive intersection when a heavy convoy in high speed passed, heading towards Central Monrovia. One of the vehicles in the heavy convoy was occupied by the ULIMO leader, Alhaji Kromah. One of the two females standing beside me cried with tears in her eyes. When I inquired why she was crying, she told me she was crying because she was elated and happy. She was crying, but she told me that her tears were actually tears of joy. She went on to say that when she thought of the days the Mandingoes were chased like chickens or goats and driven into exile, and thinking of this day, the triumphant arrival of Alhaji Kromah as head of ULIMO into Monrovia, she could no longer hide her feeling. Since she could not cry for the whole world to hear; she had to share those tears as a testimony to her feeling of happiness. She went on to re-echo time and time again that she was so full of joy and the tears were the only way to express her emotion.

Even though I did not cry with tears in my eyes, this moment was a proud moment for me as well. Like the lady who could not contain her emotion and had to shed tears to show it, I felt truly lucky and blessed to see this moment. Alhaji Kromah was a hero at that very moment and I am sure any Mandingo would feel the same. Not only was ULIMO scoring success after success against the NPFL, Alhaji Kromah had just won the endorsement of the fighters of ULIMO as their leader, thereby nullifying Raleigh Seekie and Joseph Tabior, who had earlier officiated in Monrovia as leaders of the organization. Many years after this particular incident, so much has been said and so much has changed. Just like any other leader of any organization, especially an armed faction in a deadly civil war such as ours, Alhaji Kromah is extremely loved by some while he's extremely vilified by others. To his many ardent admirers and supporters, he is a hero; to those who oppose him, he's no different from Charles Taylor, the man whose elimination was central to the goals of the movement. His opponents believe this based on the fact that at some point, Alhaji Kromah became an ally of Charles Taylor.

In their hours of hopelessness as a result of the on-going war, the Liberian Mandingoes needed a leader who could fight on their behalf. It's against this background that Alhaji Kromah emerged and ultimately became the leader of the Krahn-Mandingo resistance to Charles Taylor and his NPFL. When nobody could stand up to give them hope about their future in Liberia, it was Alhaji Kromah who came along. His interviews on BBC were a relief to the Liberian Mandingoes everywhere. He became a populist leader, very much admired by his people. Alhaji was able to capitalize on this situation to carry on massive mobilizations in Guinea, Sierra Leone, and Ivory Coast. The first effort in this direction led to the formation of MRM (Moslem Redemption Movement). At this time it was reasoned that this was necessary since the attacks by the NPFL was not limited to only the Mandingoes but Muslims as a whole. However, this name became very controversial to most Liberians. The movement later merged with another organization, United Defense Force (UDF) to form ULIMO (United Liberation Movement for Democracy). I first heard about UDF when I was still in Abidjan. One time I was listening to BBC Focus on Africa when I heard Gen. Armah Youlou speaking. He said he and his band of "freedom fighters" were going to chase Charles Taylor, even if "he goes back in his mother's womb." As already mentioned, Alhaji Kromah became the chairman of ULIMO against the backdrop of a power struggle in the movement to which Gen. Albert Karpeh was one of the first casualties. Does Alhaji Kromah had anything to do with the death of Gen. Karpeh who was the Chief of Staff of the Armed Forces of Liberia under President Samuel Doe? The answer to that question may be the subject for another book written by people who may have first hand recollection of the event. Whatever the case was, Gen. Armah Youlou went to jail in Sierra Leone for a while for the death of Karpeh.

This power struggle for the top post in ULIMO continued until the warring faction hit Po River, the outskirt of Monrovia, after dislodging the NPFL. By then, Raleigh Seekie and Joseph Tabior, Chairman and Secretary General of ULIMO, were in Monrovia meeting and negotiating with Dr. Amos Sawyer's interim government. While Seekie was in Monrovia being recognized by the interim government, Alhaji Kromah was in Conakry, Guinea. There were claims and counter-claims between Raleigh Seekie in Monrovia and Alhaji Kromah in Conakry until finally the ULIMO Military High Command issued a directive recognizing Alhaji Kromah as the legitimate leader of ULIMO and warning everyone not to do business with Raleigh Seekie or Joseph Tabior. Between Seekie and Kromah, the Interim Government of Dr. Amos Sawyer preferred Seekie, but as things turned out the Interim Government was forced to deal with Alhaji Kromah. This may be one reason why Kromah in many of his public utterances was so critical of Dr. Amos Sawyer. Even up to this point, most Kromah loyalists still view Dr. Sawyer and all those connected to him with deep suspicion and antagonism. This might have resulted in Kromah moving closer to Taylor in later negotiations that led to the formation of the first five-man Council of State and the subsequent ones.

The Mandingo/Krahn split in ULIMO was triggered when a Mandingo ULIMO representative on the Council of State, the transitional government at the time, Dr. El Mohammed Sheriff vied for the chairmanship of the Council. Thomas Zia, another ULIMO representative on the council belonging to the Krahn ethnic group, voted against him. Thomas Zia ended up taking over the vice chairmanship, which Dr. Sheriff had occupied, thereby demoting him to just being a member on the Council. This was viewed by the Mandingoes as a betrayal of the pact between the two groups. This sense of betrayal by the Krahns generated passionate discussions in our community. In the long history of Liberia, this was the closest the Mandingoes had come close to power and the Krahns had betrayed them. This was the popular sentiment among the Mandingoes.

Having been beaten with the same stick by the NPFL rebels, the two ethnic groups found a common ground to respond to their common situation. Given the status of both groups in the society before the war, it may be fair to say that what both groups wanted as an outcome of this joint endeavor might have been different. For the Krahns, the motive might have been to regain the power they had lost. For the Mandingoes, the stated interest was to come back home to bury their folks who had died, reclaim their homes and properties, or re-establish their businesses. But having seen themselves with the new found power, it seemed as if the Mandingoes wanted the same thing as their Krahn allies. This time around, Mandingoes wanted to go beyond their traditional boundary. It was with this newfound power that the Mandingoes' interests collided with those of the Krahns' as manifested by the split of ULIMO into ULIMO K and J. The Krahns might have also looked at it as a betrayal since they only expected the Mandingoes to "escort them to reclaim their throne." In the wake of all these developments, ULIMO chairman Kromah was urged by his support base to take action. The action taken was to replace Thomas Zia with another Krahn person, Dexter Tahyor. To the Krahns, this was unacceptable, and then they marched to war. All efforts to rebuild the trust among the former allies proved futile.

Long before the war Alhaji Kromah was a very high profiled personality in the Liberian society. He had served as a broadcast journalist at the Liberia Broadcasting Corporation (ELBC) years before the April 12, 1980 revolution. Under President Samuel Doe he served as DirectorGeneral at ELBC and as the Minister of Information. His popularity skyrocketed when he served as the president of the Mighty Barrolle Football Club, one of the two leading soccer clubs in Liberia. Even though he did not play any major role in the pro-democracy political agitation in the country against the Americo-Liberian regime, he became a very high profiled personality in Doe's government and enjoyed a personal relationship with the president. For the Mandingoes who were for the most part outside of the Liberian mainstream, hearing the name of Alhaji Kromah was something to be proud of. After all, one of their members had risen to a high position in government and had done so without changing his Mandingo or Moslem name. That in itself was a sense of cultural pride for any Mandingo or Moslem in Liberia.

Mandingoes used to be proud of the fact that Edward Kesselly was one of them, but with a western name, one could not be too sure as he was considered by some to be a Lormah, the tribe of his mother. But the name Alhaji Kromah was a stand-out; definitely "one of us." No one could argue who he was. Kromah's prewar reputation among the Mandingoes was further solidified in sports, as said earlier. The story is often told of a game between the Mighty Barrolle and the Invisible Eleven (IE) which was dubbed as the "Quran versus the Bible." When Barrolle won that game the talk was everywhere, especially among the Mandingoes.

A few months into the war, Moslems were getting ready for their end of Ramadan Prayer and festivity, in late April 1990. During prayer at the Antoinette Tubman Stadium, Alhaji Kromah addressed a large Moslem crowd, condemning the killing of Moslems in Nimba County and elsewhere in Liberia. This was followed by a series of meetings that were held at his residence and other places in Monrovia. Alhaji Kromah's residence became the unofficial headquarter for the Moslems or Mandingoes at that critical time. The utterances of Alhaji Kromah in those tense days gave hope to the Mandingoes everywhere. He carried the same message to the large hopeless Liberian Mandingo refugees in various places in the sub-region; the response was always unanimous. To all of these people that had been driven away from their homes and made refugees in foreign countries, Alhaji Kromah represented the hope of their returning to Liberia to regain their sense of dignity and properties.

While there were thousands and thousands of people who adored Alhaji Kromah, there were many critics who charged that he was so arrogant, too selfish and very dishonest and wanted everything for his own glorification. His critics were mostly the Mandingo intellectuals. Either for this or for other reasons, these intellectuals were alienated from the whole struggle. The high ideal for the Mandingoes to have massively supported ULIMO and Kromah leadership was besides the fact that the ULIMO struggle was a bittersweet experience for some Mandingoes. Could you support ULIMO and oppose Kromah? Not supporting ULIMO in the Mandingo community was tantamount to treason because it was seen as our war of liberation from the humiliation brought upon us by Charles Taylor. So for many people, it was hard to support ULIMO and be opposed to the chairman of the movement, Alhaji Kromah.

Those who opposed him in any shape or form were ridiculed and ostracized by the community. They were labeled as "enemies of Mandingo progress." Relatives and friends, who were bonded by family, religious and cultural ties over the years, saw themselves on opposite sides of this divide, and it was often acrimonious. People viewed each other with deep suspicion. At times those that opposed Alhaji lived in fear of being harmed by those totally loyal to him. His supporters were overzealous, fanatic and did not take kindly to any criticism of their leader. That is still very much the case even up to today. Any criticism of Alhaji is considered sacrilegious by his ardent admirers and supporters in the Mandingo community.

Alhaji Kromah, just like many African leaders, found it very difficult to resist the temptation of being dictatorial because people were paying too much homage to him. Whether the people were doing this out of ignorance or an unadulterated love for him, he took advantage of it as long as it meant more power and glory for him to do what he pleased. Whether this was done with his consent or not, his loyalists built around him such a security fortress that made him look like a typical African strong man. There were those that spied on their neighbors and reported every sentiment that was deemed inimical to him or to the movement, so much so to the point that Kromah became the organization itself with no way to separate the two.

Some prime examples of those who suffered ridicule and humiliation within the community were Sheik Kafumba Konneh, a respected religious leader within the Liberian society, and Ansumana Kromah, a former Internal Affairs Minister who was there from the beginning of the movement, but fell out with his brother the strong man. Also, there was Dr. Bangaly Fofana, an intellectual who once taught at the University of Liberia and became Minister of Commerce during the early days of the Taylor administration. These and other intellectuals and political activists such as Anthony Kesselly and Kabineh Ja'neh were branded as ineffective to do anything for their people and were considered envious of Alhaji Kromah for what he was accomplishing for the Mandingo people. With the exception of Sheik Kafumba Konneh, who has been very instrumental in the Liberian peace process and is very much respected for his role, most of the Mandingo intellectuals were completely disconnected from the every day experience and reality of the ordinary Mandingoes. Kromah capitalized on this to smear them, calling them enemies of the progress which the community was making under his leadership. He accused them of only knowing how to be followers of people like Amos Sawyer. He said they lacked vision and strength to spearhead their own independent thinking and activities. Under this atmosphere, ULIMO was like a de facto government, if not for the entire Liberian society, at least very much so for the Mandingoes.

This became very much visible when it was alleged that some ULIMO generals planned to remove Kromah from the leadership of the movement. According to some of the generals who were accused of this "coup plot," they had only met in Voinjama, their headquarters, to write a position statement to be delivered to Chairman Kromah in Conakry. The statement highlighted the grievances of the military high command of ULIMO which had chosen Kromah over Raleigh Seekie as their leader. ULIMO Field Commander, Gen. Mohammed Dumbuya, along with some elders, was sent with this position statement to be delivered to Chairman Kromah in Conakry, Guinea. This position statement was considered by the chairman as a coup attempt by those "disloyal" to him and orders were issued to have the "dissidents" arrested. Those that resisted arrest were ordered to be treated accordingly. The word "konapers," a corruption of the word "connivers" was coined to describe the "dissidents." Whether it was true that there was any serious intention on the part of the accused to remove Alhaji Kromah is hard to come by because there was no impartial investigation of the whole matter to ascertain what actually happened and how it happened. The accused made it clear it was not their intention to remove Kromah but no one would listen to them. They were condemned and it became very unpopular and threatening for anyone to come close to them. Every effort made to impartially investigate this matter was thwarted, as the judgment was already passed that the accused were guilty. It was said that they received large sums of money from Amos Sawyer's IGNU.

When the "dissidents" fled the ULIMO Voinjama headquarters to seek refuge outside, some of them made it back to Monrovia while others were arrested and handed over to the Guinean authority, falsely accused of being hired by the Guinean oppositions to overthrow the government of President Lansana Conte. Several of them including Kwamex Fofana, Solomani Sesay and Muazu Kromah were imprisoned and tortured in Conakry while those in Monrovia including Ousman Konneh, known as "Gen. Pepper & Salt", were constantly harassed. Not only were these accused "dissidents" harassed, their parents were also harassed for the "actions" of their children. The harassment of these "dissidents" and their relatives were carried out both in and outside of Liberia. Among those that were tortured at ULIMO headquarters in Voinjama was the mother of Pepper and Salt. She along with the senior brother of Sheik Kafumba Konneh, the late Gafin Konneh were detained and tortured for months. Other well-known casualties of this period of witch hunting were Gen. Ambush and Faliku Dukuly alias Blood Duke. According to some sources, Gen. Ambush was killed as revenge by another top general of the movement who accused him of killing his girlfriend. While this general who went by the name of Faraad Idi might have planned to kill Ambush, this period of whitch-hunting within the movement gave him a perfect opportunity to execute his plan without answering any question to anyone. Pepper and Salt was constantly harassed in Monrovia until he unfortunately sought refuge with Charles Taylor, the man he was previously fighting against. He died under mysterious circumstances while in Taylor's Gbarnga headquarters.

During those so called "Konapu" days, Sheik Kafumba Konneh suffered persecution in the Mandingo community. Attempts were made to kill him by some overzealous supporters of Alhaji Kromah. On one occasion, some of these loyalists attempted to burn his house. On another occasion, some attempted to burn his car. They poured gasoline on the car while Sheik Konneh was sitting in it. It was by the miracle of God that the attempts to burn his house on Clay Street and the car failed to achieve intended results. I vividly remember another occasion on Carey Street in a tailor shop adjacent to the old offices of the Inquirer newspaper. A group of Kromah loyalists had gathered with some planning to attack Sheik Kafumba physically. They were demanding to know why he was "against ULIMO." On that occasion, Sheik Konneh said, "My only sister from mother and many other relatives were killed by the NPFL. ULIMO happens to be a group that is fighting against the group that killed my sister and those relatives of mine. Naturally, most of you would expect me to support that movement which happens to be ULIMO. But the truth is that I am committed to the obtainment of peace in Liberia. I have declared my commitment to the search for peace to the Liberian people and I can't say one thing to them in the open and do something else behind closed door."

My own personal disappointment with Kromah was the day some "dissidents" were brought by their parents to apologize to him for their roles in the so called dissident activities. The accused lied down on their bellies to hold his feet. This was a traditional way of demonstrating their remorse, apologizing for their "wrong doing." Alhaji accepted their apology. While he accepted their apology, he went on to say that he was accepting nothing less from Pepper & Salt and if he could not do likewise, he would consider him and his family as "military targets." I had gone to his compound that day hoping to hear something about reconciliation. What he said caused me and my senior brother, Bangalie Konneh, to flee the compound. The attention we were getting after Kromah made that pronouncement was very uncomfortable. We felt accused and unsecured. Our only option was to flee. Not too long after this threat issued by Chairman Kromah, some group of loyalists seized a car belonging to my uncle Sekou Konneh, the father of Gen. Pepper & Salt. Another uncle, Vafomo who was driving the car had parked it on Carey Street, Central Monrovia. In broad day light, a group of ULIMO soldiers came and dragged him out of the pickup and carried it behind the line. The car was not seen again. We felt vulnerable and powerless with our own group which was meant to provide protection for all of us.

Despite this general atmosphere of fear prevailing in our

community, I encouraged the formation of an organization among the young Mandingoes in Monrovia to intervene to find amicable solution to the growing problem of division and intimidation in our community. We organized ourselves into the Youth Committee for Peace and Reconciliation. Among those who joined with me in this effort were Sekou Kanneh, now Montserado County District #2 Representative, Folebole Kromah, Hassan Bility, and Sidiki Trawally among others. I should have become the chairman of the group but I declined this position because I didn't want the stakeholders to question the motive of the group because of my family connection with Ousman Konneh, AKA Gen. Pepper & Salt who was one of the accused ring leaders of the "konapers." Folebole Kromah became the chairman. Under this banner, we had series of meetings with all the key players except Chairman Kromah. One of the things we suggested was an impartial investigation of all the charges and counter-charges so as to know where the truth lay. We did not succeed in this objective as ULIMO leadership demanded that the "konapers" must surrender and admit their guilt in a plot to remove Chairman Kromah.

Despite all the internal wrangling, ULIMO survived and grew in strength, becoming the biggest organization and the only challenger to Charles Taylor's ambition for the throne in the Executive Mansion. Kromah was the symbol of this great power. In any case, Kromah was unlike any other rebel leader anywhere in Africa. He spent more time in the air-conditioned house in Conakry than with his soldiers in the bush and the trenches on the front lines. He was a political leader, not a frontline soldier who was battle-tested on the battlefield. How he maintained a loyal following among the fighters on the battlefield can only be explained by the fact that the Mandingo family structure is a very cohesive one and no fighter, no matter how tough he was on the battlefield, would want to defy his father on any matter. So getting the solid backing from the elders whose children were fighting was very crucial for Kromah to maintain his grip on power. As long as he enjoyed the backing of those old people, the children could not rebel against him. They were organized into an elder committee that "advised" him from time to time. Then came the 1997 election in which he ran as a candidate of the All Liberian Coalition Party (ALCOP), a party he formed as an offshoot of ULIMO. Charles Taylor, his one time archrival and ally, who had formed the National Patriotic Party (NPP), won the election. With Taylor in the Executive Mansion as the president, Kromah could not feel secure in Liberia. As a result, he went into exile. He remained in exile in the United States until 2003 when Taylor was forced into exile by combined forces of LURD and MODEL.

23

From ULIMO to LURD

GIVEN THE HISTORY of the Mandingoes in Africa, having led empires such as Mali and Ghana with a long line of kings and warriors and the fact that there are several countries in Africa where Mandingoes are the rulers, it is surprising that the Mandingoes in Liberia have stood for so long on the sideline while others engaged in politics and administration of the country. It was King Sao Bosso Kamara, probably the most powerful leader in the land that became Liberia, who guaranteed the settlement of the Americo-Liberians after other native leaders had threatened to take back the lands they had already sold to the settlers. What happened to the power and influence the Mandingoes exercised during those early days of Liberia? The simple answer to all these questions is that the Mandingoes went to sleep either voluntarily or involuntarily and were only awakened by the wars of the 1990s. It is in this regard that most Mandingoes feel that ULIMO was the movement that re-awakened them from their long years of slumber. Even though they were not in power, the Mandingoes were sometimes the hidden power behind some of the most powerful leaders and chiefs back in the days. Many powerful leaders employed the services of the moli man or kamoh (marabou) who worked for them to either maintain or obtain power in Liberia. From Tubman to Tolbert to Doe and even Charles Taylor, all of them at one time or another sought the holy power of some Mandingo kamohs.

After the 1997 election, Liberians hoped that peace and stability would return. That was not to be the case as Charles Taylor still ruled by the guns, even though he had been "democratically elected." Since the Mandingoes under the banner of ULIMO were the greatest obstacle to his quest for power in Liberia, Taylor made sure to keep them in check while he was in power. Just like many leaders in Africa, democratic process for Taylor was just a matter of convenience. Since he could not get it through the barrel of the guns, he finally got what he had always wanted through the democratic process. He was rewarded for all his stubbornness.

With the persecution of the Mandingoes and the Krahns continuing unabated under Taylor, some members of these groups belonging to the defunct ULIMO regrouped under another nomenclature, Liberians United for Reconciliation and Democracy (LURD). It was LURD and MODEL (Movement for Democracy in Liberia) that broke the back of the Taylor regime thereby sending him into exile. For the Mandingoes and their allies, the Krahns, Taylor's going into exile was the biggest prize of all the wars. This victory against the Taylor regime gave birth to the democratic process that brought Ellen Johnson-Sirleaf to power. For most Mandingoes, the saying is that ULIMO started the job that LURD and MODEL ended. Even though some Liberians insist that it was President George Bush who told Taylor to leave and because of that he left, the fact is that if there was no military pressure on the ground, Taylor would not have left simply because President Bush told him to leave unless President Bush was willing to let the American soldiers do the job.

Since the early beginning of LURD, there was always news surfacing of power struggle among contending elements to head the movement. Alhaji Kromah was one of them. The logic of Kromah and his supporters was that since he led the original movement, ULIMO, he should be the one to lead LURD, which was an off-shoot of the original organization. All the maneuvering Alhaji did to take control of LURD proved futile as there were determined efforts to not give him any opportunity to take over. Even without Alhaji Kromah, the power struggle within the movement continued to the very end between Sekou Konneh and other key elements of the movement including his ex-wife, Aishai Keita and Kabineh Janneh.

Whatever power, influence and popularity Kromah enjoyed when he was in command slowly evaporated during his years in exile. All the suspicion and witch hunting that resulted from Kromah's heavy-handed leadership of ULIMO and wounds created as a result did not heal for some people. He has not made much effort to mend fences with the "enemies" he created while he exercised power as head of ULIMO. He left a deep divide yet to be mended and wounds yet to be healed. He has not been able to keep alive the momentum that ULIMO created. This is so, because he has not been able to win the trust and confidence of those he alienated and castigated as enemies of the movement. The biggest question for Alhaji Kromah presently is how he is perceived in the Liberian society as a whole. I am sure he wants to project himself as a respected national leader, even though some may object to his quest on the account that he headed a warring faction. None of such concern has stopped Alhaji Kromah from demonstrating that he is still relevant as a political leader. He is still the leader of ALCOP, the political party he formed to contest the 1997 and 2005 general elections. Since his return to Liberia after LURD and MODEL drove Taylor into exile, he has been teaching at the University of Liberia. Teaching at the university is nothing new for the highly educated Kromah. Before the war, he used to teach at the university while at the same time serving as minister in the government of President Samuel Doe. During the Peace Talk in Ghana in 2003, Alhaji lobbied for the position of interim leader but was unsuccessful. In 2005, he once again tested his political relevance by contesting for the presidency. He was among the losers who supported George Oppong Weah against Ellen Johnson-Sirleaf for the second round. His last run for an elected office was as recent as November 26, 2009. He competed for the Montserrado County junior senatorial seat made vacant by the death of Senator Hannah Brent. Alhaji did not gain enough support to win the senate seat. He came in fourth place and became one of the hottest political figures whose support the two main challengers sought. This time around, Alhaji threw his support behind the Unity Party candidate, Clemenceau Urey who lost to the Congress for Democratic Change's Geraldine Doe-Sherif. In the 2011 general elections, his party, ALCOP did very poor. Meaning, his political capital has diminished even among his people because two Mandingo candidates on Unity Party tickets defeated two candidates of ALCOP in two Mandingo dominated constituencies, Quardu-Gbonie District of Lofa County and District #2 in Montserado County. The irony of ALCOP's defeat in the Quardu-Gbonie District is that the wife of the party's US branch chairman, Mariam Fofana defeated ALCOP's incumbent representative, Mariam Jalibah. With all these political defeats, the questions are whether Kromah can ever rebrand himself and reemerge politically, or set up a private foundation to further his legacy. Despite his diminished political relevance on the national political stage, and despite all his human flaws, he along with Sekou Damate Konneh, remains a symbol of the Liberian Mandingoes' quest for national recognition and respect.

Part III
So Far Away
on the Distant Sea

24

Winning the Lottery Visa

SOMETIME IN 1994 I heard about the Diversity Lottery Visa program which gives US permanent resident status to immigrants from many countries. All you had to do was write your name on a plain sheet of paper with your date of birth, country of birth and current address. Everyone in our yard on Jamaica Road was interested in trying their luck. I became like a secretary writing more than 50 for relatives and friends. I was not eager to write one for myself. At that point, I was not in any big worry to come to the United States. I also didn't believe that writing my name and address on a plain sheet could guarantee travelling to the US to live as a permanent resident. It sounded too good to be true to me. So while everyone in my yard was crazy about the prospect of coming to America, I was kind of aloft. I was not moved. Another factor to my reluctance to fill out the form was because I had several options in Monrovia. I was the registrar of the Revival of Islamic Heritage Clinic. I was being earmarked for two possible appointments in the government. I was approached by the late Bill Frank Enoiye, a veteran Liberian journalist, to work for a newspaper he had started. I felt that anyone of these opportunities would make it possible for me to visit the US in the future.

When my senior brother, Bangalie Konneh, asked why I hadn't written anything for myself, I told him I was not interested. "I am sure one day I will travel to America by virtue of the activities I am involved in. I am a writer and if my career advances as a writer, there will be many opportunities for me to represent Liberia in many places including America." My brother was not satisfied with my explanation.

"As your big brother, I mandate you to do it otherwise I am going to beat you for defying my order." When I told him of my prospects of jobs, he said, "This is a factional government and all these opportunities are temporary. They are not enough to reject an opportunity to travel to the US and live there as a permanent resident. Because of that fear, I went ahead and filled out one for myself. Then the next morning, one of my cousins, Kalif Konneh and I went to the post office in Central Monrovia to mail the completed document. Kalif was a ULIMO soldier. He had been wounded in a fierce battle between the Mandingo and Krahn elements of ULIMO. He was badly wounded and was brought to Monrovia for treatment. Since my brother Bangalie was a Physician Assistant and head of the clinic, they brought Kalif on Jamaica Road. He was there for more than three months. Then when he heard about the lottery visa, he was so eager about it. He said that if he had the opportunity he would never go back to fight in the bush.

One day, one of my co-workers at the clinic, Musa Jabateh, and I went to town and we decided to go check at the post office. When I saw the big envelope, I was surprised that I had won the lottery visa to come to the US. When the result came in April 1994, I was the only one that had made it in our yard on Jamaica Road. My big brother and the entire members of my family were excited. My attitude was very lukewarm. I did not show too much excitement like people expected of me.

My brother's wife at the time, Mazitu Dorleh was very instrumental in the whole process. She left for the US at the time I had won the DV. When she called back three months later, I told her I didn't know where the paper was. She was infuriated. She told me she wanted to talk to my brother. After their discussion, my brother pressured me to look for the papers. Until it was sent, she would call almost every day to talk to my brother and I. Because I was afraid of defying my brother and didn't want his wife to feel bad, I went along.

It was in June 1994, I received a letter from my sister-in-law that I was scheduled for an interview at the US Embassy in Monrovia. Sekou Dorleh and Jenneh Dorleh were Mazitu's brother and sister. I had put their names in my application as my relatives, but they were unqualified to travel with me as such. Since they could not qualify to come with me as relatives, Jenneh and I got "married." With my "cousin" Jenneh as my "wife," we were scheduled for an interview which we passed. We were asked whether we were cousins or a married couple. I told the interviewer that in our culture, cousins can marry cousins.

When Jenneh and I went to the Embassy to get the sealed envelopes containing our visas, she was so excited. She could not contain her excitement. She was jumping up and down when we left the Embassy. We went to their place in a section of Monrovia called PHP (Public Health Pump) and from there we went to Jamaica Road to share the good news with my brother and other relatives. With the visas in our hands, we arrived in New York on August 12, 1995. At the JFK Airport in New York, my sister-in-law Mazitu was there to receive us. We were all excited when we met. She gave me the alternative of living in Atlantic City, New Jersey, or New York. I didn't know Atlantic City. I chose New York, the Big Apple. We drove from the airport and arrived at my first address in the US, 115th and Second Avenue. It was a very tall building which I came to know as a project. The next morning, my host, an Ivorian Mandiingo, Lasso took me to some places. We walked from 115th and Second Avenue to Malcolm X Boulevard, Martin Luther King Boulevard etc. It was then I discovered that I had landed in Harlem. I had read a lot about Harlem from Malcolm X, Marcus Garvey, Langston Hughes, James Baldwin and other prominent African American writers. I had fallen in love with the place long before I saw it with my eyes. I had developed my own romantic vision of what Harlem was supposed to be. That's why I was so excited to discover that I had indeed landed in this historic black community.

My life at 115th and Second Avenue was not to last long. My host, who was sub-leasing the apartment in this project, decided to go to the New York Housing Authority office to see if she could apply for her own place. Once it was discovered that my host, Mamayan Kanneh, was sub-leasing the apartment from the person whose name was on the lease we were told to leave. The housing authority gave us three days or they would lock all of our belongings in the house. We had to leave to find another place. My next address was 110th Street facing the north side of Central Park.

My roommate, Lasso Sangare, was a car washer. While I was looking in the employment sections of newspapers, Lasso would go to the car washing job in the morning. When coming in the evening, he would buy food and drinks. After a week, he told me to come to his working place and apply for a car washing job. I thought such a job was beneath me. I, who had come with the ambition to pursue a career in writing, should go wash cars? Lasso explained, "I know how you feel but the place where we sleep and the food that we eat are being paid for by money earned from car washing. You have to make a choice, either car washing for now or you will have to move." With that I had no option but to go with him to the car washing place. That was my first job in the US.

What made 110th Street interesting is that the apartment had a large group of African immigrants from the French speaking African countries such as Ivory Coast, Guinea, Senegal, and Mali. I was the only Liberian in their mix. They spoke more French than English. Instead of saying 110th Street, they used to call it Cent Dix (French translation of 110). They also called 125th Street in French as well. The building was frequented by prostitutes. They moved like serious hustlers. And these African immigrants, some with wives in Africa, not knowing when they were going to see their wives relieved themselves with these prostitutes. They all had some stories to tell about why they came to America. Majority of them had the preconceived notion of a place where money could be picked up from the trees. Because of that, some of them sold their businesses and their homes to come to America. Now in America, a lot of them ended up finding no job other than car washing. That was the only job most of them could do because they had the disadvantage of not having legal status, not being literate and not being able to speak English. So while going with them to the car washing place, I could not feel comfortable knowing that I had legal status, and that I could speak English. While being forced to go to the car washing place, I was always looking forward to finding another job.

25 | Are You in the Service?

I HAD GONE TO THE BANK to conduct business. I was wearing my green cruise jacket with patches of different designs and the countries we had visited during my last Med Cruise on board the USS Detroit, a navy logistic ship based in Earle, New Jersey. I was standing in a long line of people and everyone was curiously staring at me. An elderly lady asked me whether I was in the service and I said yes. Which branch, she wanted to know. I told her I was serving in the navy. She then informed me that she had relatives serving in the army, marine and the navy. The lady expressed her gratitude to all those serving in the American military fighting to protect the country "against people who are trying to destroy it." She said, "May I ask you where you're from, if you don't mind?" I answered; I didn't see any problem with that. I stated that I was from Africa, Liberia to be specific. Further in the conversation I went on to explain that I lived in Philadelphia and before then I lived in New York City. She told me that she was surprised that I was from a different country and serving in the American military. To her that could not be possible. I replied that I thought so too until I met the recruiter who convinced me otherwise. I then went on to say that even though I don't know the exact statistics, there are thousands of people in the various branches of the US military that are not originally American. Some of them have been killed in action in Afghanistan and in Iraq. Whether they are American or not, there are many that have become battlefield casualties just like the typical

Americans. Having told her all that, she then asked what made me join the military? This is one question I have been asked so many times. People who know me in Liberia as a student and writer, and those I have met in various places in the USA have asked me this question over and over again. So when this lady asked me in the bank I wasn't surprised.

I began to reflect on what answer to give her. Should I tell her I joined the navy to see the world or should I tell her I joined to get money for college? At least these are the standard answers most people expect. I responded with the truth. I joined the navy because I didn't have a job while living in New York, but now I was more committed to it to the point that I wanted to complete my twenty years serving America. She beamed, shook my hand and said, "Thank you for serving our country." I have received many of such compliments from different people, but always with the surprise of knowing that those from different countries could serve in the US military. Her question reminds me of another time when someone asked me whether I joined the navy to get a green card? I told him that before joining the Navy a person must have a green card.

This encounter with the elderly lady in the bank happened months before 9-11. Right after that infamous event, I was sitting in the classroom at the Delaware County Community College. From one thing to another, the topic shifted to 9-11. Everyone in the class had his/her take on the September 11th terrorist attacks against the US. The majority of those that spoke believed that "the Moslems are angry fanatics who want to destroy America." More than three students talked about their relatives who were deployed either in the Middle East or other places for the "war against terror." It seemed like in their minds all Moslems were guilty for the terrorist acts of 9-11. What they could not imagine was that there was a Moslem sitting right in their midst. Then I raised my hand to speak. I revealed that their conclusion was far off the mark because "I am a Moslem and I am serving in the US Navy." Every one of them was shocked to know a Moslem was in their midst. I told them it was wrong to carry the notion that all Moslems want to destroy America, as it would be wrong to say that all Roman Catholics want to destroy England because some of them may be supporters of the Irish Republican Army (IRA). Our class course was "communication." My speaking out opened a kind of dialogue in the classroom, which was an eye-opening experience for all of us. I told them that the same conclusion they had reached was no different from those of the so-called fanatics and "Islamic terrorists." I informed them that the same generalization unfortunately led the terrorists to commit the terrible acts of 9-11. At the end of the course, my fellow students were happy they had class with a Moslem, at least they got to know a thing or two they didn't know before.

Two years after September 11, my assignment was over in Philadelphia and the next assignment took me on board the USS Dwight D. Eisenhower where I spent the last two years before saying good bye to the navy. Not too long after I reported for duty on board the ship, I was hit by tragedy. My wife, Makemeh D. Konneh passed away in Guinea, Africa. She had gone to visit Africa during which time she sought traditional medical treatment for some illness which had bothered her the entire time she was in the states. She had gone and left me a three months old baby which had to stay with some family members in Philadelphia while I was on the ship. It was the darkest moment of my life but I managed to cope with the situation.

Most of the time I spent on the Eisenhower was at the Northrop Grumman Newport News (NGNN) dry dock. It was only within the last few months of my duty on board that the works on the ship at the shipyard was completed. As such the ship had to go for a series of sea trials preceded by what is known as fast cruise. Fast cruise is a long standing navy tradition, which is meant to stimulate the at sea scenarios while the ship is still berthed at port. During this evolution, training is held to review the mission readiness of the ship. Emergency scenarios the ship may encounter at sea are part of fast cruise.

March 16, 2005 was set as the first date of the fast cruise and lasted through the 20th of March. This was followed by getting underway on March 22nd through the 25th for sea trial, the first for our ship, USS Dwight D. Eisenhower in three and a half years. USS Dwight D. Eisenhower, named after the American military hero and former president, is a nuclear aircraft carrier, one of the many gigantic ships in the US Navy with 5000 people capacity.

Until two weeks before the fast cruise and getting underway for the sea trial, I had been a very motivated sailor, thinking that I would do twenty years, retire, go back home to Liberia and live off of my retirement paychecks. To reach to that milestone would take me another eleven years in the navy. In about five months, my current enlistment would come to an end and I would be left with the option of either re-enlisting or getting out. "What to do," was the question that was weighed heavily on my mind.

When I came to the US in 1996, joining the military was not on my mind. It was not a part of the "American Dream" I brought with me. As a student and freelance writer with articles and poems published in local papers and with a growing popularity in Liberia, I had hoped for embarking on a literary career. That was my American Dream. When that dream could not match my American reality of hardship in New York City, I decided to join the Navy. Before I found out whether I could join the navy, I had not thought about it. It was just one day, while looking for any job that I came across a recruiter. I was by this time going through the most difficult period in my life. It was the first time I had to rent a room or apartment. In the case of most immigrants, they would share a place with some relatives for at least six months to one year. By that time they would understand the place and be able to move on their own. I didn't have that opportunity; from the moment I got here I was on my own. I had to do anything to survive, even car washing. Through the help of some friends, I left the car washing job and moved on to the next level, a 7-Eleven convenience store. Earning a minimum wage of $4.75 was not enough at that time to handle all of my financial needs. I didn't leave Liberia to come to America, the land of plenty just to be working at 7-Eleven. I wanted something more than that in America.

Since I lived in Harlem, I sent some articles to both the Amsterdam News and the City Sun newspapers. I thought I could apply for employment with any of these papers. I contacted the Amsterdam News through Zamgba Brown, a Liberian journalist who was working as a staff reporter there. Many attempts to contact Mr. Brown failed until one day I was able to talk to him on the phone. His response was not encouraging. On the other hand, I got an encouraging response from the City Sun newspaper through their staff reporter, Milton Alimadi, a fellow African from Uganda. Through Milton, several of my articles were published in the City Sun. I also affiliated and contributed articles to the African Voices Literary Magazine. However none of those efforts could put food on the table.

After 7-Eleven, I moved on to a department store in Spanish Harlem. Later I worked at a super market in Queens as a security guard. Since I could not earn enough through any of those efforts, I trained as a Home Health Aid. I worked with a few clients but the job did not appeal to me. Either way, I had to do it because I had no options. Every free time I had, I went around looking for jobs. Most of my job hunts took place on 125th Street and other places in Harlem. It was on one of those days I went to apply for jobs and filled out three applications. At about 3pm, I started walking from 125th going to 112 and Second Avenue. I was between Malcolm X Boulevard and 5th Avenue on 125th Street when I saw a large banner with the message: **We are now hiring**. I could not imagine that the job being advertised was a military service. I got to know that when I stepped in to inquire. I met a navy recruiter who gave me the details. That very evening he wanted me to take the preliminary test in which I scored 80. He was surprised and started vigorous efforts to get me to take the ASVAB (Armed Services Vocational Aptitude Battery) test. When I passed that test, the next step was to go to Boot Camp. I was originally scheduled for Boot Camp in November 1996. Out of desperation, I pressured my recruiter to send me as quickly as possible.

At the time I was working part time as a home health aid and I hated that job. There was a client I had to run away from because one day he almost hurt me if I had not dodged him quickly enough. I was in the room with him when he took a stick to knock me with it. I had to open the door to escape his violent outburst. He was mentally unstable. Another time I had to go see a different client who was so drunk he had defecated in his pants and feces was all over him. I had to clean him up. Taking him to the bathroom was not easy. That day I started to hate that job, but I could not quit because I didn't have another job. Joining the military became my only ticket out of those difficult situations. So instead of waiting for my November Boot

Camp departure schedule, I told my recruiter I wanted to leave as early as possible. Then on August 8, 1996, I left for my basic training. We took off from La Guardia airport in Queens, New York to Chicago O'Hare Airport. A van picked us up from there to a boot camp in Great Lake. The processing lasted until 12 midnight. After processing we were sent to a building where everyone was assigned a bunk bed. When we were marching from the processing center to that building I was too sleepy and walking slow in front of others. I got a rude awakening when the chief started shouting at the top of his voice, "Motherfucker, move. This is the military, not your weak ass civilian world." I was shocked at the profanity. I can't remember when the last time someone used such a profanity against me.

I can't remember when I fell asleep but I was awakened in the morning around 5am. When the morning bell rang signaling the start of the day, I did not wake up as expected. I stayed in the bed until the chief came and started yelling at my "weak ass" to wake up.

After that rude awakening in booth camp, the rest of my time in the navy can be described as a combination of rough and smooth sailing. After almost nine years in the navy, my soul was still restless. I was not uneasy so much about being in the navy as I was about the future of Liberia in general and my ethnic group in particular. I was involved in the freedom struggle of my homeland, Liberia. I participated and spearheaded various activities in the Liberian communities all over the East Coast. I wrote extensively about what was going on in Liberia; sometimes I gave speeches, and on two occasions I organized demonstrations and participated in others. A writer, civil, human rights and community activist as well as sailor of the US Navy were what you could describe me as when I served on shore duty in Philadelphia. Being a human or civil rights activist is not a characteristic of a regular sailor. It's a violation of the Uniform Code of Military Justice (UCMJ) for a military member to participate in demonstrations. I think the only reason I did not get in trouble was because the demonstrations I led or participated in were against the brutal regime of Charles Taylor in Liberia, not against the US. I guess on that ground, no one could say I was violating UCMJ. And the question I kept asking myself was what did I want to be remembered for? I thought I was inclined to think that I wanted to be remembered in the capacity of a writer or community activist. This was because I had been engaged in social advocacy long before I joined the navy and that's where my heart and soul were. So in a way, the navy was just a stepping-stone, a transitional point in my life and experience in the US.

In another way, writing had been a dream long before coming to America; I have always written. Up to that point, I had written more than fifty articles that had been published on various internet websites here and abroad. On top of all that was the self-publishing of my first book of poetry, "Going to War for America." I considered that a realization of a dream. It was almost a year now since the successful launching of that book in 2004. Promoting and marketing that book was a great challenge for me as I served on the ship. One way or the other, I began to consider getting out of the navy to pursue a dream I had nurtured over the years. That dream was to continue my school while trying to develop a career as a writer and earn money while doing it. This was a tough challenge. Am I going to be successful out there? You never know until you try. So, try I must.

For some of my fellow sailors, the idea of leaving the Navy as E-5/nine years was not a wise one. Finding the next job outside the military was their concern. So I received lots of advice from some shipmates, who told me to think twice because it was hard out there in the "civilian world." While others suggested that I had jobs lined-up before leaving, others were checking to see if I was in the right frame of mind, as they asked, "What are you going to do when you get out?" My answer was that I was getting out in order to go to school, write, promote and sell my books; that I needed to be somewhere where I could meet and network with other creative people, find the necessary creative nourishment, thereby energizing me for the realization of my dream. With my book, "Going to War for America," I believed I could get out there to hustle towards the realization of my dream. What I had in mind before taking this "drastic step" was that no success can come without taking some risk. Fear of failure? It could be, but if it came to that I would still learn some valuable lessons while moving on to the next level. Failure is not the problem, but not being able to rise up when you fall is the problem. While some were excited by my answers and were praying and wishing me well, others were skeptical, not so sure if I was making the right decision. Creative people are a different breed of people, different from the regular folks. Lots of our thoughts and decisions are outside the proverbial box. So I was not surprised by these skeptical questions from my friends. For most of us in the military, it's not only a profession; it's also a way of life. To any "normal person," in the navy, it just didn't make sense to leave that stable way of life for a life of uncertainty in the civilian world. After all it's the uncertainty of that civilian world that made you join the military in the first place. Half of the people in the military would be out there in that civilian world if it had worked for them.

After the fast cruise, we got underway on March 22, 2005. It felt exciting going back to sea, even though it was short compared to the last time I got underway in 2000 which was before my transfer to shore duty in Philadelphia. One notable difference between now and then was that I had not taken any seasickness pills. On USS Detroit, I had to take those pills to prevent vomiting. But on this big 5000-person capacity ship, I could do fine on this first day of getting underway. I went out and about on the main deck, looking at the Atlantic Ocean. It felt so beautiful to see the ocean in its pristine color of blue, so far away from the coastline where the water is greener. Looking at it through the horizon, where it met the sky, it felt so mysterious and enchantingly beautiful.

This was just another manifestation of nature's wonderful work of creation. It felt like a dream just to sit by watching the ocean while the ship sailed. Sometimes it roared as if it were angry, rocking the ship from side to side. Other times it was calm like a sleeping lake. Nothing is more breathtaking about the sea than seeing the reflection of the morning or evening sun or the bright shining moon in the night. As I looked at the ocean from this gigantic ship, my mind took me far back to the past of where I had come from. From Saclepea, from Kpaytuo, from Beyla, and from Muandu in Africa, to this gigantic ship on the Atlantic truly felt like a long way from home. A long way from all the places I have called homes. It was a long way from home going through the Mediterranean Sea, Arabian Sea, Persian Gulf, and the Adriatic Sea etc. I sailed on all of these large bodies of water I had learned about in my geography class back in the '80s, courtesy of the US Navy. Well, truth be told, I felt great to have had this experience. Imagine being to faraway places like Palestine, Arabia and other areas without paying a dime to be there. From all those places, I did get my share of sea stories to tell my children. Sea stories from Jerusalem, Bethlehem, Bahrain, Jubal Ali, St. Thomas, Palma Majorca, France, Spain, Italy, and so on. It was only fair to say that I did see my fair share of the world, taking into consideration that some people never get the opportunity to travel beyond their own villages or towns.

Comparing my experience in the Navy to the experience of growing up in Liberia made me think of Charles Dickens' novel, "The Tales of Two Cities." While America came into being as a result of the European conquest of the Indians, Liberia came into being as a result of the campaign in America to return free slaves back to Africa. While the free slaves abhorred slavery in America, they did not hesitate, while in Africa, to subject the native Africans to the same practice. While America changed from slavery and discrimination because of Black protest and legislation that were passed, the former slave rulers of Liberia had to be violently overthrown because they were too stubborn to accept that there was a need for change. Yes indeed, when white people with their majority and economic status gave in to the demand of the minority for equality, the minority ruling class of Liberia had no intention of relinquishing power. And while today America promotes and celebrates diversity, Liberia is yet to tolerate and celebrate ethnic and religious diversity. While ethnic dialogue has made America a kind of paradise on earth for people from everywhere in the world, Liberia is a country still buried in the backward ethnic and religious prejudices. The ethnic and religious prejudice has been very apparent during the past fourteen years of bloody civil war. And it has cost Liberians more than 200,000 people and billion dollars worth of property; still, it seems Liberia has yet to learn from the errors of her recent past. Even up to this point the former minority ruling class has not seen any reason to atone for the sins of the past; instead they are trying to make native Liberians feel guilty for overthrowing their oppressive minority rule.

After the sea trial of March 22nd through the 25th, we got

underway again on March 30, 2005. This time the evolution was the flight deck certification for testing the ship's capability of launching and recovering aircraft, the mission for which she was built. Underway replenishment was conducted with the USNS Supply alongside. I had not seen an underway replenishment since 2000 when I left the USS Detroit for a shore duty assignment in Philadelphia. As someone explained to me years ago, I found myself talking to a new sailor as I told him how this kind of underway replenishment showed the level of efficiency of the US Navy. I told him that after boot camp and A-School, he was now experiencing the real navy. He said he would find it difficult to adjust to being underway. I said to him, "Nobody wants to be out here but that's something military duty requires." As I thought about it later, a thought came to my mind, which I wrote as the young sailor said, "I love the navy but I can't deal with being on the sea like this." An old sailor who was nearing his retirement after nineteen years and some months overheard him talking. He went to the young sailor and said, "Young man, you are where you're supposed to be as a sailor." He went on to say that sailors belong on the ships, and the ships belong on the water just like the army and the marine belong on the ground in Afghanistan or in Iraq." And so he told the young sailor to get used to being out there at sea and he would be just fine. Having given the young sailor the counseling, he told him, "You have a fine navy day."

Every beginning has an ending and every ending has had a beginning. Through the length of our life we embark on a journey of multiple dimensions—some physical, spiritual and emotional. We end one journey and begin another. Along the way, we rise and fall. In any case, the journey must continue till the day we depart this world. And so being in the Navy was one dimension of my personal journey in life. The journey that began in 1996 on board the USS Detroit was now drawing to a conclusion on board the USS Dwight D. Eisenhower. Before saying my final goodbye to my shipmates, we got underway one last time from May 17, through the 27th. There were lots of interesting moments during this last underway period. What made this last underway different from the ones we had in recent time was the presence of the Marine aircraft squadron, VMFA and the visit on board the ship by sailors from the French naval aircraft carrier, Charles De Gaulle. The French ship, along with those of other NATO countries, was part of the NATO's transformational maritime initiatives and was a step leading to the NATO Response Force (NRF). I had seen the Marines on other ships before but this was the first time to be in the same ship with them.

What was more exciting about these French sailors coming on board the ship was that I had just read a novel, "Task Force: Liberia," by David E. Meadow. What first drew my attention to this novel was Liberia on the cover. The book portrays some naval confrontation between two battle ships representing the navies of both France and the United States. The American battleship is steaming towards the coast of Liberia to evacuate Americans trapped in Kingsville, a fictional American expatriate settlement in Liberia. The French did not appreciate this and they made efforts to discourage America's involvement in Liberia, where some Islamic radicals had overthrown the government. France's opposition to America's war in Iraq might have inspired Meadow's novel. So seeing these French sailors coming on board in a friendly manner was directly opposite to the theme of the novel.

One last thing I wanted to do before leaving the ship was to have an opportunity to meet the Commanding Officer and autograph a copy of my book for him. So I had to put in a request chit through my chain of command. I said in the request chit, "Respectfully request to have audience with the Commanding Officer to autograph a copy of my book for him." The chit got some approval and I was even given the green light to see the Captain. A schedule was set. This is what I had planned to autograph for the Captain: "It has been a great experience to serve on this great warship under your command and able leadership." And then something happened. My request was denied because of some information at the back of my book, "Going to War for America." The information on the back of the book was this: "Nvasekie Konneh is also the founding Chairman of the National Civil Right Movement (NCRM), a Liberian pro-democracy and human rights organization based in Philadelphia, Pennsylvania" and that "Nvasekie Konneh has led two demonstrations in Washington DC..." Because of that someone within the chain of command alerted the others, "Without reading the book, I cannot recommend to the CO to autograph the book." Another one wrote, "Not sure I would support this given his bios on the left side." Talk about my book has been everywhere on the ship since an article appeared in the ship's newsletter about it.

Members of the US military are not supposed to engage in any political activity such as organizing or leading demonstrations. I had not led these demonstrations against the US government. So I did not think I did anything wrong. In any case, I never thought it would be a problem since Charles Taylor was the reason I led these demonstrations. My cousin, Kalifala Donzo, a member of the Virginia National Guard had warned me against leading demonstrations because of my status as an active duty military member. I had told him that we had the moral obligation to stand up against the ruthless dictator Charles Taylor on whose order more than twenty of our people were detained for no justifiable reason; if we didn't do anything, those people could be killed.

Since the demonstration that I was leading was not against any policy of the United States government, we needed to go ahead until somebody within my chain of command stopped me. I had done all of this without anyone taking notice of it. Now that the information was at the back of my book, someone had taken notice of it. What surprised me was, why did it take this request chit to see the Commanding Officer before someone could bring the "problem" to my attention? From the time I had been in the Navy I had not been in any trouble; never been to Disciplinary Review Board (DRB), Executive Officer Inquiry (XOI), or Captain's Mast. I had only served one time as a witness at an XOI to testify against someone for the use of the N word. Other than that I had not committed any violation against the UCMJ. If this demonstration was to be my only violation no one told me. Then it might have not been serious enough for someone to say something about it.

26

Their English, My Accent

SOME AMERICANS THINK of English as an exclusive American language, not knowing that there are millions of people around the world who either speak English as a mother tongue or as part of the European colonial heritage. I have come to this conclusion, having lived in America for some years now. I will give you some scenarios to illustrate my point.

"Elton John didn't know how to speak English when he first came to America." How could this be, knowing that Elton John is an English man from England, the origin of the English language? He is a celebrated musical star all over the world. That's why I was so shocked to hear someone making this remark about him learning English only when he came to America. Well, maybe Americans know something I don't know. Once I asked, "Who says Elton John could not speak English when he first came to America? How can you say he can't speak English, when his country produced the English you now speak?" The one I asked didn't have an answer but forced out one: "I mean the American English."

"There are two guys out there speaking some language with foreign accents," a woman told her manager at a gas station. The manager came out and having found out the language they were speaking, he told the young lady, "They are speaking English." "Well," she said, "they must have some weird accent because I can't understand what the hell they talking."

The last illustrated scenario is an adaptation of something I read in the Reader Digest some years ago. It was in the humor section. I am not sure whether it was a joke or true experience, but it is possible that someone might have truly lived it.

I said, "Hi" to a young man and asked, "I am looking for the direction to the trains going up town. Can you help me?" He could not understand what I was saying. I had to repeat myself several times before he referred me to someone who he thought might understand me better. As much as I tried in this particular situation to be understood, he still had problems understanding me. I wondered whether I was the dumb one for not making him understand me or was he the dumb one for not being able to understand me.

"I need your help to shut down the hatch," I said to a shipmate on the ship.

The man said, "Speak English to me so I can understand wha' chu saying."

"What in the hell you think I am speaking to you?"

"Wha'ever the hell you speaking sure don't look like English to me," he said.

A good reader can tell whose English, as far as pronunciation is concerned, is correct. Since I wanted to be understood, I made sure my grammar was correct. This rather makes me wonder whose English it is. Even though English is not my first language, I have spoken it from childhood up to present. Over the years as a student, I have improved on it and I trust that I speak English better than some Americans.

Each time I face situations as described above, it makes me wonder why somebody should feel that nobody speaks English except he speaks with "the beautiful American accent." How could somebody be quick to tell another "you have an accent" without understanding that there are people from different parts of this vast world, representing different cultures, that speak English with various accents? It's just unfortunate that when most Americans think of English the first thing that comes to mind is the accent, not whether or not the person's speech is grammatically correct. That is one shortcoming with most Americans.

The experiences of others and mines sent me to the dictionary and encyclopedia so as to find out what these authoritative sources define English to be. Checking first the dictionary, here is what I got: the language of the people of England (mind you, some ignorant Americans may dispute that as indicated by the Elton John story mentioned earlier) USA and many areas now or formerly under the British colonial control." According to this definition, English is an international language.

With this dictionary definition, my next step was the encyclopedia where I got a broader definition of English as it is spoken in the world today. "It's widely spoken in all the six continents of the world and has had much effect on many regions of the world in which it's not the principal language. As a result of this, there is something called Franglais, Russlish, or Japlish. These words have been coined to describe numerous expressions in different places as a result of the infiltration of English into French, Russian, and Japanese. This has much to do with the technological advancement in the world today largely influenced by English speaking scientists. Added to this could be the impact of American pop culture-music, movie, fashion as well as advances in computer technology."

According to Encyclopedia Britannica, "people who speak English are divided into three distinct categories. There are those who inherited it as a native language; there are those who speak it as a second language in a bilingual society and those who use it as a necessity for some practical purposes such as professional, administrative as well as educational." Whichever among the various speakers of the English language, there are many accents and it takes careful listening to understand people beyond the accent. Accents are part of our heritage from all the places we have come from and English has become a common language for many of us despite the many accents. I told a fellow sailor after an intense debate with him, "Next time you see me speaking, don't mind my accent, just listen carefully, you may understand what I am saying." I did as I had seen them doing if they want to make sure you understand them: "You feel me?"

27

Stereotype on Both Sides

DURING MY FIRST return to Monrovia, Liberia, some friends and relatives came to visit me. They had come for what they thought I had brought for them from America. We were sitting in the living room in my brother's house in Jacob's Town, a suburb of Monrovia. Some of them had come just to listen to the stories of America. It was a long hot day. When it became extremely hot inside, I suggested that we sit on the porch outside. We talked as we drank hatai, a Chinese herbal tea that is consumed by many people. Pretty much I was the talker and everyone was listening to me. Then there were questions here and there with many people expressing their wishes of travelling to the US or Europe. At the end of the day when I was alone, I started to analyze their thinking of America. The America that exists in their minds has streets paved with gold. Money grows on the trees and falls on the ground. All you have to do is take the broom and sweep; you can collect bags of money and store it in your house. When some relatives call you from Africa, you only need to open the bag and send some money. You are able to respond to every need of your family no matter how much the size. There is an abundance of everything in America; there is no homelessness in this paradise on earth.

In my conversation and interactions with Americans in the many years I have lived in America, the African view of America is the opposite of the American view of Africa. In Africa poverty is everywhere. People live and walk naked in the jungle. Africans have never known civilization. Airplanes don't fly there, and there is no car. The whole of Africa is one little village infested with hunger, disease and poverty. The image of the map of Africa does not register in their minds. So to them, Africa may be the second largest continent on paper but it's a little village in their mind. They believe that African people compete with animals for food and sleeping places in the deep jungle.

The above descriptions are nothing but stereotypes. But each stereotype exists in the minds of some people as reality both in Africa, Europe, America, etc. No matter how hard one tries to inform otherwise the stereotype is so solidly grounded in people's minds. This stereotype is reinforced on the daily basis by the media. If you live in Africa, you never see anything ugly about America or Europe. You only see their sparkling beauty. And if you live in the West, you never see anything beautiful about Africa. All you see is the ugly pictures of people as war victims, starving children, etc. If you are a westerner walking on the streets anywhere in Africa, you are admired and if you are African walking on the streets anywhere in London, New York City or Paris, you are loathed or sympathized with for coming over because conditions are so terrible in your country that you have to seek refuge out.

Even those people from other developing countries, who have not yet fully acquired the affluent status of the West, look down on Africa and Africans. Many Africans don't take so kindly to the portrayal of their homeland. They know there are so many issues in Africa, but most Africans would love to balance that with the fact that along with the ugliness there are beautiful things about life in Africa. There are millions of Africans who are doing so well in Africa that they don't think about leaving to come live in the West. Many times Africans are just furious that Americans or Europeans would ask them some questions that are downright stupid. Some of us have been asked all kinds of questions, enough to make one explode in anger. At times one has to try very hard to remain calm in the face of some very demeaning questions.

I remember years ago in New York City, I came across a black girl originally from Jamaica at the New York Public Library in Mid-Town Manhattan. Talking from one thing to another she asked me about lions, elephants, zebras etc. When I told her I haven't seen any of these animals except in pictures, she could not believe me. The truth is, until several years after that encounter, I had not seen any of those animals physically. I met her in 1996 and the first time I ever saw any live animal such as elephants or lions was at the zoo in Philadelphia, Pennsylvania. It was not the curiosity that took me to the zoo to see the animals. It was a class project of the school I was attending that mandated that I go there to take some pictures of the animals.

Besides the young lady, I have met countless other Americans, black and white, who have asked me similar questions. Not only young Americans are ill-informed about Africa; there are a lot of older ones as well. One time on my ship, the USS Detroit, a Navy officer, having learnt I was from Africa, asked me the same questions. Skin color is the only difference between this Navy officer and the girl described above. Sometimes, I wonder what a person can do to educate these uninformed Americans about the Africa I know and experienced before I came to America. Maybe take them to show that the Africa they have come to know about on the TV is different from the Africa that truly exists. In the real Africa they will see villages and towns that are not up to modern standard, but they will also see cities whose beauty can only be compared to some cities in America or Europe.

I have always felt that these minds need to be adequately in-formed. So one day, I decided to embark on such a mission for the benefit of some of my shipmates. During my last underway on the ship, I took some Nigerian movies. I made sure to carry those that portray the lives of the rich and powerful in the beautiful cities of Nigeria. I wanted these friends to see the parts of Africa they didn't see on TV. I wanted them to know that even in the towns and villages there are people living lives comparable to people in some towns and villages in America. I wanted them to know that Africa is not just one small village where all the Africans lived; that we are a continent of more than fifty countries with more than fifty presidents and we are so diverse in cultural and national orientations and outlooks. Since these shipmates wouldn't trust me when I told them all these things, I decided to bring those Nigerian movies for them to see. I believed that when they saw these movies, it would help to reeducate them about Africa.

Sometimes it's hard to change people's prevailing thinking about certain things. I was disappointed that my shipmates were not interested in the Nigerian movies. I put the videotape in the VCR. I expected them to express some surprise and maybe some admiration about these Nigerian actors playing the roles of rich men and women living in beautiful homes and driving expensive cars, far more than any of these shipmates could afford. My shipmates were not impressed. Since the pictures they saw did not conform to the distorted pictures in their minds, they did not pay any attention. Weeks after the screening of the movies, one of these very shipmates still asked me some dumb questions. I told him to believe whatever he wanted to believe. I told him that maybe one day he should travel to Africa and see things for himself.

The stereotypical African view of America and Europe, if we must call it that way, is a positive one but very self-demeaning to the Africans. Good life can only be lived in America, and there is money everywhere just for the picking. One does not have to do a back-breaking job to fulfill one's dream of living a better life in America. If one is to be very successful and rich, well respected and admired by not only relatives but friends as well, he or she must take the chance of going across the Atlantic Ocean. Those Africans that are "fortunate" to make the journey after many failed attempts spend several years doing jobs they would never agree to do at home. They return home with so much material things. The way they go about demonstrating their worth to everyone makes others want to visit abroad by all means.

In one of my frequent trips to Liberia, I passed through Nzérékoré where I spent three days enroute to Monrovia. My brothers and I went to speak to some people he knew. When we got there, I saw a woman who was a little girl in Liberia the last time I saw her. She had no idea who I was until I told her. The next day she went to where I was lodging and told me, "I have just come to tell you thank you for making me so proud yesterday."

I was very surprised to hear her talking like that. She went on to say, "Most people that come from America would pass people they know but they would not stop to speak to them. They walk around with so much vanity as if to say they control the world. And everybody would be bowing to them like they are the kings or queens. All because they have come from the White man country." I looked at her with great interest as she spoke. Then she continued, "The way you went to introduce yourself to me has given me the impression you are a good person. When you left, some of my neighbors could not believe you have come from America because they have not seen anyone from America that does not put on big show of vanity." When she was leaving, I gave her $10.00 for which she was very happy.

Bad governance, corruption, coups and wars that are so prevalent in Africa have reduced Africans to total helplessness and hopelessness. One group removes another group from power on the pretext that the previous group was corrupt and latter ends up being more corrupt than the previous one. The moment one group gets to power, the concern is no longer the people but how it can prolong its stay in power. Resources for the country's vital interest are diverted to serving the leaders' security concerns. Africans have seen this too many times and each time things get worse, it reinforces the belief that there is no hope in sight. The only option most people pursue in seeking for greener pasture then lies in Europe and America.

Nowadays, we hear all the horrifying stories of Africans risking everything for the journey to the other side of the Atlantic Ocean. Those risking everything, including their very lives, are the dreamers who have high hopes for Africa but do not see Africa providing that nurturing environment for the realization of their dreams. If the best determined minds of Africa, those that should be taking all the risk to make all the difference for Africa, continue to believe that only outside of Africa they can make the difference, then the future of Africa is bleak. This should be a serious concern to African leaders

Traveling to America or Europe is no small investment. It's a big investment of time and money. Either your parents are well off financially or you are very determined and hardworking to raise the money required. The misfortune of wars has been a blessing for many others whose relatives have filed for them through refugee resettlement. In any case, the Africans that make the journey to America understand that their picture of Africa does not resemble the pictures that are so frequently featured on the American or European TVs. Having landed in America or Europe, most Africans find themselves in total shock because what they have been led to believe about life across the Ocean does not correspond with the reality of what they meet there. The fortunes they spent here and there to the middlemen between them and the various embassies only to end up in some poor neighborhoods could have been used to start some investment back wherever they come from in Africa. In reality, if a man can afford to spend up to $10,000.00 to make a dream come through in foreign lands, that man is far better off than some Americans or Europeans who are homeless and living on the streets. That is contrary to the European or American perception that all Africans are poverty-stricken people.

The most disappointing thing is that most Africans who leave the motherland with the hope of acquiring all the material riches in the West end up living lives that don't commensurate with the high status life they lived in Africa. Take for instance a man or a woman who was gainfully employed in Africa, living a middle class life, leaving all that behind him, to seek for greener pastures somewhere else. He finds a job, getting paid more than he was paid in Africa. But the difference is that his job here may be taking care of some old folks, or car washing; jobs that he would not dream of doing in Africa. While he would feel insulted in Africa for someone to even suggest that he does car washing or take care of someone else's old mother or father, he is forced in the new country to do such a job. Even though he makes more money now than he made in Africa, he has to spend more money on living expenses than he would have done in Africa. To better illustrate this point, let me give you a clear picture of what I am talking about.

An average take-home pay in Africa may be $200.00 a month. A monthly rent is $50.00 or less. Compare that to the same man making $300.00 a week in America. His rent in America is $800.00 a month. Take that from his monthly wage of $1,200.00 and he's left with $400.00. After paying for his food and other living expenses, the next thing he has to worry about is satisfying the appetite of his relatives in Africa who are not aware of the reality their son or brother has to deal with here in America. All of this becomes pressure he has to deal with. Sometimes the only way to make it is by sharing an apartment with two or three more persons or doing two or three jobs. Since his relatives and friends back in Africa still believe that he must be doing so well, he will do anything to feed that notion by sending them money, even if it means denying himself some enjoyment of life in the United States or Europe. Sometimes he accumulates debt and bad credit in order to satisfy folks' expectations back home. When he's visiting the relatives years afterwards, he goes there to show that he has come from abroad but wouldn't tell the people how hard he has to work and how he has to deny himself so much to make this trip possible. He won't tell them that in America or Europe it's not easy for him to spend $500.00 on himself but would send twice that amount in a heartbeat to relatives and friends simply because they ask for it.

Before the political upheavals and wars that ravaged most parts of Africa, thereby increasing poverty and hopelessness, killing the dreams of success for many Africans on the continent, most of them only went to Europe and America to acquire education and then returned to serve their countries in various professional capacities. Nowadays, besides the desire to go to school abroad, most Africans have come to America and Europe as refugees from the never ending political upheavals and wars. Some come to seek fortune, something they have found very difficult, if not totally illusive, to achieve. So until we have good governments that will create the environment for people to pursue their dream of success in Africa, these waves of Africans wanting to seek greener pastures abroad will continue to increase. So with all the talk of relieving Africa's debts by the West, the other things that need to be done is to advocate for democracy, good governance, and eradication of corruption. That will require leadership that is guided morally.

28 | Being Black and Color Conscious

AS THE NEW millennium arrived, it was not color but ethnicity and religion that mattered most where I come from, even though, it used to be a big issue more than a hundred years ago when there was that social conflict between light and dark skin Americo-Liberians. The term Americo-Liberian refers to African Americans who went back to Africa and founded the nation that came to be known as Liberia. In these later days, people envy, hate, or even kill each other not because of skin color but because of ethnicity or religion. All because one or the other of these two make some people feel superior while thinking of the others as inferior. It could be the Moslems feeling superior to the Christians, and vice versa; or it could be the ethnic Gio feeling superior to an ethnic Krahn and vice versa. This kind of social problem, call it prejudice, or whatever, is what I have experienced and have seen others experience back in Liberia.

That color matters so much to people was a discovery for me only when I came to America. Whether it is color, religion or ethnicity, the key factor that relates to all is prejudice. Having read about it, heard about it or even experienced it, I cannot stop wondering how the complex of prejudice is present everywhere based on different factors.

Living in America and in an integrated environment (US Navy ship), experiencing life with both black and white Americans, on a daily bases, has made me come to one conclusion: African

Americans, among themselves, are as much color-conscious as their fellow white citizens. Some of them are more color-conscious than they care to admit. They will not hesitate to throw it in each other's face, like "how dark you are and how light I am." I have witnessed more black persons making references to skin color than the number of white making such references. Maybe white people like to talk this among themselves when there is no black person among them or they may be trying to avoid it for fear of being put on report. However, to put it more simply, more black persons have told me in my face how dark I am and how light they are. Some of them feel proud of their light skin to the extent of making others feel ashamed of being dark or too dark. Given this fact, I became a little color-conscious or color-sensitive than I used to be when I first joined the Navy. To make you understand what I mean, let me illustrate specific instances in different places and times.

Case # 1: My first encounter of color prejudice among black people was in boot camp during my recruit training in Great Lakes, Illinois. There was this young black man from Alabama who used to make fun of me for being "so dark" as if to say I should cuss God for making me so. He always used to say "my chocolate color and your dark color." He used to bother me so much about this color thing until one day a sympathetic white recruit told me to retaliate by calling him a "ghetto nigga or ghetto bastard." I couldn't feel right calling him any of those. However, I made my own label for him just to neutralize his constant bothering. One day I told him, "You are so ugly like a chimpanzee." From then on, I called him, "Alabama chimpanzee."

Case # 2: There was this light brown fellow from New Jersey. We met at the Navy Weapon Station, Earle, New Jersey. During our three-month mess cranking in the ship's galley, I mentioned to him one time how this black sister from South Carolina was so beautiful and asked if he was interested in her. He told me, "Man she's too dark for me."

Case #3: Back in Great Lakes, Illinois, we were on the line to cash our checks at a local bank. This light skin guy from Florida asked me, "Will I be accepted in your country if I were to go there?" Instead of responding with either yes or no, I asked him, "What makes you think you won't be accepted in my country?" He answered, "Because of this," (he touched his hand, emphasizing his skin color.) I told him that since there were some white people from many countries living in my country, "a black man like you will be welcomed to live in my country even if you are lighter than this."

Case # 4: A very dark fellow from Florida. His wife, he said, was light skinned. One day we were having some casual conversation when he asked me, "Have you got any white heritage down the line?" I told him no and why? He went on to say, "Down the line I have some white heritage because there are many light skin members in my family." I could see how proud he was because of that. I wanted to ask him why he was so dark but I didn't want to embarrass him.

Case # 5: Both of them were young black men, one from Georgia and the other from California. The brother from California was very dark and the one from Georgia was very light. The one from Georgia asked the one from California, "How come you are so dark and you are from California?" The brother from California did not respond with any feeling of pride for what God made him. Even though he was a jovial and talkative kind of person, the question at that very moment made him feel very uncomfortable and he became silent the whole while like he was guilty of something.

Case # 6: He was a chocolate colored brother in his early thirties from Kansas. One time he said to me, "Why Africans are too black like the darkest night?" I responded by saying, "Oh yeah, you look like a white man. Maybe your great grandfather was a white man." Even though this guy would not be considered light skin, he was indeed proud of the "compliment." He smiled and gave me a high five, "For real, I am light like white?"

Case # 7: He was approaching 21. He was from Louisiana. He was too comical and loved to crack jokes to make everyone laugh. One time he said to me, "Ain't no body from Africa lighter than you? Are you all black and ugly?" This young man was not light. He was dark skinned like me but somehow he liked to think of himself as lighter than me. Sometimes, I wondered what went through his mind every day. Did he feel so ugly that he wished he were white? I had this question on my mind every time I saw this brother.

Case # 8: Another brown skin fellow from Louisiana. One day he was having a ball with me and two other African Americans. He was saying things like, "You, him and Konneh look like y'all brothers or something. All you mu'fuckup too dark and ugly." I was not with them but I could hear his loud voice from the lounge of our compartment. The young men he was comparing me with couldn't say anything to counter what this loud mouth fool was saying. None of them could challenge him. Maybe they were thinking he was just joking? I could not take it anymore. For me this was more than a joke. I said to him, "Shut the fuck up you white boy. Did anybody tell you something is wrong with being black, even being too dark? What's your point in making all this noise Mr. White Man?" In our multi-racial audience, which was paying close attention to what he was saying and what I was saying, he went silent for a minute, only to tell me, "Bitch, you suck my dick."

Case # 9: He was a cool headed brother from Philadelphia. I had always had some positive conversation with him, mostly on Islam. Most often, when I use profane language like many sailors used to do, he always reminded me, "Aren't you a Moslem? You should not be cussing like everyone else." This brother was not a Moslem, but he said he had a lot of respect for the Moslems and their beliefs. One time he asked me about Minister Louis Farrakhan. I told him that Farrakhan focuses so much on race while traditional Islam speaks about mankind in general and its relationship to God. He said, "That is because race is a very important factor in this country even among people of the same kind. Actually, it should not matter, but unfortunately it matters very much." He went on to say, "Some of us are light, some of us are dark and lot of times we throw it in each other's faces."

Case # 10: From Norfolk, Virginia, there was this dark skin dude saying some of the same things to me as mentioned above. I asked him, "Tell me for real, do you hate being black?" Consciously or subconsciously he said yes. One month later the same brother said to me, "You know why, I hate you." I asked him why he hated me, "Because you are black," was his response. I said to him, "I never knew you were a white racist. Now I know you to be a white man in black skin who hates me simply because I am black."

These brothers might have been joking or serious but when I think about them, it always gives me the feeling that if African Americans were to constitute a nation with their own government, there would be a stiff competition between the light and dark skin for the power, riches and privileges of that nation. This was exemplified in Liberia when the Americo-Liberians went there and declared "independent Liberia." For a while only light skin Negros could become president. The first dark skin person to become president was Edward J. Roye. He was of Caribbean descent but was overthrown later by the light skin elites. That was the first coup in Liberia's political history, the second being the overthrow of the Americo-Liberian dominated regime in 1980 by the natives. In today's Liberia, the argument has shifted from skin color to ethnicity and religion. I grew up in a Liberia that no longer subscribed to color superiority or inferiority. Color was the thing with the settlers and that was something they brought with them from America. It's only amazing today that skin color is still very much a big part in the minds of black people in America. Maybe that is because race will forever be a matter in this country.

29

On Liberty in Haifa

WE WERE ANCHORED off Haifa, a port city in Israel. We were there for over a week. What made it so great was that it was a liberty port. Except for the duty section personnel, we were going off to the city of Haifa, walking around, sightseeing and shopping. Being strangers and extra careful because of the current Jewish-Palestinian crisis regarding the Jewish settlement in Arab Jerusalem, we had to be sure of where to go and where not to go. As such, we were mostly hanging around the United Service Organization (USO). We went to the mall nearby, walked around the zoo and passed by the McDonald's restaurant a few blocks away.

We went on tour in Bethlehem, Jesus' birthplace, Jerusalem, the Dead Sea as well as Masada. Both Bethlehem and Jerusalem were quite an experience. An experience I will always treasure.

My liberty buddies were PC3 Norman an African-American, SK3 Owusu Ansah from Ghana and EMFN Peal from Liberia. We were on our way from the ATM machine to McDonalds. When we stopped for the red light, a taxi driver stopped by, calling our attention through his window, "Come here." Without any precaution, we step close to him. He went on to say, "Girls, girls, you want me take you there." We all laughed but he did not. He looked like he was serious. We declined his offer and he sped on to the direction he was going. As he sped away, my mind ran to a similar experience in Palma, Spain. In Palma, I was with a shipmate, a white boy, who stopped a taxi and said to the driver, "Top Models."

"What the hell is Top Models," I said.

He said, "Just come with me, you will see what it is and I am sure you will like it." We rode on to Top Models and to my surprise it was a whorehouse. On the topside of the storied building were beautiful Spanish girls parading in front of us. The price to go with anyone of them was $60.00. While I declined because of the exorbitant price, my companion paid $60.00 and went in the room with one of them. For obvious reasons, I felt that $60.00 was too much to pay for a short period with any woman no matter how beautiful she was. Being with a prostitute is not the same as being with someone you know, because with prostitutes it's like come-do-me-quick-n-go so I can get ready for my next customer. With her mind set to get as many customers in one night, she will want to get rid of you as quickly as possible. So the thought of me being one of those hurried customers for $60.00 was not appealing to me. Just as I had thought, my friend went in and came out in less than 20 minutes.

At a McDonald's restaurant in Haifa, we ordered our food. We were sitting down eating when this fourteen-year-old Jewish boy walked in. He sat next to me. I could see that both of us were curious about each other and I made the first move. "Hi, I am Nvasekie, nice to meet you." Without any further explanation he tells me he knew we were American military men. I told him I was originally from Africa, living in New York City. He told me it must be a great experience to serve in the American military because America is such a powerful country. He said he was pushing to fifteen and at that age he would serve in the Israeli military for a certain period of time because every Israeli is obligated to serve sometime in the military. Like that, he said, everyone is prepared to defend Israel at any time against its "enemies."

Knowing that there are some Arabs who are citizens of Israel, I asked him whether they too were included in this compulsory military service. He answered in the negative, "They are bad people; don't have no good intention towards us." He went on to say, "The Arabs are citizens but you can't trust them with weapons."

As I listened to the young man talking, I wondered if this was what all Jewish people thought of the Arabs. I wondered how long it would take for genuine brotherhood, love and trust to develop between these descendants of Abraham, the friend of Allah. Will it take a hundred or a thousand more years or never? In my mind, I was thinking if every Jewish person is taught from a young age to distrust or hate the Arabs. These young people learning all of these ideas from their parents will grow up to be leaders in the military, politics, academia and no wonder there is this intractable conflict going on forever. How much of such teachings did Netanyahu and other hard-line occupiers of the Palestinian lands receive when they were kids? Of course there have been many complaints by the Jewish people that the Palestinian leaders, including Yasser Arafat, preach Jewish hatred to their people. Contrary to that Jewish accusation, I met an Arab Christian in a gift shop on the way to Bethlehem. He told me, "Arabs and Jews are cousins; we are all descendants of Abraham." His friend or coworker in that gift shop is an Arab Moslem and he expressed the same sentiment. I also talked to a female Palestinian police officer at the Church of the Nativity. She told me the same thing. The Arab and Jewish issues are the most complex issues in the world and fuel most of the violent conflicts in the whole of the Middle East and beyond.

I feel that both of them have wasted precious time and energy arguing, distrusting, violating and destroying each other. If both of them believe in "loving your neighbor as yourself," they can live happily in loving brotherhood and perpetual peace. I can only hope that they will overcome the distrust and hatred of each other someday. Maybe they don't have a Mahatma Gandhi or Martin Luther King. That could have been Yitzhak Rabin but he was killed by a militant Jew, who is opposed to peace with the Arabs. I love both the Jews and Arabs. I love them because they are all human beings just like me. We as human beings must extend the same degree of love to all other people from anywhere in the world. If God is one, and He is, then humanity is one. We all should be one big family.

My time in Israel inspired this poem: **Bethlehem/Jerusalem**

Here I come O Bethlehem
With the clear sky above the manger square I stand

Witnessing to the glorious past and the bleak
present.
Feel like a mystery journey in the mystery land
A mystery so complex, so beautiful, and pleasant.
I am walking on the footprints of Jesus, the son
of Mary.
Oh, I hear the Muezzin cry for prayer with the chant
Of Allahu Akbar, a clear manifestation of Allah's
power and glory.
I see the faithful gathering in the Masjid Omar
And some flocking to the Church of Nativity,
Makes me feel the unity and oneness of God.

Here I come O Jerusalem
The City of Gold and enduring Spirituality
My soul has journeyed all these years
Entrenched in the holiness of the Noble Sanctuary.
Truth is one as it was in the time of Prophet Jesus
And as Prophet Mohammad ascended to the 7th sky.
Makes me wonder why all these endless wars
Among Abraham's children.

Here I come O Lord, in search of truth and redemption
Of which my soul is thirsty and hungry.
In the fullness of the given revelation
I submit unconditionally to your power and glory.
Makes me share with all people your spiritual love
That's a common foundation for all your children
Who are lost in helplessness between the Dome
of the Rock
And the Church of the Holy Sepulcher and the
Wailing Wall.

30

Operation Desert Fox, Manama, Bahrain

ON DECEMBER 19, 1998, I was sitting with some friends in the Desert Dome in Manama, Bahrain. I was eating a cheeseburger and some fries. We were watching CNN's news accounts of the ongoing Operation Desert Fox. We had just returned there from the sea and because of this military operation against the Baghdad regime, our liberty was limited to the base. The last time we were here, we went sightseeing and shopping in Manama, the capital city of Bahrain. It's a beautiful desert city. We went to the gold souk where there was high quality gold for reasonable prices.

On the big screen TV, the British Prime Minister Tony Blair was defending Operation Desert Fox while Iraq's Tariq Aziz was criticizing what he calls an "American-British aggression" against his country. He said despite this attack, "Saddam Hussein and the Iraqi people will survive."

It had been seven years since Desert Storm in 1991. Where I was then and where I was now were not only geographically different; they were also different ideologically. The way I saw things then and the way I saw things now were different. Then I was an outsider watching from the distance. Now I was an eyewitness to what was happening. Stationed on board the USS Detroit, a part of the USS Enterprise battle group that was executing this operation, I did play my little part in the operation while bombs were dropped on targets inside Iraq. Don't ask me whether what we were doing was right or wrong. That is a question for politicians in Washington DC. It's not the military that starts the war; it's the politicians who send the order and we in the military must carry it out.

When Saddam invaded and annexed Kuwait in August 1990 and during its subsequent liberation in 1991 by the Allied Forces led by America, I was a war refugee in Abidjan, Ivory Coast. I had fled the political-ethnic-religious war in Liberia. Every morning and evening I was listening to the radio, reading newspapers and magazines and watching both the Liberian and the Kuwait events on TV. I was amazed by the Allied Forces' easy victory against the Iraqi forces. Most Liberians were asking why America, given its historic relation with Liberia, could not make similar efforts to end our war. Most Liberians hoped for this and were disappointed when America told us it was our internal affairs and only we ourselves could take care of our situation.

Although I did not support Saddam's invasion of Kuwait, I saw double standards in the way America and her allies reacted. They did not take similar actions when the same Saddam Hussein invaded Iran and dragged that country into a seven-year unjustifiable war. Instead of standing up to Saddam then for his unjustifiable aggression, the very Kuwait and other Arab countries provided material support for him. America and her western allies supported him even though they knew he was the aggressor. My feeling was that America and her allies were victims of their own hypocrisy. If they had faced up to Saddam then, he wouldn't have attempted invading another country. He would have thought twice before doing so. Since the Iran-Iraq war, I have never liked Saddam and I was praying that he would be punished someday for his unwarranted aggression against the people of Iran.

Maybe because of the victory of the Islamic revolution in Iran, the conservative Arab regimes were scared that similar revolutions could possibly take place in their own countries. They saw that as a threat and justification for supporting Saddam to wage an illegal war. Maybe America's reason for supporting Saddam against Iran was because the Iranian revolution swept the pro-American regime from power and then the hostage crisis followed. In my opinion, none of that was enough justification for supporting a ruthless dictator to invade another country. Neither America nor her allies had the moral authority to oppose Saddam when he invaded Kuwait. The fact is that God never sleeps. He made sure that Saddam would be punished one way or the other and God used his own allies to inflict punishment on him. Now, God was using America and her hypocritical allies to kick Saddam's ass. Like the saying goes, payback is a sweet thing. So Saddam was getting a pay-back for his own raw deals against other people. I won't shed any tears for him.

Now with the Operation Desert Fox, I could only wish that this ruthless dictator was removed from the back of the Iraqi people. They had suffered long enough under his cruel leadership. Such a merciless tyrant with weapons of mass destruction he was a greater menace to the world as we approached the 21st Century. Even though this was being done on the eve of the Ramadan, I didn't want to buy the claim by some fellow Moslems that it was an offense to all Moslems that a group of Christian nations were attacking a Moslem country during the Holy Month of Ramadan. Where were those fellow Moslems when Saddam was terrorizing the Iranians as well as the Iraqi people? Had it not been for these so-called Christian nations, where would Kuwait be right now? If Saddam is a Moslem, his attitude and actions towards other people, Moslems or Christians is un-Islamic.

31

I Love Paris

ONE OF THE MOST IMPORTANT highlights of my tour of duty in the US Navy was the port visit to Marseille, France in January 1999. I have had a fascinating love affair with France since I was a little boy. My mother's younger brother went to school there and he used to visit us in Liberia. Because of him, I knew about France long before I came to know about the United States. Those days, traveling to the white man's country seemed so mysterious and not often would you meet someone who had been there. So having an uncle who was going to school there always made me feel special. When it was said that during our deployment in 98-99, our ship USS Detroit would make a port visit to France and then we would tour Paris, I had looked forward to a trip with that kind of romantic feeling. When we finally got there, it was truly like a dream come true. Days before anchoring at Marseille, I dreamt about it, fantasized about it. One particular thought that had been buried in my head for years was a story narrated to me about the country. I was told that Paris was not built but was discovered by some wanderers. They were probably lost and didn't know where they were going when they came upon the city. They didn't have the slightest idea that a city of such beauty existed anywhere in the world. As a result of the expansion of Paris a nation was born. Back in those days, I believed that to be the true story of France. It was said that the scientific advancement white people have made and the under-development of our African society was decided by God. The white people's world was so beautiful and the black people's world the op-posite. One day God invited both the forebears of the whites and the blacks. God showed them two choices: a paradise on earth or hell in the hereafter. White people chose to live their paradise on earth and hell in the hereafter while black people wanted their hell on earth and paradise in the hereafter. Those were my pre-western education days. Having studied over the years and been more informed about the world, I have come to understand things differently.

The ship's company was divided into three groups to tour Paris. I went for the first one. The schedule was drawn weeks in advance before we hit the port. As the ship cruised towards Marseilles, all my attention was on Paris where I would be touring with some of my shipmates. I was longing to see and experience the beauty of this metropolis, indeed the capital of the French speaking world. I was re-membering all that I had heard about it, and then I thought about that childhood story of what made the white man able to build a beautiful city like Paris. Does Paris validate the fact that white men chose para-dise on earth and agreed to go to hell when they died? I have heard Bob Marley singing, "Most people think, great God will come from the sky, take away everything, and make everybody feel high." Bob was alluding to black people in captivity under white slave masters, thinking their paradise of milk and honey were awaiting them when they died. Bob went on to say, "If you know what life is worth, you will look for yours on earth. Now you see the light, stand up for your right." In other words, Bob was saying there is no milk or honey in the sky waiting for anyone and if we don't have anything here on earth, we may not get anything anywhere else. What Bob said is similar to the teaching of Elijah Muhammad. According to his version of Islam which is called Nation of Islam, there is no such thing as the para-dise of milk and honey in the sky or in the next life. According to his theory, both paradise and hell exist right here on earth. The symbol of hell on earth is poverty and suffering and we must strive to change our condition to paradise right here on earth. There is some connec-tion between what Elijah Muhammad and Bob Marley say on this matter and this childhood story of mine.

What I have yet to find is the origin of this "milk and honey in the sky" theory. When I heard this story in the past, I did not ask the person who told me where he heard it from. I could not investigate how widespread that thought was among our people, black people of Africa and the Diaspora. Now having listened to Bob Marley's music and read Elijah Muhammad's philosophy, I am inclined to ask: Imagine, Bob Marley is from the Caribbean, Elijah Muhammad is a black American and I am from Africa. Have we always thought this way or only when we came in contact with white people during slavery and colonization?

Having experienced both the black and white worlds, I am now convinced that there is no such thing as God apportioning the world between black and white and assigning poverty and suffering to black people. However, I believe there is so much in our world to reinforce the negativity about us and positive aspects of white people. This stereotype is prevalent among the unsophisticated folks who haven't received the opportunity of learning and traveling. We face poverty caused by wars. This is making us so hopeless that some of us feel "blessed" to live in the white man's countries in Europe or America.

I believe that we all are entitled to all the good that life has to offer, but it is a fact that black people have not taken full advantage of the opportunity we have as a people. See how many millions of dollars our corrupt leaders often stack up in the white man's banks in Europe and America. See how we have invested so much in wars as compared to what we have spent on development. It's not that God favors white people over us black people. God gave all of us equal opportunity and maybe we have yet to take advantage of what we have.

Even though it's true that the Trans-Atlantic Slave Trade and European colonization seriously affected Africa and Africans everywhere, it's about time we look within for the weaknesses we have as a people and transform them into great good for us and our children.

I was thinking of all these thoughts as we sped towards Paris in the Bullet Train from Marseilles. I was hungry to see Paris. Of all the places of Paris, I was hungriest to see the Champ Elysee, Eiffel Tower and Pigale. These are places Alpha Blondy mentioned in his song, "I Love Paris." The song gives you a kind of romantic feeling of the City of Lights. When we arrived in Paris, we got in the tour bus that took us from the Gare de Lion to Arc de Triomphe, Champs Elysee, the Louvre Museum etc. We took pictures at the Eiffel Tower and the glass pyramid at the Louvre. The focus of my curiosity about the museum was Mona Lisa, the 16th century painting by Leonardo da Vinci. I had imagined it to be something big but to my surprise, it was a small one. It may be small but the painting is very famous all over the world. According to the information provided, the true identity of Mona Lisa remains a mystery to art historians. Some believe that it is the portrait of Lisa Gherardini, wife of Francesco del Giocondo, a Florentine merchant. Because of this, it is said that Mona Lisa is known in Italy as La Gioconda. Others believe that it is the portrait of da Vinci's mistress or a self-portrait of his imagination of himself as a woman. For more than 300 years, this famous painting has been to many places, including Napoleon's bedroom. Since 1804, it has been at home in the Louvre Museum in Paris.

The tour guide showed us the place where Princess Diana died in that infamous car crash. One of the most beautiful land marks of Paris is the Eiffel Tower and it felt so special being there. We took some pictures there as well. After the tour, one of my cousins, Bangalie Donzo who lived in Paris picked me and my Liberian friend Beecee. I first met cousin Bangalie in Washington DC when I visited another cousin, Kalifala Donzo. Kalifala Donzo is the son of Alhaji Sidiki Donzo, a brother of Alhaji Amara Donzo of Saclepea, Nimba County. With Bangalie, we visited some places in the city where most Africans lived. Then we went to the McDonald's restaurant somewhere on the Champs Elysee.

We were in Paris for three days only, but the three days fulfilled my dream of one day visiting Paris. The fact that I had a personal tour guide to take me places made my stay in the city a wonderful experience.

32

Looking for Fatim Diop in Dakar

ON JULY 4, 1999, I left New York and arrived at the Leopold Senghor International Airport in Dakar, Senegal. Our arrival time in Dakar was around 0730. My final destination was Conakry, Guinea. But in Dakar, there was a delay of more than 12 hours and as a result of that we were lodged at Hotel Sunugu.

The whole day was a mix of good and bad experiences. Good because I had the opportunity of being driven around the city of Dakar where I had gone looking for an old friend Fatim Diop who I had not seen since 1991 in Abidjan. It was bad because Air Afrique failed twice to get me to my destination on schedule. I was so pissed off with this change in schedule. What pissed me off with them more was that they didn't have any manner of respect for their passengers. I was pissed to the point where I had to raise my voice against them. One of their security officers started shouting at me and I told him to go to hell or kiss my black African ass. They wanted me and other passengers to sleep at the airport with no room for accommodation. After we demanded to be treated like customers, they grudgingly put us in Hotel Sunugu. This incident caused me to hate Air Afrique. I had made the conscious decision to fly with them because it was one of our own African airlines. Plus their price was more reasonable compared to other airlines. In any case, while I was there, I decided to use it as an opportunity to look for Fatim Diop in Dakar.

Fatim was a friend I met in Abidjan, Ivory Coast, in the early '90s while I was there as a refugee from the war in Liberia. She was a student attending the University of Abidjan, majoring in English. Since she was studying English at the university and me being an English speaking person, we became good friends. When I was returning to Liberia, she and I exchanged addresses. While in Liberia and later on in the States, I wrote her several letters to which I did not get any reply. But I did not give up the hope of meeting her someday. So when I was told I was going to spend twelve hours in Dakar waiting for my connection flight to Conakry, I thought, why not use that time to do some sightseeing and look for my friend Fatim?

I showed Fatim's mother's address to a gentleman at the hotel who said it was her work place address and since it was Sunday, it would be hard to find her. I asked to look in the telephone directory. I found three Adelaide Diop names and I prayed and hoped that one of them would be Fatim's mother. I dialed the first one, wrong number. I tried the second one and luck was on my side. Someone said to hold on when I asked to speak to Fatim. Then she came on the line. At first, she could not recognize my voice. I told her it was her friend Konneh from her days in Abidjan. She was shocked that I could still remember her. She said she could not come for me at the airport because she had just given birth to a new baby. I said it would be a great pleasure to see her and the new baby. I boarded a taxi that took me to the address. We were both happy to meet again after eight years of not hearing from each other. I spent an hour with her while she offered me some soft drinks. I asked for my cousin, Mohammed Sheriff who had come to Senegal in 1991 to live with Fatim's mother. My cousin Sheriff is a traveler. When he fled Liberia, he joined me in Abidjan where we all met Fatim. When I was returning to Liberia, he said that his hope was to keep traveling until he reached to America or Europe. He said he would never return to Liberia until he was visiting from the United States. He had hoped that since Fatim's mother was working for the UN in Dakar, she might help him one way or the other. Now when I asked Fatim about him, she told me Sherif left a long time ago and since then she had not seen him.

Back in the hotel, I witnessed an elaborate wedding program of a white man and a Senegalese woman. Loud music was blasting from two large speakers. The music of Youssou N'Dour, a Senegalese national musical star, as well as music of some western musicians were playing. There were lots of people. Some were white people who I assumed to be friends and relatives of the white man who was getting married to the African woman.

33

Last Time I heard from Nicole

AFTER ALL THE ALARMING SPECULATION, the new Millennium arrived and nothing happened. The sky did not fall. The world did not come to an end. Computers did not crash. Life was still normal as it had always been since God created man and the universe. The sky remained the same as well as the sun, moon and stars. It sounded so lunatic that a group of people could say that the world was coming to an end based on their belief which was not shared by everyone in the world. The people that were screaming the world-coming-to-an-end message did not consult people of other beliefs. The fact that the world did not come to an end shows that God is no one's private agent. He is for all of us because we are all created in His image. God who made the world is the only one who knows when it will come to an end. He has not revealed that information to anyone.

These were the streams of thoughts jamming through my brain when I was sitting down in a house at the Philadelphia Navy Ship Yard as the New Year arrived. Our ship, USS Detroit was at the dry dock at the ship yard and all the sailors were assigned in houses on the base. There were two persons in each of the two bed rooms, bringing the number of persons in each house to four. I shared my room with Prince Peal, a fellow Liberian. The other room was occupied by Big Will and Zina. We had a TV in the living room. For the New Year, Peal went to New York. I had duty on the ship the day before and so I couldn't go anywhere. As I got off the ship in the morning, I came to the house on base and did not leave to go anywhere for the rest of the day. That was New Year's Eve. I was curious to see how things would turn out based on the alarming information that was floating about the world coming to an end or the computer crash.

I was not sure where Big Will's roommate was. It was the two of us sitting down watching TV. We were actually competing over the TV. He wanted to watch sports and music channels; I wanted to watch the news. We reached an understanding that I would let him watch the TV but at a certain time leading to mid night, it would be my turn. While it was still his turn, he fell asleep and I turned the TV to news stations, CNN, NBC, ABC etc. I was changing from one station to another so as to keep up with different places in the world where people were already celebrating the New Year while we were behind for minutes or hours. One minute I would be watching the count-down to the ball drop in New York's Time Square. Another minute I would be looking at another place. Besides the fireworks in different cities across America and the rest of the world, there was one interesting story that caught my attention. A reporter (I am not sure which station he represented) went to a remote part of Africa and reported that people there were not aware of all the brouhaha surrounding the New Year, the expected computer crash or the world coming to an end. They had no idea of what Y2K, the New Millennium, or the computer crashes were. They were going about their normal activities as if to say nothing special was going on in the world.

I woke up in the morning from the couch on which I was watching the news. Since it was not a working day for me, I didn't have anything to worry about except the latent feeling that things may go wrong as predicted. As it turned out, nothing changed. It was still the same old world. The sky remained the same. The computer did not crash. So the Y2K was nothing but a joke.

Perhaps the biggest surprise for me in the new Millennium was the news about the military takeover in the Ivory Coast and that the strong man who led the coup was called Gen. Robert Guei. That name sounded familiar. It instantly reminded me of Nicole Guei, my platonic friend in Abidjan in the early 90s. When we met for the first time, she told me her father was a big man in the Ivorian army and his name was Robert Guei. She once took me to her home in Deaux Plateau, a section of Abidjan, which she told me was one of his houses. Matter of fact it was the first time we met. Many times she talked about him but I did not get to meet him.

When I returned to Liberia, I kept in contact with Nicole as I promised. We exchanged letters. Then one day I received a letter from Nicole that came from an address in London, England. She called on several occasions after that to speak to me. Unfortunately, I was never around when she called. I was already in the US when she sent her last letter to Liberia. A friend of mine received that letter on my behalf. He too traveled to Germany and for a while we lost contact. When we finally hooked up, he could only give me an address and a phone number in London. I repeatedly called that number until someone told me that Nicole had moved but didn't leave any contact information. Since then I have been in limbo about my good friend, Nicole Guei.

I might be wrong, but I was telling people that the man who had just taken over power in Ivory Coast was Nicole's father. Unless there was another Robert Guei senior military officer in the Ivorian military, it had to be him. I thought if my assumption was right, then Nicole would be a member of the First Family in the Ivory Coast. If I happen to pass through Ivory Coast in the future, I will make sure to check if Nicole is still in London or if she is back in the Ivory Coast. I know at some point she was having some immigration issue in London. Now that her father was the president, I assumed she would go back home and enjoy life as one of the First Daughters. I ain't mad at her. I would do the same. What a wonderful feeling it is to wake up one day and realize that your father is the president and you are the First Daughter? There was no campaign going on and all of a sudden you hear that your father is the president. What a powerful feeling? I am sure wherever Nicole was she had to be feeling very good. Hopefully one of these days, I thought, I will meet her again.

34 | Becoming an American Citizen

IN THE YEAR 2000, several good things happened for me. I was promoted to the rank of Petty Officer 2nd Class; I completed my naturalization process to become an American citizen; my wife, Makemeh Donzo arrived in the US from Liberia, and I got transferred from the ship USS Detroit to shore duty assignment at the Naval Inventory Control Point (NAVICP) in Philadelphia, Pennsylvania. I felt blessed for all of these developments particularly the American citizenship. Up to that point I had been in the US Navy for almost four years and I felt like if I have taken the oath to defend and protect a country, and if possible I could die in that process, why not be a citizen of that country? I had other issues too such as being able to bring family members such as my wife, or my mother and the possibility of doing certain jobs in the navy which required American citizenship. If I wanted to be a navy journalist, US citizenship was the requirement. So for all these reasons, I embraced the idea of becoming an American citizen.

When it was time for me to go for my swearing in ceremony somewhere in Queens, New York, I put in a request chit on the ship which was given a speedy approval by my chain of command in appreciation for the fact that I was becoming an American citizen. It was a moment of celebration not only for me but also for members of my division. They all congratulated me when I was leaving the ship to travel to New York for the ceremony. Having spent the night at the apartment in the Bronx which I shared with my brother, Bangalie

Konneh, my wife Makemeh and I took the train to go to the ceremony. I was among more than 500 people from different parts of the world who were being welcomed into American citizenship with all the rights accorded any other American with the exception of becoming an American President. When I looked in the faces of all these people, I could see happiness and hope of becoming something they had spent years preparing for. Their reasons may be different or similar to mine. All and all, we were all happy to be inducted into American citizenship.

Becoming an American citizen is not a simple procedure; living in the country legally for 5 years makes you eligible to apply for citizenship. That's why millions of people from everywhere in the world have become Americans and this can only make America stronger. Compared to many parts of the world, becoming an American citizen is as easy as 1, 2, 3. This is one of the most important things about America, a path way to citizenship for people from diverse cultural backgrounds.

On December 25th, 2004, I was giving a speech as a keynote speaker at the inauguration of the Liberian Mandingo Association of Georgia. My topic was "Where Are We after the War?" During the course of the speech, I digressed from my prepared notes and urged Liberians to "copy America's example of tolerance and acceptance." I told my audience that there was a campaign by some Americans to amend the United States Constitution to allow a foreign born politician, Arnold Schwarzenegger, to run for the presidency in the 2008 election. I said that Schwarzenegger, who was not born in America, became a governor of the state of California, and now there was a campaign for him to run for the presidency of the United States. This shows that America is a progressive society that looks to a person's character and ability to contribute to society's progress and advancement more than his national origin. I said that this was the America that Martin Luther King dreamt of. Then I said why should some Liberians question the citizenship of people who were born in Liberia, whose mothers and fathers were born in Liberia and try to deny them their rights as citizens of the land? That was in reference to the fact that as Mandingo, I am constantly reminded by my fellow

Liberians that I am a foreigner, even though my father and mother were born there before I was even born. In America, it took a mere procedure for me to be a citizen and I am entitled to all the rights of American citizens, but in my native country, my birth record is not even enough for me to be considered a full fledge citizen. I have to constantly fight to prove my citizenship. When I made this remark, I had no idea that four years later, a black man would be elected president of the United States.

In 2006, Liberians who have acquired American citizenship or other nationalities were asking the same question. Even though I agreed with them, the context of my remark on December 25th 2004 was different from the controversial dual citizenship debate that is still going in that country. When I spoke at that occasion, I was not thinking of dual citizenship of native born Liberians with their naturalized American nationality. I was referring to the Liberian Mandingoes, because for some reason, the view that Mandingoes are "foreigners" is still prevalent in the Liberian society.

While becoming a citizen in America is as easy as 1, 2, 3, it is not so in Liberia and elsewhere in Africa. After 27 years in power, Dr. Kenneth David Kaunda, had his Zambian citizenship questioned by Frederick Cheluba, the man who succeeded him as president. Jerry Rawlings, who was the president of Ghana, had his Ghanaian citizenship questioned by some of his opponents. Then in Ivory Coast, there were millions of people, including the then opposition leader and now president of the country, Alhassan Ouattara, whose Ivorian citizenships were questioned. Interestingly indeed, Ouattara was a former prime minister of the Ivory Coast. In this postwar emerging democratic era in Liberia, the issue of citizenship has taken the front page. Especially since Lusene Donzo admitted during a confirmation hearing before the Liberian Senate that he was a naturalized American citizen.

On some occasions, I have really lost my cool when I am confronted by Liberians who regard me as a foreigner only on the basis of my ethnicity. When I was being interviewed on the radio and TV in Monrovia in 2005, I read a poem from my book of poetry which was written in response to such confrontations. I wrote that poem with all the feelings of righteous anger. The interviewer asked me if I was one of those traumatized by the war. He asked the question because of the angry tone the poem carries. I told him I was not traumatized, but sometimes I found justifiable reasons to express my anger and this always happens when some foolish fellow Liberian calls me or anyone like me a foreigner. I told him it was ignorance and I couldn't stand it anymore. I revealed that every time I hear someone calling me a "foreigner" it is equivalent to a white man calling a black man a "nigger" in America. I said I hate to be called a foreigner in the country of my birth.

In a country where people are so obsessed with the question of citizen/foreigner, it sometimes appears as if everybody came straight from the sky and fell within the borders of Liberia. It appears as if only the Mandingoes come from a place called Guinea. In the country that is so obsessed with the question of citizenship, only two groups of people can openly say where they came from. These are the Americo-Liberians and the Congos. At least we know they either came from America or they were recaptured slaves. Other than these two groups, no one wants to talk about their distant relatives across the borders in Ivory Coast, Guinea or Sierra Leone. Before the lines were drawn by the European colonizers, it is only natural that the Manos in Guinea and Liberia are family. Same can be said of the Gios and Krahns in Liberia and Ivory Coast. This makes me think of Ivory Coast in the early 90s when the war was going on in Liberia. When the news spread that Prince Johnson had captured and killed President Doe, many people might have been happy, thinking that was to be the end of the war. If you were among those who were happy that Doe was dead, you could not show your feeling in the Yopougon Sicogi neighborhood where I lived. A few doors down from my aunt's house were some members of the Ivorian side of President Doe's family. There was loud crying in their house. They were crying because their relative, who happened to be the president of Liberia, had been killed.

I first knew of this family during my first visit to Abidjan in 1985. A young man from the house, having realized I spoke English and was from Liberia, befriended me. He was a high school student wanting to perfect his English in anticipation of a travel to Liberia after his secondary school study. His main goal was to travel to the United States of America and in the process he would obtain a Liberian passport and US visa; all through the influence of cousin Doe, who happened to be the president of Liberia. He told me he was following in the footsteps of his sister who came to the US in the same way.

It is said that the father of the late Commanding General of the Armed Forces of Liberia, Thomas Quiwonkpa was an Ivorian Gio? There is a saying that during the funeral service of his old man, during which time General Quiwokpa was still a big man in the Liberian government, someone was eulogizing his father. The moment the eulogizer began to talk about how the general's father came from the Ivory Coast, he was shut down. They didn't want him to talk about the general's family connection in Ivory Coast because they didn't want anyone questioning the Liberian citizenship of the top general of the Liberian army.

In countries like America, the idea of a person having family members who are citizens of other countries is normal. In Liberia, we don't talk of family members across the borders because to do so is to be called "foreigner." So for fear of being called a foreigner, Liberians don't want to talk about cross border family ties. That's why we walk around with the notion that we come from the sky and found ourselves within the border of Liberia and only the Mandingoes come from that place called Guinea; such a big fat lie of course. This is a big lie that cannot erase the fact that long before the borders were drawn, all of us were families interacting with each other.

While some fellow Liberians have all hateful thoughts of Guinea and the "foreigners" they associate with that country, they on the other hand are very proud of their connection with the United States of America. The Liberian obsession with their American connection is ironic given the fact that most Americans can't differentiate between Liberians and any other Africans. As long as you are a black man, you are an African or Jamaican, most Americans think. When in actuality, we are just some of those poor people from Africa and elsewhere in the world who came to America seeking opportunities we couldn't find in our own countries. So many Liberians, including myself, have obtained the American citizenship. We brag about it and sometimes keep quiet about it when necessary because we don't want to make it public in Liberia for political reasons. We have adopted the "don't ask don't tell" attitude. This was always the case until Lusene Donzo's public admission before the Liberian Senate during his confirmation hearing. Since then, the issue of dual citizenship has become a controversial issue in many Liberian forums.

When I was in Liberia in 2006, I went to the Foreign Ministry to investigate a story that was circulating around regarding some Liberians who were being denied Liberian passports because they were Mandingoes. I went with journalist Mike Jabateh of the Analyst newspaper. The Foreign Minister, Hon. George Wallace, welcomed us into the spacious conference room of his ministry. After asking several questions and hearing some responses from Minister Wallace and his staff, I told him in a side comment that I was a nine-year veteran of the US Military. He told me that by serving in a foreign military, I have lost my Liberian citizenship. Until then I didn't know that serving in a foreign military automatically nullified my Liberian citizenship. So by serving in the US Military and naturalizing myself as an American, according to the minister, I have lost my Liberian citizenship. He told me I could reverse the situation by renouncing my American citizenship. I told the minister point blank that I will keep both. I can't stop being Liberian because I was born there and all of my people are there and I can't renounce my American citizenship for all the benefits it accords me.

One benefit, I will always remember, of my US citizenship was filing for my mother from Liberia to seek urgent medical treatment in the US. Even if there was no other reason for becoming a US citizen, bringing my mother at such a critical moment was sufficient enough. The question that keeps popping up in my head is how can I stop being Liberian when every day I think Liberia, live Liberian, love and am very much concerned about Liberia just like any other Liberian. I may be living outside of Liberia but my mind is there always. Even if I want to stop thinking about Liberia it is impossible to do so because my mother and the rest of the family are there. I have to keep in constant contact with them to know my mother's condition. By thinking about and caring for my mother, by extension, I am thinking about Liberia. It never stops to amaze me how in one place one can become a citizen by paper and have the natural born citizens congratulating you for becoming one of them and in other places, not even your birth is enough to make you a full fledge citizen.

35

Voting for the Losing Candidates

IN MY LIFE I have voted in five presidential elections. The first was the 1985 election in Liberia. The second and third elections in 2000 and 2004 were in the United States. The fourth and fifth were the 2008 and 2012 elections both of which were won by Barack Obama. My common experience in all these elections except 2008 was that the candidates I supported and voted for did not win. In the 1985 election in Liberia, I supported and voted for one of the opposition politicians, Edward B. Kesselly. Samuel Doe, the incumbent former military leader was declared the winner, but many people thought the election was rigged in his favor. In 2000, I supported and voted for Vice President Al Gore. Governor George Bush was declared the winner against the fact that he lost the popular votes to the man who would not be the winner. Then in 2004, I supported and voted for Senator John Kerry with so much passion; he too did not win. The 2000 election made me think about the 1985 election in which there was a report of massive fraud to deliver victory to President Doe. Even though George Bush became president on the technicality of the Electoral College vote, most people felt that it was not fair. The election outcome was finally decided in the court and made more people feel cheated. In 2004, it looked almost as if Ohio was going to be a repeat of the Florida fiasco of 2000, but I guess Senator Kerry didn't want to repeat the 2000 fiasco, because he graciously accepted defeat.

The events of 2000 seemingly defied most of the world's

perception of the US and democracy. America is celebrated by its movies and music as the place where everything is perfect compared to most parts of the world. Some say America is a paradise on earth. Some say it's the land of milk and honey. And it proudly calls itself the "home of the brave and the strong." Because of all these, America had been held in high esteem in the rest of the world.

If what happened in 2000 defied that world perception of America, the way the whole development came to finality equally defied the world's perception of itself. Anywhere else, especially in the Third World, blood would have flowed on the streets. The man who should have been the president graciously accepted "defeat?" Only in America can that happen. It shows something very interestingly unique about America.

The 2000 election only showed that human society in general is not perfect no matter how it projects itself. The fact that America, compared to most parts of the world, was able to resolve its issue without a single bullet being fired and without a single person dying is something praiseworthy.

During the 2000 election, I strongly supported Vice President Al Gore but at the same time, I didn't have any strong dislike for Governor Bush. Whoever won would be my Commander-In-Chief. But when the Supreme Court decided the election, whatever feeling I had about Bush was turned into a strong dislike for him. As someone from the Third World where election irregularities are common practice, the 2000 election did not conform to the picture perfect democracy that we have come to admire the United States for. If democracy cannot be perfect in America, how much can we expect it to be in the so-called Third World countries? Dictators in Africa and elsewhere would love that because they could always use that as one example to prolong their stay in power. There have been so many electoral frauds in Africa in favor of dictators in power and the results have for the most part caused massive suffering and sometimes intractable civil wars. We have presidents in other countries whose biggest worries are to keep themselves in power and don't give a damn about the ordinary people. It's against this background that I could not feel comfortable with the fact that the man who won the popular votes could not be the president while the man who lost the popular votes became the president. Against this background, I strongly wished to support anyone against President Bush. When John Kerry finally won the democratic nomination, I prayed and hoped that he would beat George Bush. Being in the Navy meant I could not carry on any open political campaign for my candidate. The only thing I could do was to vote for him. Even though my vote was just one vote, I was so passionate about it that I sometimes felt guilty at the thought of not being able to vote because of the fact that I was away from my voting district, serving my military duty on the Navy ship. I followed every campaign activity with great interest.

While I was passionate about the election, most of my shipmates didn't really care. Most of them had other things on their minds and surely the election was not one of them. Most were not voting because they thought that whoever won wouldn't make any difference because "politicians are all the same" and "nothing will change." Those that showed any interest would say that they supported Bush because his winning is good for the military pay. Their reasoning was that every time a republican entered the White House the military got paid better than when democrats got in. Many times I told them that regardless of who was in the White House the military would still get the annual pay increase.

When I read the Navy Times a few months before the election, it said that the majority of the military members in and outside the United States supported President Bush; I began to think about those military members I talked to. If the views of the officers in the military were not different from those of the enlisted, I would think that the media was making so much out of the military votes than it really was. Those in the military are committed more to their jobs than the ups and downs of the electoral season. Whether or not they support a candidate, most of them are not so passionate about it like I was in my support for my candidate. It is common knowledge that young people in America didn't care much about politics back then. The same young people from the various communities all across America are the very ones in the military and if they couldn't give a damn in those communities, surely they won't give a damn in the military. This is the feeling I got all around the military bases I have been assigned to.

My electoral district is in Pennsylvania. I was on military assignment in Virginia. Absentee ballot was my only chance for voting in 2004. Where to get the absentee ballot from or where to send it was the problem. I went online to read more about it. The form I expected did not arrive on time through the mailing system. When I received the email from the voting officer on the ship, I went to find him to get some forms from him. I got the forms and asked him some questions. This was just two days before the election. With the form filled out, the question became whether it would get there on time to be counted. Part of me was telling me to forget it because the form would not get there on time. Another part of me was telling me to send it any way.

It all boiled down to exercising my civil responsibility as a voting citizen. While many young people may not care, for me voting is a serious matter. I know many people died in this country to give all Americans the right to vote. There are many people around the world who don't enjoy this right. They are either denied the right to vote or if they vote their votes don't make any difference because some lunatics will do anything to keep in power. So having that right in America means so much to me. I felt this compelling need to cast my absentee ballot. It may not be counted among the ballots on Election Day but not putting it in the mailbox did not make me feel good. With this guilty feeling, I finally put it in the mailbox just a day before the election. I consoled myself with the feeling that even though the election results are given on voting date, the results for the various states are formally certified on different dates. So I hoped that my vote would form part of the certified votes in my state of residence. Whether or not it was counted is something I will never know.

36 | Friday Prayer in the Chapel

IN THE WORLD of the three Abrahamic religions, Friday, Saturday, and Sunday are very important days and are observed accordingly by the faithful. For the Moslems, it's Friday. Saturday is for the Jews, and Sunday is for the Christians. The Mosque is to Moslems what the Synagogue is to the Jews and what the Church is to the Christians. Most members of those faiths would rather be in their official prayer centers on their days of reverence than anywhere else. However, due to our engagement with life's busy activities such as earning our living, we may find ourselves in different places other than our mosques, synagogues, churches or for some people their temples.

In some settings, it may be necessary or expedient for people of different faiths to use the same facility to conduct their prayers, of course on different time schedules. In order to do so, they must negotiate with each other, thereby recognizing their differences but agreeing to the principle of mutual respect. Such is the reality if you are in the US military on shore base or on the ship.

On the ship, I was one of the few Moslems. With no mosque to conduct my daily prayers, I used to go to the ship's chapel. To the best of my ability, I was able to conduct my five daily prayers sometimes in my work center (depending on where I was working), berthing or in the chapel. Compared with the work or berthing spaces, I found the chapel to be much more relaxing with a undisturbed atmosphere. At least in there, I didn't feel like I was invading someone's space like it would be in the work center or berthing. With all the talks about Moslem-Christian confrontation as we read in newspapers, magazines, books or as it may appear on TV, I felt a different atmosphere of tolerance while I served in the military. It was not a traditional Islamic mosque, but since it's purposely set up as a place to worship God, I would rather conduct my Islamic prayers in chapel than not praying at all.

Even though there were not many Moslems here on board the ship, the folks at the ship's religious ministry, who operate the chapel, made sure there were enough materials on board to satisfy the religious needs of the sailors because while we were all serving the country, we must all serve our God in ways we see fit.

When I first told the folks at the ship's religious ministry that I was a Moslem, they gladly told me about the prayer rugs and the copies of the Holy Qurans they had available. Since then going to the chapel to pray or read the Quran gave me a sort of liberated feeling and a sense of belonging.

In my first ship, USS Detroit, I used to do most of my prayers in the berthing. I used to feel more comfortable in there than in the chapel. Whatever once made me feel uncomfortable in the chapel had now been overcome. So when the Islamic Friday schedule was included in the ship's plan of the day (POD) as I heard it being read at the morning quarter, I felt very good about it. I felt very included despite my minority status. Seeing Friday listed in the POD and hearing the announcement on the 1-MC, "Islamic Jumah prayer is now being held in the ship's chapel. Maintain silence in the vicinity," made me feel more devoted. It made me feel good about the fact that religious diversity has been promoted by the command through the religious ministry. If only this were the reality in the real world, we would be at peace with all people. Yet, I realized that although the military environment may represent the bits and pieces of everything out there in the civilian world, it would be very difficult to achieve that reality in the real world.

What came to my mind every day when I saw myself in this environment was the need to let the world know about it with the hope that in some little way, it would make us understand and appreciate each other. Maybe we may want to join Alpha Blondy in singing, "some call him Allah, some call him Adona, some call him Jesus... Like a tree with many branches God is one." As the reggae singer goes on with the same song, "we get the sun rise, we get the sun set, and no one can understand Jah mystery."

We were four Moslems on the ship, two African-Americans, an Arab, and one African (me). Every now and then we tried to encourage each other in the practice of our religion. This was necessary because in an environment where you were only four among thousands of people, it takes an extra commitment to keep the faith and practice it regularly. That sometimes affected the other three Moslems and instead of us coming together to strengthen our faith in fellowship, I was most of the time in the chapel by myself. When the Friday prayer schedule first appeared in the POD, I went out looking for them in their various work spaces on the ship. I suggested that because our prayer schedule had appeared in the ship's POD, we must compel ourselves to make use of the time. I told them we should see this as recognition of our presence as Moslems on the ship but we would be failing in our duty if we didn't make use of the time. It's easy for a weak Moslem to find an excuse for not performing his religious duty and the reason will obviously be the, "well, this is not the right environment," excuse.

One night, I came to the chapel to pray. As I talked to the personnel to get the prayer rug, one of them told me the chaplain wanted to see me. She went to check for him in his office but he wasn't there. The shipmate told me the chaplain was not available but he wanted to talk to me. I learnt later that he wanted me to lead the Islamic prayer on the ship. This was recommended to him based on the fact that I was the only one among the Moslems frequenting the chapel for prayer. Two days before the next Friday prayer, I went around looking for my fellow Moslems and told them it was a challenge and we had to meet it. They all promised that they would make it and I should go get them if necessary. On Friday, I informed the shipmates at my work center that I was going to the chapel to pray. Together with the brothers, we went to the chapel to conduct the Friday prayer. They agreed that I lead the prayer as an imam. Since it was the Friday prayer, they insisted that I read the sermon, which I did by reading some passages of the Holy Quran.

37

If Saclepea Could Speak

UNTIL MY VISIT IN 2005, my last time in Saclepea, my birthplace, was back in November 1989, just a month before the war started. As the rumor became a reality, my folks fled the town, with some coming to Monrovia and others going to Guinea and Ivory Coast. Most of them left, thinking that things would be over soon and they would return home. Since then, many have not made it back. Some like my father, Ngoamilleh Konneh, died longing for the home they couldn't go back to. Some went back to settle when Taylor became president, hoping that the war was over and that peace and reconciliation would be the order of the day. At the end of the day, they were chased out. This made headline news in Liberia but no action was taken to address the problem.

August 2005 made it ten years since I left Liberia. During those ten years, I visited Liberia once and for only two days in 1998. Since then, I had always hoped to spend some time in Liberia. I couldn't think of doing so while Charles Taylor was in power. Since I was serving in the U.S Navy at the time, I could not get a leave approved to visit Liberia because of the unfavorable security conditions. Going there would have also been a personal risk. This, plus the fact that I had written articles that were critical of the Taylor regime and had participated in demonstrations against the regime convinced me that I would be arrested if I had visited. Given the current political climate, I visited Liberia in October 2005. Even though my visit coincided with the campaign season, my visit to Liberia was primarily to visit families and friends I had not seen for all these years. Maybe I wanted to experience the place and feel at home once again. As it's obvious, my visit to Liberia wouldn't be complete without visiting Saclepea. As I have mentioned earlier, the reason was that it's the place of my nativity, a place more than any other place in the world that holds my childhood memories. Enough reason to visit there to see how different it is now from what it was 15 years ago when I last visited.

Another important reason to visit was to see with my own eyes as to what extent the issue of illegal occupation of homes and properties belonging to the Mandingoes was true. As a writer and editor in chief of the Limany website at the time, we had written many editorial pieces about that illegal occupation, condemning it in the strongest terms possible. Now that I was in Liberia, I deemed it necessary to go there to be able to tell my readers if what we had written about in the past was still the same. Some people had accused us of exaggerating this confusion over land in Nimba County. For these people as well, it was extremely necessary for me to visit my hometown.

Still, there was another important reason for my trip to Nimba, a visit to Tengbenye, a village about a 45 minutes drive from Saclepea. Tengbenye is the birthplace of my grandmother, Tolor, the mother of my father. I had been curious to know how Grandma's people were doing. It was to be a kind of family reunion between the Mandingo and Mano sides of my family. My father had enjoyed a very good relationship with his uncles. Since he was no longer alive, I wanted to rekindle that relationship as a tribute to his memory. I was curious as to how my father's uncles would receive us after these many years of animosity between the Manos and Gios on one side and the Mandingoes on the other.

Given my multi-ethnic heritage, I had in mind that my visit to Nimba County, particularly in Saclepea and Tengbenye, and my interaction with the Mano side of my family could in one way or the other help bring about a greater understanding among our people leading to the resolution of the land problem. With all of these thoughts on my mind, I and seven members of my family left Monrovia on the evening of October 7, 2005, three days before the historic election of

October 11 in Liberia. My four aunts also share the same multi-ethnic heritage of Mandingo and Mano backgrounds.

We were caught up in a long traffic at the Red Light. By the time we were clearing out of the traffic jam, we met the convoy of candidate George Weah, triumphantly entering Monrovia for the "Million Man March" the next day. He was waving to his supporters from the open top of his Hummer jeep. The crowd was going wild for him and he was just smiling and waving. We waited for the candidate to leave before we could pull on. As we went, our first stop was Kakata. It was so lively with so many people. Since all of us were fasting, we went to a restaurant to break our fast. While we were walking on the street looking for a place to eat, we heard a group of people speaking Mandingo and we went and greeted them. We sat and ate with them in a local restaurant. We continued our journey after forty-five minutes. Between 10:00 and 11:00 p.m. we were in Ganta. Whereas before the war one would see many Mandingoes on the road, this time you came across them as passengers passing through town. The shops that used to belong to Mandingoes were either occupied or demolished and new shops were built in their places. I visited the home of one of my deceased aunts and could not see any familiar faces. I could see the vivid signs of the war on a mosque that was badly desecrated. Efforts were being made to renovate the mosque but those efforts had not produced any dramatic improvement. Nevertheless, I saw a few people praying in there. I didn't ask if they were passengers passing through or if they were residing in Ganta.

As we left Ganta, my memory took me back to the days before the war. I was talking and my traveling companions were confirming where so and so person's house or shop used to be. Someone else was occupying them while the owners were either in Monrovia or Guinea, afraid to come to claim ownership of their properties. Some of the occupiers, I was told, had entered into a lease agreement with the legitimate owners to keep some of the properties.

We passed Yasonoh, the home of the famous Nimba County senator, Johnny Voker, in whose honor my Alma Mater, Johnny Voker High School in Saclepea is named after. As we passed through there, my mind went to Vamunya, a friend who died during the war in

Monrovia. Yasonoh was his birthplace. I looked to where their houses once stood. Since it was night time, we did not stop to inquire as to who lives there now. May his soul rest in peace.

Another town along the way that brought me some memory was Karnwee, the home of the late Gen. Robert G. Saye, one time Superintendent of Nimba County, and one time Director of Staff of the Armed Forces of Liberia. Gen. Saye was one of those that became an early casualty of the instability that finally swept the whole nation. I remember Karnwee because of two other people. It was the home of one of my teachers during my elementary school years, Mehwonkeh, and of Gen. Mohammed Dumbuya, the late ULIMO Field Commander who was once Chief of Staff of the Armed Forces of Liberia. Gen. Dumbuya died during the April 6 crisis. May his soul rest in peace.

When we got to Mehnpa, I started breathing the air of Saclepea. This was because Mehnpa is just a stone's throw from Saclepea. As we passed through Mehnpa, I was reminded of some controversy I stirred up at Johnny Voker High School about Mehnpa. Our class, 11th grade, had a program in which I served as the keynote speaker. I delivered a very controversial speech that upset some fellow students at the school. Among the things I said was that a Mandingo man started Mehnpa and that's why it's called "Mehnpa." The Mano people call us "Mehn." In that sense the literal meaning of Mehnpa is Mandingo town. I used that as my reason for saying that Mehnpa was originally a Mandingo town. This really upset some guys at my school. As I passed through the town this night, my mind went back to that experience.

After Mehnpa, we passed the Moslem cemetery where so many people I once knew had been laid to rest. I was sort of wondering if those dead people could be aware that their living folks made an involuntary journey out of town and have not returned since then. I wondered who might have been the last one buried there before the mass exodus of the Mandingoes from the town. That would probably be Aleo Foday, the only Mandingo casualty of Saclepea. It wasn't the rebels' bullets that killed the man who used to call prayer for our mosque, rather it was an AFL soldier assigned to protect civilians. While the AFL soldiers were in town "providing security," some of them went to grab a goat that belonged to Aleo who protested. A scuffle developed and he was shot dead. That was months before the Mano folks of the town advised their Mandingo folks to leave town to avoid calamity. Most Saclepea Mandingoes considered that advice a kind gesture by their Mano neighbors. Because of this kind gesture, Saclepea was spared from the massive Mandingo hunting and killing that took place elsewhere in Nimba County and in other parts of Liberia. If my father had any choice as to where he would like to be buried, his choice would have been this graveyard. He couldn't have imagined that he would die in Monrovia in 1994 and be buried there, instead of Saclepea.

After the graveyard, we passed the place where Grandma Matian used to farm. I often came there to help her plant or harvest bitter balls, tomatoes, potatoes and other garden produce. Grandma Matian is a Mano from Karnwee. Her daughter, Aunty Mamadia, the oldest living daughter of my grandfather was traveling with me. After passing where Grandma's farm used to be, we crossed a creek that we used to swim in when we were little. Many times we accompanied our brothers or uncles to wash their cars. We kept on going, passing the big building where old man Donzo used to have commercial rice machines. Before reaching the city center of Saclepea, I saw the police station where on many occasions we went to settle cases or witness thieves being flogged. I remember one occasion that happened right after the November 12th failed coup. I was in my mother's shop when this army guy came in and started taking things without paying for them. When I protested, he got mad. He hauled me from behind the counter and dragged me to the police station. There was no policeman on duty when we arrived at the station. He locked me up without any investigation. After an hour, one policeman came in and I made some noise with the hope that he would know I was in there. He opened the door and told me to come out. He asked what I was doing in there. I told him that an army man had brought me in there because I wouldn't agree for him to take things from my mother's shop without paying for them. He told me to go home and to come the next morning. I did not go back and no one bothered me thereafter.

We got to the center of Saclepea where I grew up as a child. We used to play hide and seek, sometimes with the girls, other times with our crowd of boys. I could see familiar places but since it was past 12 midnight, the town was quiet and that wasn't the time to be looking for any familiar faces. At such time of the night, our main concern was to find a place to sleep. So we headed straight to Grandma Mawa Voker's place on Tappita road. As mentioned previously, Grandma Mawa was a relative of the legendary Johnny Voker. Through her marital relationship with my grandfather, she gave birth to a son, Vafuomo, named after the father of Sheik Kafumba Konneh. Grandma Mawa was very resourceful and this was evidenced by the quantity of land and houses she owned in Saclepea. It was in one of these houses we spent the night. By the time we got to the house, it was some minutes past 1 a.m. The other house next to the one we slept in holds some more childhood memories for me. It was rented and used as a Madrassa, which later on became a bilingual school of Arabic and English learning. The Moslem Union School, headquartered in Sanniquellie, Nimba County, administered the Madrassa. Our first English teacher was Mr. Lincoln G. Nyah. Throughout the time Mr. Nyah taught us, many of us admired him. He was a strict disciplinarian. The last time I saw him was 1998 during my two-day brief visit to Liberia.

Having gone to bed from around 1:30 to 2:00 am, we woke up to a bright Saturday morning. The first time in fifteen years I had wakened up from sleep in Saclepea. We all took a bath and prayed. There were two things that we wanted to accomplish on this day. One was to walk around Saclepea visiting our neighbors and other people we knew in town. The other thing we wanted to accomplish was to visit Tengbenye. We agreed that the first order of business was to visit Tengbenye. But we were told that the road was in disrepair and not good for the van we had carried. Fortunately for us, a brother-in-law of mine had a pick-up truck and he decided to take us there. My sister Mawa is married to him. Mawa is the daughter of Uncle Vafuomo but she has spent most of her adult life with her Gio mother and her people from Kpaytuo. While we call her Mawa, her mom and other people from Kpaytuo call her Martha. Interestingly indeed, Sister Mawa or Martha's current husband is a Guinean Mano. He proved to be very hospitable as he drove us to Tengbenye. He talked about the deep-rooted ties between the Manos from Guinea and those from Liberia. He named many towns in Guinea and Liberia that have identical names, suggesting that Manos from the original towns in the place that became Guinea migrated to the land that became Liberia and named the new towns after the old ones. That is just another effect of the European balkanization of Africa, drawing lines to divide families into separate countries. In this case, a family member on one side of the imaginary line became a Guinean, and the one on the other side became a Liberian. This effect of colonial division is evidenced everywhere in Africa today and it's the source of most of our conflicts. Immigration authorities in Africa don't take into consideration the family ties that existed before the colonial division, and have only enforced that division, thereby making a mockery of all our talk regarding African unity.

When we got to Tengbenye, we were warmly welcomed. Since it was the campaign time, some of the family members had gone to Gawompa to attend the campaign functions of some candidates. Among the family members we met, there was only one surviving brother of Grandma Tolor. It was he who I turned to for some information about my grandmother. I told him and the crowd that had gathered in the living room that I had come from the United States all the way to Tengbenye to reconnect with this side of my past, the past that connects me to Tengbenye, the birthplace of Grandma Tolor. I told them about my experience in the US Navy and as a writer who had written a book of poetry. I presented two copies of the book to the public school of the town. I told them whenever they read the book they should remember that it's written by someone who has a connection with them and the town.

In response, they said they were surprised but truly happy that we made it to Tengbenye. They said we were welcomed and that they would always remember this day. They said that the fact that I could come from America and consider coming to Tengbenye, with the road condition being so terrible was beyond words. They said that Tengbenye is our home since it was the home of our grandmother. They said we were protected in Tengbenye as any native born person of the town. They even showed us some Mandingo nephews and nieces who continued to live with them. These were the children of the late Muesiamana Koisia who lived there and had children by a Mano woman. When the war came and the Mandingoes fled, the Mano woman and her Mandingo children remained. And they survived the war and have no intention of leaving Tengbenye to go anywhere. One of their father's sons, Small Man, wasn't so lucky as he was one of the early casualties of the war. He had left Saclepea to visit another village at the time the war was still in its infancy. He and another passenger on a motorbike did not make it back to Saclepea.

My father's uncles urged us strongly to sleep so we could meet other town folks who had gone to Gawompa. Earlier when we came, they said they had just left. Someone was sent to let them know about our surprise visit. They were already at a program so they sent a town chief, who happened to be much younger than what town chiefs used to be, to meet us. He came and spoke on behalf of the town people, saying that we should spend the night so that other people could meet us in the morning. We said that we had other engagements in Saclepea and we had to leave. We told them to extend our greetings to everyone in town.

It's a tradition among the Manos for their visiting nephews to grab a chicken or goat. This is a sign of hospitality. As tradition required, we were given two chickens. They said they would have given us a goat if we had agreed to sleep.

After all of the formalities, we said goodbye and headed back to Saclepea. Upon reaching to Saclepea, we stopped in Tonween to speak to old man Sammy Dahn, former Nimba County representative in the House and a brother of one of Liberia's many political figures, Marcus Dahn. I saw something remarkably different with the old man and his house. In days gone by, Sammy Dahn's house was the most beautiful house in Saclepea. This time, I could not see that beauty. The last time I saw the house was fifteen years earlier. I had been to Abidjan, Monrovia, America, Europe and other places and had seen so many beautiful buildings. Was that why the most beautiful building in Saclepea didn't look so beautiful in my eyes anymore? The old man's health condition was not the best either. My aunts and brothers told him we were the children and grandchildren of Bolekayfa, my father's father. From the way he looked, he had much to say but the condition would not allow him to say it. The last time I saw Sammy Dahn, he was much healthier and energetic. This time, old age and bad health were taking their tolls on him. We left Tonween and headed for town.

After climbing down the hill from Tonween, we reached to the place we Mandingo people used to call "Macanisunboula," meaning a mechanic place. We had named it that way because most of our tribal people who lived there were mechanics. I can't remember now how the Mano people call it. As we passed there, my mind went to two friends that died in the war. One was Junior Mamie, a Mano and the other was Losene Bamba, a Mandingo. Both of them lived right in this neighborhood and their houses were opposite each other. While Junior Mamie was one of the victims of the Lutheran Church Massacre in Monrovia, Losene Bamba was killed behind the rebel line outside of Monrovia. While Junior Mamie was killed because he was Mano, Losene Bamba was killed because he was a Mandingo. May their souls rest in peace.

Another person that lived not too far from where Junior Mamie and Losene Bamba lived was Mohammed Kamara. His mother was Mano. When the war came, Mohammed fled to Sierra Leone. When Taylor's loyalists crossed the border to Sierra Leone, one of them who knew Mohammed is said to have killed him simply because he was a Mandingo. I wonder if his killer knew he was the son of a Mano woman.

Not too far from Mohammed Kamara's parent's house, my aunts took me to another house. Some family members live there. I was introduced to them. They were the children of one of my grandmother's younger sisters. After the usual greetings, they told me that two of their brothers live in the US and I should establish contact with them when returning to the States. They told me these were my father's direct cousins. Their names were Magnus Saye and Raphael Saye. They gave me their numbers. When I arrived back in the states, I contacted Uncle Magnus and his brother Raphael Saye who recently passed away on January 1, 2013. They were surprised to hear from me. I told them we should be happy that we have discovered each other. They asked about my father and his sister Bendu Kenneh and I told them both had died.

By this time we decided to just walk in town as a matter of exploration. From around Saclepea Inland Church, we walked as a group, passing familiar places but seeing unfamiliar faces. People we knew to own certain places no longer lived there, and people we didn't know now lived there. When we got to the center of Saclepea, where we once had a big store with a gas station, another store stood in its place. Uncle Amara Donzo was the richest man in Saclepea before the war, and his store, once the biggest store in town was now occupied by someone else. There were three other houses built on our family land. The house in which I was born and raised was occupied by some people. The mosque my grandfather had built had been demolished and his grave that used to be in front of the mosque had been desecrated. The remnant of the mosque was being used as a carpenter shop. The last time there was a problem between the Manos and Mandingoes during Taylor regime, I understand that it was caused by someone who was desecrating Grandpa's grave and someone from the Mandingo side protested. It resulted in a conflict in which several Mandingoes were killed and others fled the town. Since that incident, most Mandingoes have been afraid to come back.

Opposite our yard I saw a nightclub built in the Bility family yard. This is the birthplace of Musa Bility, a prominent business man in Monrovia and is also the birthplace of Hassan Bility's father, Alhaji Lassana Bility. Other people's houses were also destroyed to build that nightclub.

We then went further down on the street that divides our yard from the Bility's yard. While walking on the street, I saw some of the old people we were planning to meet. Among them were Cooper Toh, a former Town Chief, and Sekou Cooper, a former Paramount Chief of Saclepea Mah County District. With them was another elder of the town, John Gborley. They were keeping conversation at Evan Koah's mother's shop. Evan was one of the senatorial candidates of Nimba County in the 2005 election. His sister's father is a Mandingo. I had forgotten about her until one of my brothers told me "this is Gboyo's (Aleo Bility) daughter."

Aunty Madeaba spoke in fluent Mano, telling the gathering the purpose of our trip to Saclepea. She introduced me as "our son has come from America and was interested in coming to see his home." By this time now a small crowd had gathered to witness what was unfolding. In this crowd, I met many friends I had not seen in all these fifteen years. There was Betty Mehn, a classmate from 10th grade through 12th. She and other friends told me how proud they were when they heard me on Voice of America reading a poem about growing up in Saclepea. Hearing them tell me that made me proud too; that despite everything, these Mano friends could express some pride in me. Their simple joy of seeing me convinced me that despite everything, there was a possibility for reconciliation among the tribes in Saclepea and the rest of Nimba County.

Having been introduced, I told the gathering that as a child of Saclepea, I have always lived with the burning desire for this place. That the fifteen years absence from the town feels like living in forced exile. That in all those fifteen years I have remembered and celebrated Saclepea in my writings. I told them that I have romanticized my childhood experiences of Saclepea in poetry that have won me many admirers. I told them that Saclepea was a home that nurtured me and those childhood memories will remain with me wherever I go. This had been the case even when I had been stationed in the US Navy ships cruising the high seas of the Atlantic, Adriatic, Mediterranean or the Persian Gulf. Because of this strong feeling, it felt like I was on a pilgrimage to the past that I feel so strongly about. This is my heritage as much as it is theirs and the same way they are proud of it, so am I. The place was very quiet and everyone was very attentive to what I was saying as it was being interpreted in Mano. At the end of my short speech, I presented two copies of my book to the Johnny Voker High School. I would have been glad to have made the presentation on the campus while school was in session but it was Saturday. That being the case, I gave them the books to be given to the school on my behalf. Coincidentally, the chairman of the Parent Teacher Association of the school arrived. The books were presented to him.

I could see that the old people felt some emotion in my speech. I could tell from their faces that my speech had taken them on memory lane. For them, Sekou Cooper did most of the talking. He talked warm-ly about my grandfather and his historic contribution to the making of Saclepea. He enumerated some of his personal encounters with the old man. He said Grandpa was like his own father and he treated him like his own child. He said the reason he is called "Sekou" is because his birth coincided with the arrival of a respected Mandingo man. The man requested that since his coming coincided with the birth of a child, the child should be named after him. He went on to say that to see "Old man Bolekayfa's children's coming to town is a happy oc-casion which deserves celebration." While he was talking, everyone could tell that he was on a long memory lane, trying to connect the past with the present.

Grandpa Nvakaifa Konneh is also known as Bolekayfa. While the Mandingoes call him Nvakaifa, the Manos call him Bolekayfa. He was an Islamic scholar who built a mosque to propagate Islam. He is said to have performed "mole" work for some people that became very powerful and prominent. Among them were Dahn Gbonwee and Johnny Voker. He also became a government official, a market-ing coordinator for Saclepea and the surrounding towns and villages. It is said that in that capacity, Grandpa used to go around the mar-ket, which was held in his yard, to inspect the goods brought in by various towns and villages within the district. He would levy fines on any town or village that failed to bring its share of goods to the market. Accordingly, that was one way the government was trying to bring the native people under its control. As a prominent religious leader among his people and being very active in local tribal poli-tics, Grandpa is well respected by everyone. Our Madrassa was later named after him.

As a sign of hospitality, Sekou Cooper and the other people of-fered to buy us some soft drinks to cool our thirst. But too bad it was Ramadan and we were all fasting. So we said goodbye and left. Our last stop in Saclepea was to old lady Mary Yongah. We went to her place. We met her and her son Joseph Marshall whose biological fa-ther, Alhaji Sekou Koisiah, was one of the prominent Mandingoes of the town. In the past, Mah Yongah was what we used to call a "civi-lized or kwi woman." She was beautiful, very energetic and powerful.

One could tell that by the way she dressed and the house she lived in. I remember one time one of her sons died in Monrovia in a car accident. As a young boy growing up in Saclepea, it was one of the most colorful funeral services I had witnessed. That was the first time I entered her house to view the body. I was amazed by the big "kwi" house. Looking at Mah Yongah during this trip was a testament to only one thing; no matter how energetic we are at one point in life, there will come a time when we have to slow down. Sickness and old age will take over. There had been fifteen years since the last time I saw her and now seeing her again was indeed a happy occasion. We all expressed how we missed each other over the years.

After that meeting with Mah Yongah and her son Joseph Marshall, we headed for Monrovia. In another time, instead of visiting Saclepea just for a day, I would have spent at least a week or two with my family. But since my family had been dislocated as a result of the war and are still afraid to return because of the illegal occupations of their homes, my visit was brief. During Taylor's time, some Mandingoes came back to town, hoping that the war was over. Their dream of living peacefully in their homes was shattered in a brutal attack. As I understand, there have been some peace and reconciliation talks and most of my family and others were only waiting for the seating of the new government. By that time the expectation was that things would be better and people would get their homes and other properties back.

In spite of the illegal occupation of properties, I felt a high degree of hospitality during the entire trip. In the eyes of the people, I could see hope of finding lasting solution to all the problems. I felt really satisfied that despite everything we could still be nice to each other, recognizing and celebrating our multi-ethnic heritage. It's my hope that my experience in both Tengbenye and Saclepea could be replicated in other parts of Nimba County, indeed in all of Liberia.

With all of these thoughts going through my head, I was left wondering if Saclepea could speak. More than likely it would encourage all of us to come together and rebuild our lives and relationships as they were before the war.

38 | The Phenomenal Rise of Barack Obama

IN EARLY 2008, I went back to work as a canvasser for Working America, an affiliate of the AFL-CIO. I worked for the organization back in 2006 doing a membership registration, canvassing and campaigning for several democratic candidates in the mid-term election that year. We went from door to door registering people as members. The issues we were presenting to the people in their homes were the outsourcing of jobs to other countries and the problem facing more than 40 million people without health insurance in the US. With these issues, many people were excited to sign on. While we met many people who were happy to sign on, there were others who told us "I am not interested but thank you any way."

After our 30 minute daily briefing and training which started around 1:30pm and lasted up to 2:00pm, we would divide into teams heading to different areas within and around Philadelphia. While heading to our turfs, we had van training which began with an ice breaker. We talked about our favorite movies, music, political candidates or whatever we did the last weekend or planned to do over the next weekend. After the ice breaker we practiced our rap, the way to present our message to the people we met on our turfs.

Sometime in January 2008, we were seven in the van, four whites and three blacks. I, a native African, and the other two blacks were African-Americans. When our field manager asked who our favorite candidates in the race were for the White House in 2008, one of the four white canvassers said Dennis Kucinich. When I told him that Kucinich had been out of the race a while back, he said he "may consider" Barak Obama. Our field manager, a white male, said for him it was "definitely" Obama because his message is "refreshing and inspiring." He believed that Obama had a clean record; had never been involved in any scandal. Another one said he was still undecided between Hilary and Obama. The young white female among us also said she was undecided between Hilary and Obama. The two young African Americans said they didn't care much because "all politicians are the same and no matter who became president they couldn't expect any 'difference.'" For my part I said that Barak Obama was my first choice but I would support any of the two candidates that would finally win the nomination because my primary concern was to drive the Republicans out of power or deny them another four years after all the mess George Bush had put the country through.

I am proud that Obama is African like me. I am aware of his multiracial backgrounds but since his father was a son of Africa, I consider him to be an African. To see a black man, indeed an African becoming the most powerful person in the world is very inspiring. Good news about black people or Africa does not get reported often in the western media. As Africans, we have been beaten down for so long. We have been enslaved, colonized, and even in 2008, we have not fully recovered from the negative effects of slavery and colonization. Even as independent nations in Africa, as freed people in America, Europe and the Caribbean, our world is still defined by wars, poverty, hunger, disease, etc. That's the only picture of Africa portrayed in the western media. Yes we have suffered too many years of humiliation but we have always hoped for better days to come. Against all the negativity, it was refreshing to see a black man, indeed an African man becoming a source of inspiration for America and the rest of the world. This was good news worth celebrating and that's why I was supporting Barack Obama.

A few weeks afterward, I was watching TV with an elderly relative of mine. She is not literate and couldn't understand what was being said about Obama or what he was saying when he was talking to adoring crowds here and there on the campaign trails. She said to me, "I feel proud every time I see Obama on TV and I am praying day and night for him to be president. I am sure God will answer my prayer." Another relative of mine living in Las Vegas was one of the early Obama supporters. He was even fanatic about him. According to him, he used to love the Clintons to death but with the emergence of Barak Obama, he's found a new hero. He has switched over to Barak Obama because he represents something new for America and the world. He was fired up even before Obama's first victory in Iowa. He went on to say that "For White people in Iowa to have voted for him, I am convinced that he will make it all the way." He believed that these white people saw him as a unifier; they saw him as a redeemer of the nation from "Bush's nonsense" and the terrible history of racism. He was even mad at the Clintons for "badmouthing Obama." He went on further to say that for "many years we have been there for the Clintons, we have been their loyal supporters, at some point calling Bill the 'first black president.' We have supported them through all the scandals." With all these, my cousin believed that "our time has come and the Clintons should give us a chance because they had been there for eight years already."

I tried to calm him down, telling him it was politics. I told him that as much as we love Obama and are eager to see history being made, Hilary too represented another historic reality. For the first time in American history, Americans were closer to electing either a first black president or a first female president. So this race was much more about race and gender as it was about who had the experience or who was inspiring. While each one of them was eager to make history, I could understand why Hilary was so desperate because this might have been her last chance and because of age being on his side Obama may have had another shot at the same opportunity down the years. Probably Bill and his wife might have thought it would be an easy ride back to the White House. Maybe they could not imagine that what they thought would be an easy ride would be challenged by a man called Obama, a black man.

As I pondered all these in my mind, I came across two young Liberians in Philadelphia talking about Obama. One of them said that he believed that Obama was America's next president. His friend responded, "If Mandingo man can be president in Liberia, then Barak Obama will be president in America." This reminded me of Obama's native Kenya where his people were locked up in ethnic conflict as a result of a flawed election. In Kenya, the accusation was that the Kikuyu wanted to monopolize power. It was only ironic that while Barak Obama was inspiring people in America to transcend race and consider the common good of humanity, his people in Africa were still locked up in ethnic conflicts. One can only hope that Obama's success in the race to the White House will help us to understand that we too must transcend ethnicity for the sake of peace and prosperity in Africa.

39

My Own Personal Barack Obama Moment

FAST FORWARD TO OCTOBER 11, 2008 and all the signs were pointing to an Obama victory against the Republican nominee, John McCain. Right before our eyes, he was making history many of us could not imagine some months ago was possible. When I heard about his rally not far from where I live, I deemed it necessary to attend. I wanted to see this living legend with my own eyes. His uplifting story is worth telling my children and grandchildren to come. Will he be the next president? I prayed and hoped so. But before then, I thought it was good to see him at one of those rallies. I had seen his pictures in newspapers and magazines as well as on TV. I read his books. Seeing him in person was the next thing. He was scheduled to make four appearances at four different rallies in the City of Brotherly Love on October 11, 2008. The one on 52nd and Locust streets was closest to me and I didn't want to miss it. I had received emails informing me about the event two days earlier. I shared the emails with folks on two of my community email listings. The emails said gate would open at 11:00 am and the candidate would be arriving at 1.10 pm. A day before, I planned to arrive early so I would be able to see Sen. Barack Obama up-close. As I shared the email with friends who I thought might be interested in coming to the rally, I certainly planned to be there on time to see the man whom I was praying and hoping by January 2009 would be inaugurated as the next president of the USA; indeed the most powerful man in the world.

Due to some unavoidable circumstances, I could not be there on time. When I finally got there, I could see the sea of people that had already gathered to see candidate Barack Obama.

As I already mentioned, the rally was at 52nd and Locust streets. I drove up to 53rd Street and Locust where the police sealed off the area with a "Do not cross" duct tape. I drove around but could not find any parking spot. The nearest place I could find to park was five blocks up at 58th and Locust. I parked the car and walked towards 53rd Street. I was among the massive crowd that had gathered there. According to news report, there were 25,000 people. Fortunately, the Obama convoy came down on 53rd street, passed us and made a left turn on Locust towards 52nd. I saw him up close through the car window. I also saw Philadelphia Mayor Michael Nutter in another vehicle following Sen. Obama.

Since the police wouldn't allow anyone to follow the convoy, I had to walk around to find my way to 52nd Street by way of Spruce Street. I pulled and shoved through the massive crowd hoping to reach a close distance to the candidate. I went as far to where I could see him but not close enough. At least I could see him in the distance talking and the fired up crowd was just roaring with approval after every word Sen. Obama spoke.

There were many people, black, white, etc, but since this particular rally was being held in the predominantly black neighborhood of South West Philly, majority of the people were black. It was an exciting feeling of pride that one of their own had come this far. No black person had come this far before. Barack Obama being the first had fired up black people everywhere, even in Africa. You could see this sense of pride on the faces in the crowd.

He said many things but some of the words have stayed with me since then. Among them he said that he wasn't "born in wealth." He credited many people, those who struggled before him, and praised his mother who gave him love, made sure he got education and said that "everybody has a story like that to tell." He urged the people to "stand up for justice, education, and freedom." He said the American Dream is being tested by his candidacy and promised that change is under way. He went on further to say, "That's the story of America.

Each successive generation working hard. I'm here because some-body somewhere stood up for me. And because they stood up, a few more stood up. And then a few thousands stood up. And then a few million stood up. And because they stood up, America became a place where dreams were realized"

As I made my way through the crowd to come back home, I felt much more energized, inspired, and lucky to be a witness to this great historic moment in America. Being at an Obama rally felt much more positive as compared to the hate-fest John McCain's rallies had become. The whole time I was at the Obama rally, I was basking in the glory of positive energy. Even when Obama had some words of praises for McCain for telling his angry supporters that Obama is a "decent man" who he just happened to disagree with, no one booed him. The Obama Rally was more like a celebration of peace, love and harmony. What was a bit of a surprise to me was seeing an African-American female Moslem dressed in her Islamic garment with hijab dancing with two white guys. That image stayed with me. I couldn't stop thinking that Obamamania had made them to overlook their skin color and religion. What they had in common is the fact that they all had been inspired by the uplifting message of one man, Barack Obama and they all hoped for the change Obama had promised. What a great moment in the American history.

Besides being a witness to this incredible historical moment, I tried to find out what little contribution I could make. The best I could do was to sign-up as a volunteer for the campaign. Even though my job schedule had been tight, I managed to formally register with my cell phone and received text messages of things and events that were taking place in different places. Like millions of volunteers, I did my share of knocking on doors, making phone calls, dropping flyers here, and talking to people there. With that I can now say that we all made history on November 4, 2008.

On the day of the election, I did some more knockings on doors, pairing with an African brother from Nigeria. But before going out to knock on any door on November 4, I went out to cast my vote. Having cast my ballot, I felt truly energized and motivated to go out there to knock on other people's doors or see someone on the streets and ask if he or she had already voted or if he or she knew their polling centers. My partner and I made sure to reach every house listed on our GOTV sheets. Having completed our tasks for the day, I went home to wait for the results.

Visiting us was a relative from Paris, France. She is a distant cousin of mine from Guinea and now holds French nationality. This was her first visit to the states. She had been following the process in France and felt very lucky to be here witnessing the incredible possibility of a black man becoming president for the white man's greatest country on earth. She told me she had been praying for Obama's victory ever since she heard he was running to become president of the United States of America. Comparing Europe and America, she said black people are doing far better in the US. She said white people in Europe have not shown any indication that they may give similar chance to black people in Europe and that black people in Europe are too powerless to even dream of becoming president of any country in Europe. Even though she could not understand English, she was watching TV around the clock about the whole electoral process.

We had our own mini party in our house when the final results came in putting Barack Obama all the way to the top and when John McCain conceded. For most people, Obama's victory was one of those things you couldn't believe until you saw it happen. With his concession speech and Obama's inaugural address, we joined millions of people in the US and around the world to celebrate the change that had truly come to America. As far as we, black people are concerned, the world will never be the same again after the victory of Barack Obama, a son of an African immigrant and a white woman became president of the US. If Jesus ever died to wash away the sins of the Christians who believe that to be the truth, then every black person in the world can say that Barack Obama's election as the president of the most powerful nation in the world, thus becoming the most powerful person on earth has erased all our shames and humiliation in the world. Having been enslaved and colonized, and being looked down upon by everyone including the Arabs, Barack Obama's election meant black people are not subhuman as has been portrayed throughout history by people who enslaved and colonized us. Now we all can agree that the United States as a nation has lived up to its creed that all men are created equal. When Bush's presidency was decided by the Supreme Court in 2000, many people doubted that America was the bastion of democracy she proclaims herself to be. For all those who doubted America's democracy, like Obama said, this victory is their answers.

Crowning Moment of Many Years of Struggle- While we are witnessing today what would have seemed impossible yesterday, we have to consider and appreciate the history of the long years of struggle for racial equality in the United States of America. These long years of struggle by so many people made today possible. Over these years, the struggle has taken so many forms and produced different leaders with different ideologies but with common agenda. It is now easy for us to celebrate some of those leaders while diminishing the contribution of others. From my perspective as an African, all those who at one time or another stood up and demanded freedom, justice, and equality for black people should be respected, appreciated and celebrated. Whether it's Frederick Douglas, W.E.B Du Bois, Booker T. Washington, Marcus Garvey, Martin Luther King, Malcolm X, Louise Farrakhan, or Jesse Jackson; their collective objective was to make America a society where black a man could be judged on the content of his characters rather than the color of his skin. After some of these men have been dead and gone while some are still alive, the struggle had now reached a point where victory was in sight. To reach that final point required a leader eloquent enough to speak in such a language that everyone would feel comfortable with. The leader that stepped forward in this regard is Barack Obama. Not only do we as black people feel liberated by his words, I believe white people can feel the same sense of liberation without feeling any guilt about the past that demonizes them in the eyes of us black people.

All along the white and black dialogue has been about black people speaking of all the terrible things white people have done and continue to do to them. On the other hand, white people want to remind black people that things are better now and instead of dwelling on the past, they should take advantage of the current opportunities that even those recent immigrants are taking advantage of. White people don't want the guilt of the past to be rubbed in their faces all the time and black people don't want to forget the past that defines their history of slavery and Jim Crow in the US. Maybe the dialogue needed to be taken to another level that will give some comfortable feeling to both blacks and whites. Perhaps Barack Obama understands this more than other black candidates that ran for the presidency in the past. Obama acknowledges the past when he said, "I'm here because somebody somewhere stood up for me... And because they stood up, America became a place where dreams were realized." While he acknowledges the past struggle for freedom, justice and equality, he also agrees that America has changed and still is capable of further change as a result of the past struggle.

Another reason for Obama's mild manner campaign could be attributed to the fact that he shares a dual-heritage of both races. He owes more in his life to the generosity of his white mother and grandparents. It is that white side of his family that raised him and sent him to school. The African side of his family was completely absent in his life. But for the love of the African side of his family, he maintained his "funny name," and instead of seeking jobs on Wall Street after graduating from Columbia University he decided to work with the poor housing projects in Chicago as a community organizer and then went all the way to Kogelo in Kenya in search of his identity. He might have not talked in the same way as Malcolm X or Jesse Jackson yet he has demonstrated his love for his African heritage without offending the white side of his family. And it is the white supports for him that motivated the massive African-American supports in the first place.

Only in America As an immigrant, I have been fascinated by the stories of immigrants and their children who have found success in the mainstream of the American social, political and economic environments. Among those stories I have often mentioned are those of Henry Kissinger, born in Germany and served as Secretary of State, Madeline Albright, born in Czechoslovakia (now the Czech Republic) and became the first female Secretary of State, and Arnold Schwarzenegger, born in Austria and then governor of the state of California. Until the phenomenal rise of Barak Obama, I have always felt that stories such as these were possible "Only in America." If one is amazed by the stories of Henry Kissinger, Madeline Albright, and Arnold Schwarzenegger, one should even be amazed by the story of Barack Obama, the son of a Kenyan immigrant and a white woman from Kansas. Compare that to the West African country of Ivory Coast where Alhassan Ouatara was banned from running for presidency because they said one of his parents is or was Burkinabe.

The fact that naturalized Americans and the son of an African immigrant can rise to the highest positions such as governor, secretary of state, and president speaks volumes about America being a melting pot and a land which gives everyone an equal chance to succeed at anything. One does not hear about these kinds of stories anywhere else in the world, only in America. Obama himself has said it over and over again. America has shown to the world its ability to adopt change based on reasoning and this is the image of America that inspires people everywhere in the world, causing people to risk everything to come to the land which has limitless possibility for everyone irrespective of ethnic or national origin.

What we are witnessing in America today is the realization of Martin Luther King's dream of a nation where "people will be judged based on their characters" rather than the "color of their skin." The fact that that dream has been realized by the election of a son of Africa and America is a historic moment not only for America but the whole world. This shows America to have become a very tolerant society. This is the picture of America many people could not imagine was possible. King's dream has been romanticized in literature, films, music, etc. It's been commercialized as well. This time around, it's been made a reality. For those of us from different parts of the world who have to deal with the issues of ethnic, racial, religious or any type of discrimination, Obama's victory gives us hope that we too can overcome any social limitation imposed on us based on our ethnic or religious identity.

When Barack Obama says no other country in the world is his story remotely possible, this is true even in Kenya, the country of his father's birth. Either ethnicity or youthful age would have disqualified him if he had run for the same position in Kenya. Taken this into consideration, it is very hypocritical in parts of Kenya and Africa to celebrate Obama's victory, because they will not allow the growth of a political culture that made the phenomenal rise of Barack Obama possible. While we are celebrating the election of a black man as the president of a white majority country, we are at the same time tolerating the likes of Robert Mugabe of Zimbabwe, or the late Omar Bongo of Gabon, or the late Lansana Conte of Guinea. These leaders are lording over corrupt and ineffective political cultures that have bankrupt their countries, resulting to massive poverty.

Listening to the concession speech of Sen. John McCain, and the victory speech of Barack Obama, one can hear inspiring words from two men who during the campaign went after each other so fiercely. This is another good and positive example of tolerant political culture I wish people in other parts of the world, particularly in Africa, can learn from. When McCain said in his concession speech, "In contest as long and difficult as this campaign has been, his success alone commands my respect...," it increased my respect for the American political culture. In the part of the world where I am from, losers don't make gracious speeches about people they have lost to. Neither can the victors be humble enough to say something good about the person they have defeated as can be seen in these words of Barack Obama: Sen. McCain fought long and hard in this campaign. And he's fought even longer and harder for the country he loves. He has endured sacrifices for America that most of us cannot begin to imagine. We are better off for the service rendered by this brave and selfless leader. I congratulate him."

CPSIA information can be obtained at www.ICGtesting.com
Printed in the USA
BVOW010431040313

314587BV00004B/9/P

9 780578 113005